Connecting
Peace, Justice &
Reconciliation

Connecting

Peace, Justice

& Reconciliation

Elisabeth Porter

LYNNE
RIENNER
PUBLISHERS

BOULDER
LONDON

Published in the United States of America in 2015 by
Lynne Rienner Publishers, Inc.
1800 30th Street, Boulder, Colorado 80301
www.rienner.com

and in the United Kingdom by
Lynne Rienner Publishers, Inc.
3 Henrietta Street, Covent Garden, London WC2E 8LU

Library of Congress Cataloging-in-Publication Data
Porter, Elisabeth J.
Connecting peace, justice, and reconciliation / by Elisabeth Porter.
Includes bibliographical references and index.
ISBN 978-1-62637-235-1 (hardcover : alk. paper)
ISBN 978-1-62637-236-8 (pbk. : alk. paper)
1. Peace-building. 2. Transitional justice. 3. Reconciliation.
    4. Post-war reconstruction—Social aspects. I. Title.
JZ5538.C6685 2015
327.1'72—dc23

                                                        2015000925

British Cataloguing in Publication Data
A Cataloguing in Publication record for this book
is available from the British Library.

Printed and bound in the United States of America

The paper used in this publication meets the requirements
of the American National Standard for Permanence of
Paper for Printed Library Materials Z39.48-1992.

5 4 3 2 1

Contents

Preface

Why am I interested in the themes of peace, justice, and reconciliation? I have always steered clear of aggressive conflict, and even as a child I had a strong interest in justice and supporting the struggling underdog, even if it was a losing sports team. But it was through living and working in Northern Ireland for more than eight years at different stages of the conflict and ceasefires, during the negotiations that led to the 1998 Good Friday Agreement and afterward, that I became interested not only in conflict, but importantly, in how to move toward peace. As a research director at INCORE, an international conflict research center at the University of Ulster, I engaged with a wide range of local peace activists, both ex-combatants and aspiring politicians from other conflict-affected countries, and peace practitioners. I learned what it means to live in a society where sectarianism, bitterness, and deep hatred threaten to crush those who are working for peace. I also learned how inspiring peace activists are at both grassroots and political levels, even when their own lives and those of their families are in danger because of their activities. Since returning to Australia, much of my research has been on women, peace, and security in the Asia Pacific region. I have met people living in this region who courageously take a bold stance on peace and security that goes against the status quo and makes their lives risky. Their life narratives grip me. Their commitment to making a difference in diverse communities is moving. I am a strong advocate for peace, justice, and reconciliation.

Many books have a focus on "war and peace." This book has an explicit focus on "peace and war." This deliberate emphasis helps us to rethink how we might respond as concerned citizens—students, researchers, members of community groups or nongovernmental organizations (NGOs)—to some of the pressing issues of the twenty-first century. Prioritizing peace over war presupposes that, despite the massive tensions and violent conflicts raging in different parts of the world, it is possible to work toward dialogue, coexistence, peace agreements, and eventual reconciliation. This work is never easy. However, it is my firm belief that peace with justice is possible when there is open dialogue and sufficient mutual respect between parties. Antagonistic, sectarian, and hostile relationships dominate conflict zones, but I believe that it is possible also to analyze what is needed to develop sufficient trust between former opponents for reconciliation to begin. Thus my chief goals in the book are twofold. One goal is to highlight ways in which peace, justice, and reconciliation are interconnected. My position is idealistic, but I offer reasons why I am optimistic about individuals, groups, organizations, and nations working cooperatively to build a more peaceful, just, and secure world where relationships can flourish. And it is through providing examples where peace, justice, and reconciliation come together that my second goal emerges. I seek to show how, in understanding peace narratives and in exploring the stories told about what happens when people actively work to build peace and justice, typical assumptions about peace and war are challenged. In drawing on stories to highlight fundamental peace concepts, I maintain that the immense richness of people's experiences springs to life.

In connecting peace, justice, and reconciliation, I draw on a wide range of disciplines as part of interdisciplinary peace and conflict studies and transitional justice. I have taught courses on "peace, war, and international politics" in two Australian universities since 2000 and a course on "peace, justice, and reconciliation" since 2011. While the theories that I present in those courses help students to understand and interpret conflicts, it is the stories I tell about fighters for peace that bring the courses to life. In anonymous feedback surveys, students stress how much they gain from listening to my firsthand experiences. These include my research in troubled zones and stories about the amazing people I have met at conferences or through fieldwork. I have also gained enormous insight from listening to the stories told in class, particularly by refugees studying in Australia. Coming from war zones, many of these individuals spent long periods in refugee camps. Some received education there, others did not. Most were separated from family, and all lost loved ones. Throughout this book, I highlight the impact of such stories and first-person narrative statements on diverse individuals and groups in shedding new light on theoretical interpretations of peace, justice, and reconciliation.

* * *

A book takes a long time to write. During that time, reading, experiences, discussions, and reflections abound. I pay tribute to the wonderful community of scholars who produce thought-provoking literature on the topics written about in this book. Students at Southern Cross University and the University of South Australia who have taken my courses on these topics have inspired interesting reflections and lively debates. Often, it is their questions or skepticism about my optimism that peace can prevail over destructive conflict that has triggered the most useful ways to clarify my thoughts. Lynne Rienner is an excellent publisher to work with. I appreciate her bold clarity and encouragement of independent thought. I am grateful to the University of South Australia for a Division of Education, Arts, and Social Sciences research fund, which assisted the progress of this book. The fund enabled me to gain perceptive research assistance from some excellent students: Zöe Darling, Elise Fantin, Phoebe Haynes, and Shari Reid. My sincere thanks also go to Kate Leeson, formerly at the University of South Australia's Hawke Research Institute, for providing insightful editorial advice. My greatest thanks always go to Norman Porter, my dearest friend, creative cook, soul mate, and loving supporter of my writing endeavors.

1

Connecting Peace, Justice, and Reconciliation

Are peace, justice, and reconciliation connected? Certainly, it is difficult to talk about one without talking about the other. I argue in this book that peace, justice, and reconciliation are bound intricately. Rather than adopting a conventional approach of starting with theories of peace, justice, and reconciliation to explain practices that occur in conflict societies, I explore what happens to our understanding of these concepts and practices when we begin with a real-life story, such as someone's account of experiencing injustice, or another person's sense of feeling that they are moving closer to being reconciled with their former enemy.[1] Can people's narratives illuminate understandings of peace, justice, and reconciliation? I suggest that they can. This starting point of a personal story puts the spotlight on the human effects of peace, justice, and reconciliation for people in myriad conflict situations. Theory comes alive. Personal accounts of experiences of peace, justice, and reconciliation show the extent to which these concepts and practices are connected. In this chapter I show how wars have changed the way we understand peace, justice, and reconciliation, making their interconnections fascinatingly complex. I outline a range of ways to define peace and justice and explain why I defend broad notions of peacebuilding. I situate the book within transitional justice contexts and stress the need for a just peace.

How Have Wars Changed?

Individuals' experiences in conflict-affected countries where there has been violent political conflict and armed aggression, or combat between the military forces of states or warring groups, has changed as the nature of wars have changed. Civil wars between opposing groups in the same country and fighting by rebels against the government break out more frequently then wars between states. Violent conflicts within states "now make up more than 95 percent of armed conflicts" (Mack 2005: viii). Since 1900, at least 750 armed conflicts have been waged, and between 1989 and 2008 only 7 of the 124 active armed conflicts were interstate warfare; the rest were civil wars within states (Kegley and Blanton 2010: 377, 378). War is defined as "an armed conflict with at least 1,000 battle-related deaths in a given year" (Bastick, Grimm, and Kunz 2007: 23).

The record of war is alarming. *Peace and Conflict 2012* is a ledger that examines the drivers of wars, regime collapse, and the prospects of rebuilding states. The ledger shows that, since the end of the Cold War, approximately half of the civil wars "ended in negotiated settlements and power-sharing," but stalemate or defeat are common (Hewitt, Wilkenfeld, and Gurr 2012: 2). The challenges of living in failed or failing states where the government does not govern effectively are enormous. The consequences include having politicians who mismanage policies, are corrupt, and sometimes endorse military coups, or having a dictator who has ruled for so long that citizens defy longtime repression to rebel and large-scale civil strife erupts. As a consequence of living in a failed or failing state, as well as enduring the ongoing violence, basic needs of citizens like food, water, shelter, healthcare, education, and security are not met. Instead, there are massive economic repercussions, including costs often borne by neighboring states, some of which are failing states themselves. The authors of the peace and conflict ledger had not foreseen the wave of mass protests that flowed through countries in the Middle East and North Africa from the spring of 2011 and led to instability and, in some cases, significant regime change. Africa remains a serious concern in terms of the risks of instability. "Of the 46 African countries covered in the ledger, 20 (43%) qualify for the high or highest risk categories" (Hewitt, Wilkenfeld, and Gurr 2012: 5).[2] One danger of the growth of the number of failing or nearly failing states is the likelihood that civil wars lead to waves of refugees and internally displaced persons who struggle with corresponding outbreaks of disease and famine.

The nature of these wars has changed. Politically, since 1945, we see the rise of what Mary Kaldor (2007) calls "new wars," where traditional distinctions between war, organized crime, and large-scale violations of human rights are not easily drawn. In these wars, the conditions that contribute to an escalation of violence, namely "fear and hatred, a criminalized economy that profits from violent methods of controlling assets, weak illegitimate states, or the existence of warlords and paramilitary groups," become more pronounced during and after periods of violence (Kaldor 2007: 185). Typically in these wars, ethnic and religious differences are more important than political ideology. Also, civilian casualties and forced displacement increases, and in the breakdown of state authority, the distinction between combatants and sympathizers blurs. Further, former warlords or rebel leaders often gain political positions in transitional governments as part of the compromises needed to gain a political settlement. Their positions mock their victims, who remain in positions of powerlessness and intense suffering.

Undoubtedly, the war zone has changed from the battlefields of World Wars I and II to ordinary living spaces where people go about their everyday lives. These spaces include markets, villages, schools, churches, temples, mosques, public transport, theaters, and homes. Usually, these new wars draw on the ease of gaining small arms and light weapons such as pistols, handguns, rifles, and grenades. Gangs, militias, and paramilitary groups can use these weapons readily to conduct ambushes and raids, and children can use the weapons easily. Civilians make up a substantial number of casualties of contemporary violent conflicts, with about ninety civilian deaths to every ten military losses (Kegley and Blanton 2010: 509), a reversal of the statistics from World War I. The general focus in this book is on trying to understand some of the impact of violent conflict on people's everyday lives, and to show the way that war alters the social dynamics of communities. I focus specifically on the postconflict phase and the role of transitional justice within this phase. What it means to talk about "postconflict" is important, given that, even when conflict has officially ended, often a culture of militarized violence remains that particularly affects many women in households and villages.[3] I explain the postconflict concept below.

What Is Peace?

Having explained that wars typically are civil wars that impact harshly on local communities, I now explain the key ideas of this book. In this introductory chapter I provide definitional explanations for the key concepts and practices of peace, justice, and, to a lesser extent, reconciliation. These explanations are an important foundation to my larger goal of exploring their interconnections. For my purposes, the convergence of all three concepts and practices is both desirable and necessary for sustainable peace with justice and reconciled relationships to hold, for reasons that unfold progressively through the arguments I develop in each chapter. The complementarity of peace and justice is clear in the Nuremberg Declaration on Peace and Justice when it states, "Peace and justice, if properly pursued, promote and sustain one another. The question can never be whether to pursue justice, but rather when and how" (UN General Assembly 2008). My main argument is that peace, justice, and reconciliation are interconnected, and while bringing them all together is immensely difficult and rarely realized in full, the task is worth striving to achieve. Implicit in this argument is the view that degrees of enjoying peace with justice and reconciliation are to be valued, even if the realization is only partial. For example, there can be degrees of peace without justice, where the temporary lull in violence is a welcome relief and permits, for example, aid relief to be brought in, but the peace will always be fragile because of the underlying feelings of injustices that abound. Such fragility of peace is clear in a statement made by Carolina, a combatant with the Faribundi Martí National Liberation Front in El Salvador. In relation to peace, she says that "building it, making it, and not allowing it to collapse is very difficult to do. Peace is like something made of glass: if you drop it, it breaks" (in Bennett, Bexley, and Warnock 1995: 196–197). Similarly, justice without peace rarely is possible, because peace provides the conditions in which law and order can be restored and all forms of justice considered. Reconciliation, in the strongest sense possible, can only thrive in a context of peace, where former antagonists feel safe to come together for dialogue, but without justice reconciliation can never mean much because victims feel injustices deeply and old antagonisms prevail.

Why is it difficult to define peace? Part of the answer lies in the range of ways to understand peace. In 1978 Kenneth Boulding presented the idea of "stable peace," which is "a situation in which the probability of war is so small that it does not really enter into the calculations of any of the people involved" (1978: 13). Elise Boulding describes the active nature of "peaceableness" as a concept directed toward "shaping and reshaping of understandings, situations, and behaviors in a constantly changing lifeworld, to sustain well-being for all" (2000: 1). Influential Norwegian peace theorist Johan Galtung (1964) explains how understandings of peace have expanded from "negative peace" as merely the absence of war, armed conflict, or violence, which is always a weak or fragile peace, to "positive peace," which requires the resolution of root causes of conflicts in order to develop and maintain sustainable peace. Root causes of conflicts are multiple and include conflicts over ethnic rivalries, long legacies of mistrust, failures of earlier peace agreements, unfinished business of decolonization, high levels of human development deprivation, and fights for territory and resources. The effects of these root causes of conflicts are manifest at multiple levels, including political, cultural, economic, social, psychological, and human well-being. In order to realize positive peace, those root causes that lead to injustices need to be tackled. Galtung's view is that positive peacebuilding, as an active, ongoing process, is more than negative peace or the direct stopping of violence. It involves changes to indirect violence, such as when children are killed; structural violence, such as when children die as a result of poverty and malnutrition; and cultural violence, where violence feels normal and is accepted, given prevailing prejudice, ignorance, and discrimination. This expansive view of what is needed to realize peace is helpful because Galtung's emphasis is on finding the structures that can remove the causes of war and offer alternatives to violence.

Forty years on from these early influential views, Galtung (2004) suggests two opposed discourses about violence: the security discourse and the peace discourse. The security discourse assumes an evil party presents a danger, so strength is needed to deter it as a way to produce security as "the best approach to 'peace'" (Galtung 2004: 1). In contrast, the peace discourse is based on an unresolved conflict, a view of violence as an impediment to conflict resolution, and conflict transformation as "empathetic-creative-nonviolent; producing peace, which is the best approach to 'security'" (Galtung 2004: 2). These discourses produce contrasting paradigms that ask two different questions: Does security produce peace, or does peace produce security? In using the voices of victims and survivors of violent conflict to highlight multiple answers to these questions, the human implications of discourses and paradigms come to the fore. In the next chapter I make the specific link between human security and peace. Suffice it to say now that this link is important because, in addition to the global prevalence of conflict and insecurities, many conflicts relapse. Statistics on the frequency of relapse vary. Some argue that about "one third of peace agreements ending civil wars collapse within five years," and ensuing violence after failed peace agreements is often more extreme (Call 2008: 1). Other researchers suggest that "nearly 60 percent of all civil wars between 1946 and 2004 ended and recurred at least once" (Hewitt, Wilkenfeld, and Gurr 2012: 22). To prevent a setback into conflict, how is peace built?

Postconflict peacebuilding includes actions undertaken after the termination of armed hostilities. The main goal is to prevent a return into conflict through creating a sustainable peace. The point is to create gradually those conditions that ensure that there is no reason to resort to destructive means again. The postconflict stage of peacebuilding refers to the "long-term process that occurs after violent conflict has slowed down or come to a halt" and happens after formal peacemaking and peacekeeping (Maiese 2003: 1). It is an ongoing process, because the term "postconflict" is somewhat of a misnomer. "Postwar" may reflect the situation more accurately. During the postconflict period, despite an official end of hostilities, underlying antagonisms, sectarianism, tensions, and emotions of anger, bitterness, and hatred prevail, making reconciliation between former opponents a very difficult task.

Significant changes have taken place in the way the United Nations understands postconflict peacebuilding. In 1992 former UN Secretary-General Boutros Boutros-Ghali wrote *An Agenda for Peace*, where he referred to structural peacebuilding in postconflict societies as "rebuilding the institutions and infrastructures of nations torn by civil war and strife; and building bonds of peaceful mutual benefit among nations formally at war" (1992: 8). Boutros-Ghali distinguished between preventive diplomacy to avoid a crisis, peacemaking as a lead up to peacekeeping, and "postconflict peacebuilding," which he writes is the rebuilding of institutions, infrastructures, and relationships with an emphasis on preventing recurring conflicts (1992: 5). In 1995 he presented the *Supplement to an Agenda for Peace*, where peacebuilding involves broad "responsibilities in the economic, social, humanitarian, and human rights fields" (Boutros-Ghali 1995: 9). Former Secretary-General Kofi Annan in *Prevention of War and Disaster* writes that "postconflict peacebuilding seeks to prevent the resurgence of conflict and to create the conditions necessary for a sustainable peace in war-torn societies" (UN Secretary-General 1999: 101). The UN views peacebuilding as both preventative and as a postconflict necessity. Lakhdar Brahimi, in his *Report on Peace Operations*, acknowledges complex interrelationships between peacebuilders and peacekeepers (2000: 5).

Since the creation of the UN Peacebuilding Commission, convened in 2006, the idea of peacebuilding cuts across all sectors of the UN's work in international security, sustainable development, and human rights. This book's focus is on the complex nexus of these interrelationships. The point here is to emphasize that UN notions of peacebuilding embrace multiple sectors of activities that include political, legal, military, diplomatic, human rights, child protection, and gender issues, as well as humanitarian concerns. Indeed, some writers include a vast range of values, skills, analyses, and processes in defining peacebuilding (Schirch 2006: 66).[4] My emphasis is not to analyze these peacebuilding activities conceptually, but rather to recognize how these activities impact differently on victims of conflict, and thus to highlight how this recognition enlightens conceptual and practical understandings of peacebuilding.

Broad Notions of Peacebuilding

Further clarification of the reach of the discussion beyond UN definitions is warranted given the diversity of views on peace. Roland Paris is explicit: "Peacebuilding begins when the fighting has stopped. It is, by definition, a postconflict enterprise" (2004: 39). But violence and the threat of violence do not end when arms are laid down or peace accords are signed. The violence of a regime produces a general culture of violence, with significant impact on women and girls. The signing of peace agreements signals significant progress, but there are many different stages of transition, including security sector reform, political democratization, economic transformation, capacity building, legislative changes, rebuilding of social structures, healing, and varying degrees of reconciliation. The short-term goal of peacebuilding seeks to prevent the outburst or recurrence of widespread, systematic violence, while the long-term goal is to build the economic, legal, social, and political foundations of lasting peace. The best means to accomplish these objectives is open to question. Rob Jenkins suggests that the key contentions refer to the "when, what, how, and who—that is, the period during which peacebuilding takes place, the type of peace sought, the methods employed to attain it, and the key actors in the peacebuilding enterprise" (2013: 19). Expansive notions of peacebuilding underlie the examples used in this book, because they extend the ways through which we can see the effects of peacebuilding on people's lives. Additionally, an expansive view of peacebuilding that addresses multiple insecurities, including gendered insecurities, is "more likely to recognize women's informal activities as peacebuilders" (Porter and Mundkur 2012: 29), because much of women's peacebuilding activities tend to occur in ordinary everyday ways, rather than in formal, acknowledged settings.

John Paul Lederach also calls for an expansion of our understanding of peacebuilding to be "more than post-accord reconstruction" and understood in a comprehensive manner that "sustains the full array of processes, approaches, and stages needed to transform conflict toward more sustainable, peaceful relationships" (2004: 20). Lederach speaks of conflict transformation as a holistic approach to managing violence. This signifies an ongoing process of change from negative to positive relations, behavior, attitudes, and structures. Negative emotions can include anger, dehumanization, despair, destructive tendencies, hatred, humiliation, fear, and misunderstandings. "A sustainable transformative approach" works with multiple relationships "at the psychological, spiritual, social, economic, political, and military levels" (Lederach 2004: 75). With this approach, what it means to think of peace holistically "is not to argue that it will be achieved completely but only that its components are interdependent and require integration" (Philpott 2012: 5). Daniel Philpott's clarification is fundamental to my argument on the difficulty but desirability of bringing peace, justice, and reconciliation together. Lederach and Scott Appleby, in extending holistic conceptions of peace, maintain that "peacebuilding nurtures constructive human relationships" and, to be effective strategically in initiating constructive change, it must operate at every level of society, particularly across "potentially polarizing lines of ethnicity, class, religion, and race" (2010: 22). According to these authors, certain hallmarks of these constructive relationships rely on the encouragement of interdependence, support of transparent communication, and integration of "resources, programs, practices, and processes" (2010: 23). Mats Berdal (2009: 173) makes some similar suggestions when he highlights the need for sensitivity to the historical, political, cultural, and linguistic contexts within which peacebuilding takes place. Broad definitions of peace are geared to addressing structural causes of violence and are oriented toward creating revitalized relationships during long-term peacebuilding.

Hence, throughout the book I adopt a broad understanding of peacebuilding developed in an earlier work. "I argue that peacebuilding involves all processes that build positive relationships, heal wounds, reconcile antagonistic differences, restore esteem, respect rights, meet basic needs, enhance equality, instill feelings of security, empower moral agency and are democratic, inclusive, and just" (Porter 2007a: 34). This is a comprehensive concept of actively building peace as an ongoing process. It involves a vision of constructive relationships, an inkling of the possible, and I intend to argue that such relationships are a prerequisite for furthering reconciliation. Peace hits different people differently. Chairman Bishop Humper of the Tonkolili District, Sierra Leone, told an interviewer, "We can sense, we can smell, we can experience a peace. . . . The experiences of the ten-year civil war can never and must never be forgotten. But we can put the past behind us" (in Kelsall 2005: 380). Peace is not an abstract concept but an active practice that affects the lives of diverse people in varied embodied ways. As we will see, a focus on narratives shows how people interpret the concept of peace differently and practice peace in multiple culturally distinctive ways.

What Is Justice?

There are many faces of justice. Different cultures, religions, and eras have different ideas on what constitutes justice. Justice is explicit in most religions. For Muslims, the requirements of justice include being good to others. For Christians, there is the requirement to "do justice and love mercy." The question "What is justice?" is a central question in political thought. Other political ideas like rights, equality, and freedom are related to ideas and practices of justice. Conflict increases where there are injustices, inequalities, repression, and human rights abuses. In Plato's *Republic*, Socrates asks, "Is not justice the standard of human excellence?" (1971: Part 1, Book 1, 334)—that is, it is the way we judge good character. In Aristotle's *Ethics*, justice is defined as that which is "lawful and fair" (1977: Book 5, 1129a21–b6). Like Plato, Aristotle links justice to moral character because it "implies a relation to somebody else—justice is the only virtue that is regarded as someone else's good" (1977: 1129b30–1130a18). The importance of relationships in this Aristotelian notion of justice is central to the purpose of this book in highlighting how peace, justice, and reconciliation affect people's everyday lives and their connections with others.

John Rawls in *A Theory of Justice* takes justice to be the "first virtue of social institutions" (1972: 3). A public concept of justice is needed to regulate social cooperation. Where this regulation falters or is nonexistent, we readily find that "injustice is not just a *consequence* of conflict, but is also a *symptom* and *cause* of conflict" (Mani 2005: 25).[5] Dealing with justice is pertinent, particularly in transitional justice processes, where a society is trying to move out of its violent past into a new, just context. As Galtung (2004) explains, structural violence is a conspicuous form of injustice, which means there are correlations between the injustices that accompany poverty, environmental degradation, discrimination, exploitation, militarization, and violence. Like the expansive notions of peace outlined above, throughout the book I give broad-ranging attention to injustice and justice because of their massive and diverse effects on human lives. Also, as will become clear, people's experiences of injustice and what is needed to realize justice differ.

Yet there is good reason for caution. Richard Goldstone was justice of the Constitutional Court of South Africa, and chief prosecutor for the International Criminal Tribunal for the former Yugoslavia (ICTY) and the International Criminal Tribunal for Rwanda (ICTR) when he wrote, "One must not expect too much from justice, for justice is merely one aspect of a many-faceted approach needed to secure enduring peace in the transitional society" (Goldstone 1996: 486). The merit in securing justice lies in providing a procedure to expose the truth, thereby enabling a society to move beyond the pain of the past. Goldstone (1996: 488–490) suggests positive contributions that justice can achieve in postwar contexts. He suggests that the exposure of truth individualizes guilt, thereby avoiding any imposition of collective guilt. With this exposure, justice ensures that victims receive public and official acknowledgment of crimes committed against them. Public disclosure of the truth is essential to ensuring that history is recorded accurately. A systematic pattern of human rights violations can be exposed. Also, an official criminal justice system is needed to curb criminal activity. In the Nuremberg Declaration on Peace and Justice, "'Justice' is understood as meaning accountability and fairness in the protection and vindication of rights, and the prevention and redress of wrongs" (UN General Assembly 2008). Protection of rights and prevention of their abuse assists justice.

Transitional Justice

Differing ideas of justice come to the fore in transitional justice processes. The academic study of transitional justice began in the 1980s and 1990s with countries in transition from dictatorship to democratic rule, such as in Argentina, Brazil, Chile, East Germany, Greece, Hungary, Poland, Spain, Uruguay, and critically, South Africa. More recently, it focuses on countries emerging from violent conflict, such as the Democratic Republic of Congo, Liberia, Sierra Leone, Sudan, Timor-Leste, and Uganda. The objectives of transitional justice are twofold: to deal with the past in confronting the legacies of human rights abuses and human suffering, ensuring accountability for past injustices while maintaining peace, the rule of law, and democratic processes; and also, to move into the future, including fostering reconciliation.[6] The questions raised by Chilean playwright Ariel Dorfman sum up well some of the difficulties in achieving these objectives:

> How can those who tortured and those who were tortured coexist in the same land? How to heal a country that has been traumatized by repression if the fear to speak out is still omnipresent everywhere? And how do you reach the truth if lying has become a habit? How do we keep the past alive without becoming its prisoner? Is it legitimate to sacrifice the truth to ensure peace? And what are the consequences of suppressing that past and the truth it is whispering or howling to us? Are people free to search for justice and equality if the threat of military intervention haunts them? And given these circumstances, can violence be avoided? And how guilty are we all of what happened to those who suffered most? And perhaps the greatest dilemma of them all: how to confront these issues without destroying the national consensus which creates democratic stability? (in Harris Rimmer 2010: 5)

These are massive questions, highlighting the enormity of the scope in which people's lives are affected by the lies and injustices arising during violent conflict.

For the purpose of this immediate discussion, within transitional justice there are many different ways that justice is jeopardized. In periods of violent conflict, there is a massive breakdown of the rule of law; political manipulation of the legal system; corruption by lawmakers, law enforcers, and judges; and lack of legal redress for injustices and grievances experienced. Within a transitional justice process, creating the institutional framework for legal justice is an imperative.

There are also different categories of justice. *Rectifying justice* seeks to remedy the injustices that are the direct consequences of conflict, like abuses committed against civilians. *Social justice* addresses the structural and systemic injustices and distributive inequalities that underlie many causes of conflict. In *retributive justice*, lawful punishment of the perpetrator by the state is required. *Customary justice* involves traditional ways of dealing with conflict resolution and injustice. *Gender justice* refers specifically to ways to repair gender-specific damages caused to women, girls, men, and boys. *Restorative justice* accepts that court procedures alone rarely prompt a healing response, so it focuses on the well-being of the victim, and usually on reintegrating perpetrators of the abuse into community norms and events. Restorative justice processes see the community, the offender, and the victim as connected participants in the outcome of the justice process. My emphasis in this book is primarily on restorative justice, with its cultural variances, because it takes into account complex relationships that are a central component of reconciliation; thus fleshing out the differences in types of justice a little further is important.

Retributive and Restorative Justice

One argument holds that the only acceptable response to gross violations of human rights like genocide or ethnic cleansing is criminal prosecution and punishment—that is, retributive justice. The rationale is straightforward. Retributive justice deters abuses in the future. The Nuremberg Tribunal and the Tokyo Tribunal, as well as the ICTY, the ICTR, and the International Criminal Court (ICC) are examples of retributive justice. Retribution "reflects a belief that wrongdoers deserve blame and punishment in direct proportion to the harm inflicted" (Minow 1998: 12). Wilhelm Verwoerd, the grandson of Hendrik Verwoerd, the architect of apartheid, signed up as a member of the African National Congress and was a researcher for the South African Truth and Reconciliation Commission (TRC).[7] He maintains that people's everyday concept of justice is "a (passionate) protest against wrongdoing as well as a demand for rectification" (Verwoerd 2003: 253). Retributive justice is appropriate for crimes of genocide, war crimes, terrorism, and torture, which should be punished because of the extent of harm inflicted on others.

It might seem controversial to suggest that retributive justice can help reconciliation. Luc Huyse gives examples of how this result might occur through avoiding unbridled revenge, protecting against the return to power of perpetrators, fulfilling an obligation to victims in taking their suffering seriously, individualizing guilt rather than blaming an ethnic group or a political party or a clan, strengthening legitimacy in the democratization process, and breaking the cycle of impunity where crimes go unpunished (2003: 98). Yet sometimes punishment and prosecution destabilize a fragile peace settlement by provoking hostile subcultures and networks, and crippling governance. For example, in the early political leadership of the newly independent Timor-Leste, then president Ramos Horta and then prime minister Xanana Gusmão decided not to proceed with prosecution of the Indonesian militia as a priority, but rather to face the immediate, urgent practical needs of the majority of Timorese people through addressing the structural violence of poverty. Their assumption was that in prioritizing the need to improve the social conditions of poor people over retributive justice, reconciliation was more likely to be seen as a viable long-term option. However, this approach left many victims and relatives of victims feeling that past injustices hovered unaddressed.[8] Sometimes, justice is compromised or set aside momentarily for other ideals. By developing a holistic approach in this book, I seek to integrate peace with justice and reconciliation. Such integration is never easy, because sometimes peace or justice *are* more pressing prerequisites to reconciliation because people's lives and livelihoods are at stake. Nevertheless, I aim to demonstrate progressively why this integration is desirable: that reconciliation built on a foundation of peace and justice is likely to be more substantial than one reliant on peace without justice.

In contrast to retributive justice, restorative justice views violence as a violation of people's rights and relationships that entails an obligation to set things right. The emphasis of restorative justice is on acknowledgment of the needs of victims. In particular, restorative justice seeks to rebuild broken relationships and communities. Restorative justice requires perpetrators of injustice to be accountable by making redress to their victims for harms that they have caused. Restitution does not always happen, or it happens partially without properly fulfilling victims' needs. The emphasis of this type of justice is on restoring dignity. In international affairs, demands for restorative justice are a form of restitutive justice that arise in situations such as when nations seek the return of territory seized from them by acts of aggression, or states require reparations from a defeated enemy for losses incurred in fighting a war assumed to be a "just war," or people seek compensation for injuries done to them by the officials or citizens of another state. Restorative justice draws strongly on indigenous mediation-based ideas and practices from Africa, Australia, Canada, and New Zealand and constitutes an important paradigm shift, moving the emphasis from individual blame and punishment to restoration (or sometimes the creation) of relationships in order to forge new possibilities. In reconceptualizing crime, the victim, the role of the community, and the purpose of justice itself are all central.

Restorative justice responds to the shortcomings of criminal law that ignore or understate the victim and the social context. Traditional legal notions of impartiality tend to be blind to human differences. Yet justice requires judgments that demonstrate care toward both the victim and perpetrator of violence that are "principled as well as responsive to differences" (O'Neill 1993: 311). Obviously the nature of principled care toward a victim differs from the care of respect of basic rights that a perpetrator of violence requires. People who advocate the benefits of restorative justice seek to restore losses to the victim and to the community that result from crime. Sometimes this restoration occurs "by reconciling the transgressor to the victim and the community" through the active participation of all parties involved (Digeser 2001: 41). Attention is given to the victim who has been wronged. This attention requires a two-way process, where the offender expresses shame and remorse at the wrongdoing, and the victim takes some step toward forgiveness. As we see later in the book, regret and forgiveness are complex, and neither come easily. Restorative justice deals with the relationships between the perpetrator, victim, and community, contributing to the restoration and maintenance of peace in many ways. This type of justice establishes individual accountability, deters future violations, establishes a historical record, promotes healing, gives victims a means of redress, and supports a capacity-building approach to the rule of law (Kerr and Mobekk 2007: 4).

For harms that reasonably can be addressed in this way, there are good reasons to support restorative justice. The harms must not be so extreme that retributive justice is required. Restorative justice focuses on healing wounds; it is concerned with the humanity of the victim and the offender. Narrative storytelling is fundamental to restorative justice. Rina Kashyap suggests that restorative justice "identifies the opportunity to tell the story of what happened, as a primary need of the victim" (2009: 453). This storytelling emphasis is primary in this book. With stories told in a restorative justice context, the need for accountability for wrongdoing is recognized, but the target of justice lies in achieving a right relation between the victim and the perpetrator—that is, some degree of reconciliation. This rarely is easy, but its rationale is clear. Restorative justice embodies a standpoint that violence violates "relationships that entails an obligation to set things right" (Walker 2006: 87). While offenders clearly have responsibilities toward redressing injustices or being punished, with restorative justice, "The harmful act, rather than the offender, is to be renounced" (Minow 1998: 91). Building the connections between remorseful offenders and victims in forging workable ties across the community takes priority over punishment. In the next chapter I make the case more fully to explain how storytelling can play a central role in creating these ties.

Different views of restorative justice exist. For example, José Zalaquett, a member of Chile's National Commission for Truth and Reconciliation, interviewed thousands of relatives of people who were killed or who disappeared under Pinochet's regime and reported the following:

> Certainly, many of them asked for justice. Hardly anyone, however, showed a desire for vengeance. Most of them stressed that in the end,

what really mattered to them was to know the truth, that the memory of their loved ones would not be denigrated or forgotten, and that such terrible things would never happen again. (in Walker 2006: 88)

Similarly, Pumla Gobodo-Madikizela, a psychologist on the staff of the South African TRC, explains "the victim's resolve that 'I cannot and will not return the evil you inflicted on me' not only as 'the victim's triumph' but as 'a kind of revenge'" (2003: 117). This is a powerful resolution. The restorative justice approach can provide the context in which the courage that the victim needs in order to formulate such a resolution can arise.

Individuals respond to justice differently; hence, their different stories provide insight into the concept and practice of justice in postconflict societies. Researchers on motivations for justice in Bosnia and Herzegovina, Croatia, Iraq, Rwanda, and Uganda found that people's perceptions about justice are strongly influenced by a wide range of issues, including "experience of the violence, prior experience with those on the other side, beliefs in retributive justice, access to accurate information, cultural beliefs and practices, and identity group membership" (Weinstein et al. 2010: 39). Pertinent here is the impact of personal experience on views of peace and justice. The ethnographic studies of these researchers show that some victims believe that "the greatest justice for me would be to let me live and die in peace there where I was born," yet others state that "punishing criminals would bring satisfaction" (2010: 39). The chief point these researchers reiterate is that, if one fails to recognize what victims need, their unique differences are suppressed and their moral agency is diminished. For some victims, simply having their suffering recognized and receiving practical help with shelter, medical resources, and basic education is meaningful justice. Given the many different types of victims of conflict, there will be many different interpretations of what version of justice is personally meaningful. Through adopting a narrative approach to differences, explained more fully in the next chapter, I hope to show how the distinctions of victimhood and justice emerge in clearer form, because this approach highlights the personal need for particular types of justice.

Just Peace

Having briefly considered meanings of peace and justice, and particularly ideas of restorative justice, what does it mean to bring them together? Pierre Allan and Alexis Keller, in asking the question "What is a just peace?" respond that it is "a process whereby peace and justice [are] reached together" in conditions where parties recognize each other's identities, renounce some chief demands, and accept the need to abide by common rules that are developed jointly (2006: 195). Allan and Keller describe this process as a bottom-up approach whereby negotiators seek to build a common language about the recognition of different identities and each party is willing to compromise in the interests of the common good. In Chapter 8 we see how crucial this dimension of finding shared ground is to building reconciliation. In this accommodation process, participants seek to agree on the conditions for a fair peace in a way that all protagonists deem just. This process is always tough. Peace achieved in this way "is just because it is expressed in a shared language that respects the sensitivities of all parties" (Allan and Keller 2006: 196). A just peace is demanding; it expects a lot from parties that are more accustomed to fighting than agreeing. How might it be reached?

Allan and Keller outline four conventions that satisfy the requirements of a just peace. First, with "thin recognition" both parties recognize the other as fundamental to solving the conflict (2006: 197). This early step is significant in appreciating the common humanity that exists despite diverse narratives. Given that this step is taken by former enemies, its value cannot be underestimated. Second, with "thick recognition" all parties seek to understand the fundamental aspects of others' identities, akin to a mutual empathy.[9] The point of this stage is to reach "an intersubjective consensus of what each side profoundly needs to remain 'self,' and thus, satisfied, should be developed in a just peace process" (2006: 199). Again, this stage is demanding because it involves intense listening to the voices of others who previously have been ignored, ridiculed, or despised. The personal identity claims that are part of this thick recognition of all parties are a crucial aspect of subjective and intersubjective meaning. We form our own narratives about ourselves, but these narratives interact with how others understand us, and sometimes others' views conflict with our own understanding. Complicated narrative constructions are made up of the continual interaction of one narrative with others' complicated narratives. When parties that once were antagonistic are seeking a just peace, conflicting identities rise to the fore as each group tries to grasp "a minimal understanding of the internal support a proposed just solution would have" for each group (2006: 199). Often this thick recognition of differences does not occur and misunderstandings grow. Third, the "renouncement" convention involves all the concessions, costs, and compromises that are needed when vastly different parties begin to demonstrate respect for each other. Examples include obvious factors like territory, sovereignty, and power, and also symbolic issues such as "religious freedom, constitutional reform, and the role of language" (2006: 202). In examples such as Canada, Kosovo, or Northern Ireland, these factors and symbolic issues have justified violent disagreement for many, so giving them up or making compromises does not come easily. Fourth, just peace cannot simply be in the sentiments of the people, but its articulation needs to be made in the open public sphere with explicit settlements, legitimacy of behavior, and benchmarks to approve solutions.

In practice then, Sanam Naraghi Anderlini asks the question, "Can there be peace without justice" (2007: 186)? Her answer is clear. "Yes, it happens every day. Is it a lasting and positive peace? Certainly not for the survivors of violence. Justice is essential, but not courtroom justice alone" (2007: 186). Anderlini suggests that listening to, hearing, and responding to the voices of victims are crucial activities to furthering sustainable peace, which is my position also. In listening to diverse voices in the context of their life narratives, we hear that "justice pursued violently contributes to further injustice," but without justice, peace is unlikely to meet people's needs (Schirch 2006: 64–65). Articulating these needs is a localized matter. Western notions of peace and justice do not always translate well into different cultures. This notion of a just peace relies on a wide array of actors and endeavors, at all levels of society, and is directed toward dealing with the past, adjusting to the present, and revisioning the future. Each of these stages needs to be culturally appropriate. The end goal of peacebuilding is a just peace, which always is dynamic, "in which the reduction and management of violence and the achievement of social and economic justice are undertaken as mutual, reinforcing dimensions of constructive change" (Lederach and Appleby 2010: 23). Throughout the book I argue that justice and peace are not either-or options, but both are integral to building a sustainable just peace that is likely to contribute to meaningful reconciliation.

My arguments in the following chapters are bold in seeking ways to understand how courageous people work toward creating an often elusive just peace. Such a just peace is not easy to achieve, because "political requirements of peace" and "moral demands of justice" (Biggar 2003: 3) sit in tension, such as when there is an amnesty or a political prisoner is released. I hope to show that this tension is not a simple choice between peace or justice, but rather that the making of peace involves justice in order to draw closer to reconciliation. The underlying rationale for this claim is that remembering victims in their suffering is part of the practice of justice. This practice acknowledges fundamental human dignity, and I try to show that it is best understood by learning more about the actual stories that make up victims' life narratives.

As I explain in the next chapter, my emphasis in the book is not primarily on victims but on victim-survivors, in order to show how it is possible to overcome the victimhood of violence and contemplate reconciliation, particularly between former enemies or between a victim and penitent offender. By "victim-survivor," I mean someone who, despite severe suffering and harm to self-dignity, has experienced some healing and begun to deliberate and make choices about their particular fulfillment of capacity. I am leaving the meanings of reconciliation to emerge progressively throughout the book, and in particular in the final chapter. Suffice to say that postconflict reconciliation involves building or rebuilding relationships that are not haunted by old conflicts and lingering hatreds. At both individual and communal levels, reconciliation involves supporting meaningful collaboration between former adversaries. Trying to understand processes of reconciliation involves trying to understand the inner, emotive complexities of relationships between former opponents.

Intrinsic to my argument that peace, justice, and reconciliation are connected is an approach similar to Lederach's view of the moral imagination, which he defines as the "capacity to imagine something rooted in the challenges of the real world yet capable of giving birth to that which does not yet exist" (2005: ix). As he restates this simply:

> The moral imagination requires the capacity to imagine ourselves in a web of relationships that includes our enemies; the ability to sustain a paradoxical curiosity that embraces complexity without reliance on dualistic polarity; the fundamental belief in and pursuit of the creative act; and the acceptance of the inherent risk of stepping into the mystery of the unknown that lies beyond the far too familiar landscape of violence. (Lederach 2005: 5)

That is, I am suggesting that it is not specific techniques about peace and conflict, or prescribed methods of conflict resolution, that bring significant change to cruel conflict situations, but a willingness to step outside of typical, narrow structures to await the unexpected, and realize the creative and surprising outworking of human inspiration. Lederach suggests that, in relation to peacebuilding, this moral imagination is situated in daily challenges of violence and entails "the capacity to imagine and generate constructive responses and initiatives that . . .

transcend and ultimately break the grips of those destructive patterns and cycles" (2005: 29). He suggests further that the disciplines that form this moral imagination include "relationship, paradoxical curiosity, creativity, and risk" (2005: 34).

Each of these disciplines needs some explanation because they recur in the following chapters. First, the centrality of relationships contextualizes "the space of recognition" that "recognizes that the well-being of our grandchildren is directly tied to the well-being of our enemies' grandchildren" (Lederach 2005: 35). I contend that revisioned relationships are fundamental to reconciliation. Second, it is easy to draw simplistically on dualistic polarities of either-or categories in cycles of violence so that people are classified as being wrong or right, violators or liberators, enemies or friends, or oppressors or the oppressed. Refusing to be contained within these categories requires what Lederach calls a paradoxical curiosity that muses on the rich diversity that is evident in human complexity, and thereby sees the unexpected potentiality in people. I add that this complexity interacts with culturally diverse understandings of peace and justice. Third, activating the moral imagination requires "the provision of space for the creative act to emerge" (Lederach 2005: 38). As we see in the following chapters, these spaces are many and varied. Sometimes the space emerges unwittingly when the conditions are ripe. Generally, time, thought, and resources are needed to create rich spaces. Fourth, an element of risk is always involved in stepping into the unknown, of engaging with those who have a radically different perspective on life or are considered as an enemy. I maintain that without taking such risks, reconciliation won't happen or will be flimsy. I have outlined these ideas of the four disciplines that cultivate the moral imagination fully because they overlap with many of the arguments developed throughout each chapter.

How Is the Book Structured?

In this introductory chapter, I have set out the context for understanding the interrelationships between peace and justice in dealing with a traumatic violent past. Foundational to this understanding is acceptance of the multiple and contested definitions of peace and justice. For example, negative peace or the cessation of war is preferable to no peace at all, but it lies far short of a positive peace that addresses root causes of conflict and thus can be sustained. I concentrate on restorative justice rather than retributive justice because I give priority to victims in need of healing, and my focus lies on building or restoring reconciled relationships. Perhaps the most elusive concept to define is reconciliation. Given that the book's context is postconflict transitional justice, with its dual goals of confronting the legacies of human rights abuses and ensuring accountability, as well as moving toward the future in fostering reconciliation, I stress the relationship dimensions of these goals as they are manifest through diverse narratives. Transitional justice must deal well with the past in order to move into the future where reconciliation between former opponents can be visualized as possible. My main argument in this introduction is that peace, justice, and reconciliation are interconnected and, while enormously difficult to achieve, are worth striving for.

In Chapter 2 I explain why everyday stories of war can aid in an understanding of the relationships between peace, justice, and reconciliation. To explain this puzzle I elaborate on how a human security approach to peace and conflict changes our thinking. I show that it does alter the focus of attention from national security concerns to the security of people's everyday lives. In the main I highlight positive stories, not to underestimate the enormity of the horrors that abound in violent conflicts, but to show how women and men, boys and girls act in ways that overcome enormous obstacles of insecurity to build peace or to deal with their tragic past. Sometimes this agency is deliberate; occasionally it is unintentionally spurred by the experiences of conflict, when someone is motivated to transform their local situation, often for practical reasons like the need to open a marketplace or find shelter for people displaced by war. I am interested in highlighting the story behind contrasting acts of agency. A related purpose is to test how well theories of peace and conflict stand up in the light of such stories. I am building on Lederach's idea: "When we attempt to eliminate the personal, we lose sight of ourselves, our deeper integration, and the source of our understandings—*who we are* and *how we are* in the world" (2005: viii). This idea acknowledges the messy personal processes in which complex life narratives emerge. Each story of suffering and each story of breaking cycles of violence is part of a unique life narrative. This narrative understanding of human agency frames my arguments because it places the focus clearly on human security and lived experiences.

How war damages humanity is my focus in Chapter 3. I begin by exploring enormous central questions. Why does evil prevail? What exactly is the nature of evil? Why do crimes against humanity continue? Crimes against humanity are human rights violations so gross that they undermine our dignity as humans and for which redress in transitional justice is necessary. Some violations are not suited to restorative justice processes. Examples include genocide, ethnic cleansing, and war rape. Surrounded by such horrors, the majority of people can feel like victims, and thus I explore vulnerability, pain, shame, and guilt. In seeking to balance the stark awfulness of violent atrocities with the hope of justice and reconciliation, I look at what is entailed in calling someone a victim or a survivor. Clearly, the best way to respond to suffering is to work to prevent it, and the "responsibility to protect" principles are paramount. These principles confirm sovereign responsibility to protect citizens and defend an ethical obligation by the international community to protect life and human dignity, when a state fails in its fundamental responsibility to protect citizens. My main argument in this chapter—an obvious one—is that the evil of war creates multiple layers of suffering that serve as major obstacles to progress in healing damaged humanity in transitional justice contexts. This chapter sets up the case further for why strategies to develop peace, justice, and reconciliation are vital in order to respond to overwhelming suffering caused by war.

I look at the complex notion of truth in Chapter 4, exploring what happens in the process of telling the truth. Before focusing on what truth commissions achieve, it is necessary to explore obstacles to the truth, such as the refusal to acknowledge the truth, something that happens when people are stuck in the past or deny personal culpability. I explore the significance of different types of truth that lie behind personal stories, noting the emotional impact of telling stories in truth commissions and also in witnessing the telling of stories. Each truth commission shares the need to ascertain a historical record of the truth, but truth comes in many different forms. Truth is not merely presented from a victim's or survivor's perspective, because in most truth commissions there is also a public platform for perpetrators' accounts of their violations, whereby victims may become witnesses to the truth as well as narrators of their stories. No discussion of truth telling would be complete without some examination of the controversial issue of amnesties, which frequently are used to broaden the extent of stories told in truth commissions. An amnesty is a political pardon given in exchange for truth told about politically motivated wrongdoing. Generally, amnesties prioritize truth and negative peace while compromising victim justice in a broader call of reconciliation. Do truth commissions work? It depends on the historical context and the commissions' mandates. Different rival groups have different stories as to what happened during the violence. Listening to these accounts and dealing with the consequences are fundamental responses in moving toward a just peace and the possibility of reconciliation. My argument is that the more the local community is engaged positively with the truth-telling process, the more likely the community will realize the long-term benefits of truth telling as a means to furthering reconciliation. Telling the truth has a powerful snowballing effect.

In Chapter 5 I examine whether trust can be built in divided and conflict societies. Sometimes trust has never existed between opponents, so asking why it is broken down or how it can be rebuilt is not a clear-cut approach. There are numerous obstacles to building trust. Extremist nationalism and fundamentalist forms of religion contribute greatly to violent uprisings, so understanding why clashes between different ethnic and religious identities can lead to violence and radical distrust is important. I explore examples of "othering" such as occurs in sectarianism, where people hold such extreme views that everyone not belonging to their group is seen as other, a justification to exclude or fight them. The atrocities of othering are fundamental to people's wariness toward those perceived as the enemy. In depersonalizing the other, a terrible disruption to dignity takes place. Building trust thus requires a reciprocal process of dialogue and listening, which is initially awkward for its pure novelty; then comes the recognition of the value of difference, gradually overcoming fear of the other, and in the strongest cases of reconciliation, a celebration of difference. My argument is that building trust is a crucial first step toward a mutual recognition of difference. Trust takes time to build and is easily broken. Given the power of memory to hover, often unwelcomed, the embrace of difference is rare. It requires overcoming fear of the other and a willingness to compromise, a venture that is always risky.

I explore ethical issues surrounding apology and forgiveness in Chapter 6. Central questions in this chapter include the following: What is gained or lost in apology and forgiveness when the acts involved are so traumatic and distressing? Are acknowledgment, apology, and forgiveness all needed for reconciliation to occur? Obstacles to these practices include a desire for revenge or a refusal to show remorse. I offer some discussion of the significance of public, political apologies for acts of discrimination or offense that happened before political leaders came to power, but my emphasis is on trying to understand narratives of exceptional instances of individual apologies and forgiveness. I then trace steps that lead toward political forgiveness as well as fleshing out the relationships between acknowledgment, apology, and forgiveness. Undoubtedly, forgiveness is a gift, bestowed by the victim and sometimes withheld for understandable reasons. The potential healing power of forgiveness is crucial in rebuilding new relationships. My argument is that an apology can be a powerful restorative tool, and forgiveness can never be assumed, because it is like a peace offering. I show why acknowledgment, apology, and forgiveness need to be present in order for strong reconciliation to occur.

In Chapter 7 I address compassion, asking what role it can play in postwar and transitional justice contexts. This theme might appear surprising, particularly given that obstacles always remain in divided societies, where hard hearts and stubborn tactics are barriers to moving on to new relationships—hence the need to highlight those practices that might exhibit compassion, including giving examples of sympathy and empathy. Underlying my argument that practices of compassion assist healing for traumatized people is a defense of feminist ethics. Feminist ethics defends universal ideals of personhood, justice, equality, and rights, and a "particularized practice of care" (Porter 2007a: 43) that is focused on meeting the specific needs of individuals such as those who are seeking to build peace or recover from trauma.[10] I show that, against common thinking that relegates compassion to private, personal relationships, a compassion that combines justice and care can play a crucial public, political role in responding to the human cry for help in postconflict contexts.

I draw a picture in Chapter 8 of what it means to create reconciliatory spaces. I explore questions such as the following: What happens in reconciliation? What are reconciliatory spaces? Can these spaces accommodate justice and peace? To answer these questions I contrast differing notions of reconciliation. Throughout many of the previous chapters I discuss the ideal of reconciliation, but in this chapter I flesh out what it entails. Many different conceptual views exist on what reconciliation is, as do many different narrative expressions of its practice. I summarize four ways to understand reconciliation: as relationships, a process, a culture, and a spectrum of possibilities. I support Lederach's (2004) notion that we find reconciliation where truth, mercy, justice, and peace meet. If there is a space where we find reconciliation, the point is to search for and take advantage of this space. I draw closely on personal interpretations of what happens in these reconciliatory spaces to discover what is needed to foster them. It is important to pay close attention to cultural differences in meanings and practices of reconciliation. My argument in this chapter is that peace, justice, and reconciliation interact in complex spaces; the point is to work collaboratively to find culturally meaningful practices, places, and processes in which reconciliation can flourish.

A short conclusion completes the book. In it, I reiterate that my position is idealistic, but I offer reasons why I am optimistic about individuals, groups, and nations working cooperatively to build a more peaceful, just, and secure world. Like others before me, I make a case for giving serious consideration to approaches to conflict transformation "that stress win-win outcomes, reconciliation, and stable peace" (Hauss 2010: 7).

Notes

1. I refer consistently to peace, justice, and reconciliation as both conceptual ideas and also as practices that occur in everyday lives.

2. The countries at highest estimated risk for instability during 2010–2012 in ranked order are Afghanistan, Democratic Republic of Congo, Burundi, Guinea-Bissau, Djibouti, Ethiopia, Pakistan, Nigeria, Mali, Sierra Leone, Somalia, Central African Republic, Iraq, Mozambique, Chad, Zambia, Benin, Bhutan, Zimbabwe, Bangladesh, Haiti, Kenya, Gabon, Cameroon, and Malawi (Hewitt, Wilkenfeld, and Gurr 2012: 8). The list and order change every year.

3. I have expressed reservations about the use of the term "postconflict" elsewhere (Porter 2007a: 28–32; Porter and Mundkur 2012: 30), given the remaining culture of violence that prevails even when there is a ceasefire or peace process. "Postwar" is a more accurate term. However, given the wide acceptance of "postconflict," I continue to use it.

4. In the peacebuilding nexus, Lisa Schirch (2006: 66) lists conflict transformation; restorative and transitional justice; legal and judicial systems; environmental protection; human rights; humanitarian assistance; early warning responses; civilian and military peacekeeping; economic, social, and political development; education; activism and advocacy; research and evaluation; trauma healing; military intervention; and governance and policymaking.

5. Throughout the book, all quotations containing italics reflect italics in the source text.

6. David Crocker (2003) outlines a helpful normative framework called "Reckoning with Past Wrongs." He suggests that eight goals identify the ethical issues that must be addressed in reckoning with past atrocities: truth, a public platform for victims, accountability and punishment, rule of law, compensation to victims, institutional reform, reconciliation, and public deliberation. He stresses that, while these goals have prescriptive dimensions, they permit latitude in application to historical, local contexts.

7. As I write, he is working with former combatants in Northern Ireland.

8. See Porter (2012a) for a fuller account of these priorities in Timor-Leste.

9. These authors suggest that the liberal view of peace cannot always accommodate this notion of thick recognition. They stress that all parties must be able to understand intrinsic differences that need to be respected in order to remain true to oneself.

10. While feminist ethics is grounded in responding to the inequalities that women suffer because of their sex, my usage of it highlights the applicability of practices of care and justice by and toward both women and men. Feminist ethics is discussed explicitly in Chapter 7 but is implicit in the other chapters.

2

Why Are
War Narratives Important?

War, armed violence, and conflict affect people deeply. Increasingly, reliable political journalists highlight the human dimensions of wars, but many media representations of the daily horrors of violent conflicts are reported in a matter-of-fact manner as if they are a normal part of global politics. The television media may present several minutes of news on a celebrity wedding and then flash to a few seconds of reporting on the numbers dying in a hostage siege or a battle between warlords. Headlines scream about how many are killed in a bombing or how many children are killed at a school, but the human impact of the tragedy can get lost under the layers of political debate. We hear and read reports of numbers of casualties, but until something of the personal story behind the statistics is known, the factual presentation of war can hit the reader, listener, or observer as abstract, something from which we can readily distance ourselves. Once we know a little about name, age, gender, family relationships, and cultural and political context, our perceptions of what is occurring may change. Suddenly the person on the news is not just a civilian casualty but a person with a particular life narrative.

Not all media reports are dispassionate. A *Sunday Times* veteran journalist like the late Marie Colvin, writing from the besieged city of Homs in Syria in 2012, told her fellow journalists, "They are killing with impunity. . . . I should stay and write what I can to expose what is happening here" (in Pollard 2012: 15). Her final story told of the heartbreaking, desperate situation of families trying to cope amid sniper fire and exploding shells. Three days later she was killed, along with citizen journalist Rami al-Sayed, who posted eight hundred videos online

25

recording the atrocities occurring in Syria. His final message was directed toward the international community: "Baba Amro is facing a genocide. . . . I will never forgive you for your silence" (in Pollard 2012: 15). Journalists who bear witness to the devastation of war play a crucial role in bringing the distressing stories to the world's attention. When Colvin was asked whether the risk in doing so was worth the story, she replied, "Burned houses. Mutilated bodies. Women weeping for children and husbands. Men for their wives, mothers, children. Our mission is to report these horrors of war with accuracy and without prejudice" (in Pollard 2012: 15). She paid the ultimate price in doing so.

The central question that I pursue in this chapter is as follows: Why are war narratives important? The answer is precise. Simply because they pay attention to lived experiences. Specifically, I ask: To what extent does a narrative approach to understanding stories told from within postconflict and transitional justice settings expose aspects of human security and agency that would not otherwise be revealed in orthodox accounts? What do war narratives reveal? My overall argument is that through a narrative approach to understandings of peace and conflict, the particularized human security needs of war-traumatized victims become evident. What also becomes clear is the rich depth of resilience of survivors and their active agency. This chapter sets the groundwork for establishing the importance of war narratives in revealing lived experiences of working to build peace, beginning with highlighting human security.

What Is a Human Security Approach?

National security targets a nation's sovereignty, territory, borders, defense capabilities, reputation, and political institutions. Typically, academic books steer clear of the personal dimensions of war, with notable exceptions to be explained shortly.[1] In doing so, "Individual pain and suffering are concealed, and the atrocity of modern war, the awesome destruction of bodies by the power of modern weapons, becomes invisible" (Humphrey 2002: 47). Michael Humphrey's point is that casualty figures are important to note, but they often displace accounts of the actual, individual suffering. Undoubtedly, the emphasis on human security in international relations theory, development studies, and peace and conflict studies has increased since the United Nations Development Program (UNDP) began publishing the annual *Human Development Report* in 1990. This report is significant in drawing greater attention to people's particular plights. This report seeks to reinvigorate "the legitimate concerns of ordinary people [for whom] a feeling of insecurity arises more from the worries about daily life than from the dread of a cataclysmic world event" (United Nations Development Programme 1994: 22).

People often sense approaching insecurities and react to these intuitive feelings. Abrupt population movement is an indicator of an escalation of violence and can make people feel anxious. For example, in 1992 in the weeks preceding the outbreak of violence in Bosnia and Herzegovina, large numbers of Muslim women and children began scrambling from their homes, leaving to protect their families from danger. With the 1994 Rwandan genocide, there were early warning signals, the government imported arms and commercial organizations imported large numbers of machetes as farming implements which could be used as weapons. Rwandan president Juvénal Habyarimana's government let the world believe they were importing arms to protect themselves from insurgencies staged by the Rwandan Patriotic Front, while effectively arming a militia with machetes for the planned genocide. In 2001 in Afghanistan, an indicator of potential conflict brewing was the Taliban preventing girls from attending school. There is sufficient evidence to indicate that women's illiteracy compounds poverty, which is a significant driver in wars. Given that the battlefields of civil wars are everyday locations such as marketplaces, villages, and small towns, security and insecurity hit people directly.

An appreciation of human security is thus vital in responding to feelings of insecurity and in attending to people's needs. It also is foundational to establishing my case that a narrative approach to peace, justice, and reconciliation reveals deep insight into how violent conflict really affects people's lives. A human security approach responds to this insight based on several underlying principles. One is that individuals and communities sense when they are safe and also when they are feeling insecure; listening to people's stories thus exposes what is troubling them or what might assist in their safety. A second underlying principle of human security that builds on this first one is that listening to local accounts of concerns leads to a greater understanding of the root causes of insecurities. Chapter 1 showed how dealing with these root causes is essential for positive peace to develop. Prioritizing the attempt to understand people's narratives and their own understandings of insecurities makes it possible to see the multiple levels in which people feel unsafe and the reasons for such feelings. These reasons include the violation of human rights, all types of inequalities and injustices, poverty, disease, organized crime, political corruption, sexual or human trafficking, environmental degradation, all forms of sexual and gender-based violence, and the fear of terrorism. Validating all felt forms of insecurities goes far to recognize the common worth of human dignity. To act on these insecurities by intensifying prevention of violence and protection from violence strategies is to respond to the particularity of human security needs. Understanding war narratives leads to more meaningful responses. A human security approach is interested in individuals in their communities, while a national security approach is concerned with the much bigger picture and is not engaged with everyday lives.

John Paul Lederach (2004: 13) shows that, in situations of armed conflict when people feel threatened, they understandably seek security in familiarity, particularly in narrow, localized groups such as clan, ethnicity, religion, or regional affiliation. However, this identification often leads to violence against other narrow, localized groups, furthering insecurities. Also, security assumes different forms for refugees, displaced persons, raped girls and women, and maimed or traumatized individuals. For women with young children, finding security can mean obtaining practical remedies such as milk for babies or basic medical care for themselves. For displaced persons, security can mean finding out whether separated family members are alive, and if so, where they are. After essential survival needs have been met, security still takes practical forms such as access to education and skills training that lead to the security that comes with some form of employment or sustainable livelihood. Marlies Glasius and Mary Kaldor provide a strong ethical defense of human security based in the "right to live with dignity and security, and a concomitant obligation to help each other when that security is threatened" (2006: 8). The explanation of this defense connects a commitment to not do harm to others with the development of dignified policy decisions that restore security and are connected with furthering empowerment.

Heidi Hudson, who writes about "doing security as though humans matter," suggests that human security is "a critical project aimed at interrogating the sources of people's insecurity" (2005: 164). Personal feelings of insecurity come about through a wide range of experiences, including facing inequalities, injustices, domination, exploitation, and human rights abuses. Gender analyses of insecurity in particular attempt to rework understandings of security in such a way that they become "open to the voices of those who in fact experience insecurity in all its variations" (Hoogensen and Stuvøy 2006: 211). The extent of this reworking is significant, because women and men often have different experiences of insecurity, whether as combatants, former combatants, civilians, or peacebuilders. Hence, a "human security approach implies that *anything* that threatens security is a violation of human rights," which includes violations often "considered to be normal, private, or inevitable outcomes of war," such as partner abuse and war rape (El Jack 2003: 22). I contend that adopting a human security approach necessitates responding to differing ideas of insecurity, including different perceptions of what is needed to feel safe. Stories about insecurity and particularly about security help to reveal deep layers of understanding about the gender-specific, age-specific, and culturally particular ways that violence affects human lives. War narratives are important because they show these particularized differences.

Human Security Stories

Stories about what constitutes security emerge in a range of ways. Sanam Naraghi Anderlini confirms how women across the globe from all walks of life, despite different motivations and ideologies, often tend to adopt a similar holistic view of peace and security that is not defined solely in military terms but is "rooted in a combination of political, economic, personal, community, and environmental factors" (2007: 9). She maintains that many women link a personal peace—that is, a peace of mind—"to their need for a peaceful society predicated on principles of social justice, equality, rights, and responsibilities, and the most basic universal human needs: health, education, security, freedom of movement, and legal and political rights" (2007: 74–75). This understanding of peace and security is broad-based, consistent with a human security approach.

The peace table is one conspicuous place to address underlying structural causes of insecurity as part of progressing toward a peace agreement. For example, in talks between Israel and Palestine, politicians such as Hanan Mikhail Ashrawi and Naomi Chazan from the beginning unburdened themselves of "historical, existential, human luggage" in order to address the peace process openly (in Anderlini 2007: 76), bringing what Ashrawi calls "the underbelly of war to the peace table" (in Anderlini 2007: 78). A similar story could be told of the Northern Ireland Women's Coalition in the 2006–2008 peace talks.[2] Monica McWilliams and Pearl Sagar were key women who presented the human face of conflict to the peace negotiations. I highlight women's voices as documented in feminist literature because it has a keen eye for grounding the epistemological basis of research in lived experience, as a notable exception to abstract academic norms that depersonalize war's impact. Carolyn Nordstrom (1997) writes specifically of stories of war in Mozambique. Cynthia Cockburn (2004) worked with women across ethnic divides in Cyprus. Other feminist writers, whose starting point is the everyday experiences of women's lives, bring to the fore the direct impact of violence on women and girls across the globe (Anderlini 2007; Porter 2007a; Olonisakin, Barnes, and Ikpe 2011; Porter and Mundkur 2012). Olivera Simić writes of her "journey of memories, flashbacks, particular narratives, history, and conversations," trying to make sense of her experiences of the Bosnian war "by telling stories about it" (2014: 4) as a survivor of peace.

Then there are other significant authors like John Paul Lederach and Angela Jill Lederach, who, while not writing from a feminist perspective, are unafraid to "write from an intuitively adventurous and experimental standpoint" (2010: 14) when they write on lived experiences in local communities disturbed by violence. Lederach and Lederach's writings resonate with the arguments developed in this book, in the way that they present human security stories that shows the importance of listening to war narratives. They took on the challenge of opening pathways into an exploration of the unspoken and unspeakable. They sought insight into "the multifaceted nature of reconciliation and social healing" in both lived knowledge and local communities (2010: 9). They draw on a range of stories that are worth explaining.

Their first story concerns Morris, who was a child soldier and a commander in the Liberian and Sierra Leonean civil wars. Morris says that "facing the past is too hard" (in Lederach and Lederach 2010: 20), and to cope he built a farm where former child combatants nurture the soil, growing vegetables and fruit. Morris works with Jake, a former rebel, in using dance, music, drumming, and theater to tell the stories of war and displacement. Other stories tell how reconciliation requires long, engaged discussions. Lederach and Lederach present Christian and Muslim women meeting to form the Women of Liberia Mass Action for Peace Campaign in 2003. When then president Charles Taylor could no longer resist the persistent pressure from the women, he met with the rebel facilitators, but the women were excluded from the peace talks. When war erupted in Monrovia the women looped arms and refused to let the male negotiators out until the peace agreement was signed. Leymah Gbowee, lead organizer of this campaign, said, "We are all victims. *And we all have a Voice*" (in Lederach and Lederach 2010: 30).[3] The next story talks of Maria, whose husband "disappeared" from his coffee farm in Colombia. Years later, Maria's brother-in-law found his bones on the land. Maria's victimhood was established, an important status for verifying widowhood.

One of the points these authors highlight with these stories is the nonlinear nature of healing and reconciliation, which occurs in dynamic, unpredictable, fluid, and ambiguous settings. What this means is that textbook, tick-box manuals on peace and reconciliation can act as guidelines only. Within lived experiences there is a "seed-like quality of reconciliation" that draws on people's capacities for "survival, resiliency, and flourishing" (Lederach and Lederach 2010: 53). Sometimes, the seed potential of reconciliation withers or is not nurtured for all sorts of reasons. These authors suggest that "place, safety, and voice" give insight into the horrible reality of violence and the ability to demonstrate resiliency (2010: 58). The significance of place lies in people's need for "belonging and connection" (2010: 60) as a source of rootedness. The need for safety includes physical protection and a sense of trust. Victims of violence typically feel powerlessness and a loss of humanity. In reflecting and writing on such deep hurt, "We enter the terrain of the *Unspeakable*, the search for finding ways to name experiences and events that are beyond words and comprehension" (2010: 66). In this book I pay attention to this voice and unspeakable loss. In listening to what individuals say, or sometimes cannot say, about the impact of loss, displacement, torture, maiming, and death of loved ones, the human cost of conflict becomes powerfully manifest. Yet there are also stories of great courage, with individuals and community groups demonstrating successful stories of building peace (van Tongeren et al. 2005).

Human security "stories offer insights that are missed in forensic reports" (Verdeja 2009: 37), which document quantifiable facts. Consider the story of Chanrithy Him in the aftermath of a Khmer Rouge attack on her town in 1975. She describes in blunt, vivid imagery what she saw and smelled. "I am nine years old. Never have I seen so much death. For a moment I am hypnotized and spellbound by the ways these soldiers have been killed," and then she becomes dizzy and vomits (in Verdeja 2009: 37). This is not merely one particular war narrative; the story connects with broader narratives to deepen an understanding of the Cambodian genocide. The takeaway point is, "Stories matter. They have gravitas; they are grave. They have weight. They are concrete. They materialize policies, institutions, relationships, and identities that circulate locally and globally, anywhere and everywhere" (Cobb 2013: 3). For example, as Sara Cobb explains, the stories told by Israelis or by Palestinians are not merely sets of words but stories that are told, retold, and reformulated, not only about complex conflict issues, but also about essential aspects of life and legitimacy. The complexity surrounding these stories is replicated in many conflicts, but in culturally different ways.

On the global stage, the post–September 11, 2001, "war against terrorism" "rests on the (rather incomplete) story on either side about the Other" (Cobb 2013: 4). The West creates its story about the "enemy" and why "they" hate us and views the largely undefined category of "Muslim terrorists" in places like Afghanistan, Gaza, Iraq, and Southeast Asia as opponents. "In a terrible cycle of irony, the narratives create the evidence for their own presence and persistence" (2013: 4), and stereotypes are uncritically cemented. However, while there have been attempts to understand the heart and mind of the other, Cobb argues that diplomacy does not focus enough attention on the way the dynamics of cultural narratives shape conflicts and ideas on the other. For example, in the Niger Delta region, with its interplay between militias and multinational oil companies, criminal, social justice, environmental, and multiple ethnic narratives all struggle for legitimacy along with local, national, and international actors. There are competing and banished narratives where "violence fills up the spaces where words are not allowed" (2013: 5). Stories form intersecting narratives. In this book I do not view the stories that individuals tell about self and other as simply the interpersonal, everyday accounts of their lives, but as struggles for meaning and interpretation between conflicting groups in violent or postconflict contexts. In such conversations, power imbalances, misunderstandings, and ironies abound.

So far, I have used the terms human security "stories" and war "narratives" as if they are interchangeable. Abbott (2008) offers a useful distinction, where *story* refers to the sequence of events being told and *narrative* to the way the story is told—and, I add, retold, elaborated on, queried, and incorporated into individual life narratives as well as into communal narratives. But really I mean a little more than this distinction. I refer to *story* as an element of the broader narrative. That is, looked at holistically, our life narratives are made up of a series of stories. As social constructivism stresses, the social world is created through lived and told narratives. Our cultural context affects these narratives. The meanings that matter to us emerge through intersubjective contexts where narratives can contribute to the escalation of conflict and sometimes be a resource for its transformation. Hence, the idea of a narrative identity "is shaped by a subjective relationship to one's whole life story" (Smyth 2008: 75) that constitutes one's lived narrative. Storytelling thus is used increasingly in peace and reconciliation work as a way to respect speakers for whom conflict has had a major impact. We turn now to see how stories fit in a life narrative approach to understanding the interconnections between peace, justice, and reconciliation.

Why Are Narratives Important?

What is the importance of narrative in understanding peace, justice, and reconciliation? Narrative has always been strong in certain disciplines.[4] There is an increasingly interdisciplinary approach to using narrative as a central methodological tool in diverse research fields. "The narrative turn encompasses more and more disciplines concerned not just with story as story but with storied forms of knowledge" (Kreiswirth 2005: 380). What does this mean? The war narratives cited in this book are stories about particular people in specific social and cultural contexts. They are brief anecdotes or first-person statements about what it means to suffer war trauma and, importantly, to move from victimhood to being a survivor, with hope for a better future. These short statements of first-person reflections, or of someone else's reflections, tell tales of people's everyday lives.[5] While narrators have an individual interpretation of their personal stories, the spoken, or in this case written, word is open for interpretation. Written narratives act as imaginative prompts because "the narrative does not speak for itself but needs to be articulated through our reading/engagement with it" (Wibben 2011: 27). Different readings of the narrative will occur, but this is not a worry, because there are different types of engagement with the narrative. Each engagement has the potential to expose novel ways of viewing the story. Some readings resonate with the narrators' meanings; others diverge drastically. They all contribute to different ways to understand war and peace.

People's stories are a stimulus for exploring what stand as obstacles to peace, as well as proposals for alternative answers to complex questions on the relationships between peace, justice, and reconciliation. This narrative approach validates the contribution of theoretical scholarship in responding to some of the crucial needs of the twenty-first century in addressing how divided communities can reconcile, and how peace with justice, while always difficult, is not impossible. Peace and justice are both understood within particular lived realities, where individuals and collective groups rework their own understandings of peace and security with justice to be personally and culturally meaningful. In prioritizing the personal, local, particular, social, and mundane everyday responses of individuals and communities, the limitations of conventional abstract understandings of transitional justice become more obvious. Abstract accounts relate facts and theories, which certainly play crucial roles in deeper analysis, but the actual ramification of these accounts on people's lives does not come fully to the fore.

As Hannah Arendt put it so eloquently, "The story reveals the meaning of what otherwise would remain an unbearable sequence of sheer happenings" (1973: 106). Meanings occur in a context—that is, in a narrative framework. Arendt, writing of "the darkest times," suggests that often "illumination may well come less from theories and concepts than from the uncertain, flickering, and often weak light" that men and women kindle (1973: 9). Gaining this type of illumination is precisely the aim of the narrative framework I take in this book. Lederach uses a similar approach in *The Moral Imagination* (2005). He uses four stories that tell of the human ability to transcend violence. One story from Ghana is about creating a space for dialogue between representatives of two ethnic groups, another of Somalian women creating a zone of peace in the marketplace, one of Colombian peasants who pursued civilian resistance without weapons, and another from Tajikistan of dialogue between warlords and a professor of philosophy. According to Lederach the moral of the stories lies in finding that crucial moment that can transform a protracted conflict, when there is a glimmer of hope. As we saw in Chapter 1 he calls this moment the "moral imagination," which involves "the inherent risk of stepping into the mystery of the unknown that lies beyond the far too familiar landscape of violence" (2005: 5). The transformation of conflict into the hope of peace does not always occur, but I deliberately highlight examples where it does. Martha Minow also suggests that "between vengeance and forgiveness lies the path of recollection and affirmation and the path of facing who we are, and what we could become" (1998: 147). My method in this book shares a similar strategy of imagining what could occur in reconciled relationships, using a wide range of short stories from war narratives to bring to life conceptual understandings of peace, justice, and reconciliation.

Narrative Theory

Given that we are exploring the questions of how we can understand war narratives and why they are important, we first must grasp what is entailed in narrative theory. I extend the work of Sara Cobb's (2013) critical narrative theory.[6] Her motive in developing this theory is to go beyond interest and needs as the bases for peace negotiations, to stress "the stories that the extremists themselves would tell, the stories that require violence and the generation of fear" (2013: 11). While Cobb's emphasis is on the contribution of narrative to conflict resolution, mine is on understanding what lays behind, underneath, and enclosed within narratives of conflict transformation that contributes to realizing peace, justice, and reconciliation. What we share is the desire for a focus on the narrative that encourages "the development of an ethics of practice equipped to favor the development of stories that redress marginalization and anchor people's capacity for moral agency" (2013: 12). Through this notion of agency we can reflect deeply upon clashes between our desires and motives, and we "deliberate and make choices on the basis of reasons, choices that both express and determine 'who' we are" (Mackenzie 2008b: 9). In Chapter 5 I explain the importance of dialogue as part of these deliberations and the importance of recognition of the other in confirming different ethnoreligious nationalist and political identities. We will see that giving attention to the type of stories that are composed in a dialogue process provides a method for tracing whether recognition of the other is reciprocal and not merely used as an instrumental means of exchange. Cobb also contends that, while peace-making and peacebuilding ostensibly are aimed at relational development, the former can be co-opted by insurgents, and the latter, being associated with nation building, can too readily be aligned with the narratives of the occupying forces. Both would "benefit practically and ethically from a redefinition anchored in narrative theory, tuned to the features of stories that populate a given conflict" (2013: 13). I suggest that the benefit comes when narrative provides a lens to understand the meanings that anchor conflict, thus hopefully also supporting the changes necessary for its transformation.

A qualification is needed. Discourses also tell stories about individual, social, and political realities. A discursive approach focuses on how narratives construct meanings, beliefs, and identities. My approach is not a discourse analysis that problematizes and challenges the ways in which realities are accepted as real or assumes necessary power relations. Certainly, I accept that language in texts constructs meaning, so that social texts construct a version of reality. Texts "do not describe things, *they do things*. And being active they have social and political implications" (Jabri 1996: 95). A focus on stories and narratives and the construction of meaning necessarily requires an interpretive epistemology, one that is open. As stated already, this openness inevitably leads to different readings of the war narratives. How the reader receives published narratives varies. Those who tell or publish their stories of war trauma and loss cannot dictate how their story is accepted and interpreted. Given that narratives and discourses create and shape the meanings not only of war narratives but also of peace, justice, and reconciliation in intersubjective contexts, open interpretations of meanings enlarge the moral imagination, showing diverse ways to understand human security and meaningful peace.

Cobb argues for the importance of exploring the structure as well as the dynamic of conflict narratives; both affect the way people are captured in stories, because some stories are made by others, and often people "are victims of their own stories" (2013: 47). They become defined by one traumatic part of their lives. Stories have plots and themes and, importantly, characters. Parties to a conflict develop a narrative that anchors themselves in relation to their opponents. Alterations to the narrative can destabilize identity and relationships across networks of people. In Chapter 5 I explore the issue of identity more fully. Suffice it to say here that "identity is a question of how *others* understand what I am doing, as well as how *I* understand what I am doing" (Nelson 2001: 22). This relational aspect to conflict and to transforming conflict is my central concern. The narrative frame attends to the speaking voice in a way that ensures that the voice is heard and thus incorporated into peace agreements, justice frameworks, truth commissions, and reconciliation processes. Later chapters give attention to the unspoken, the voices that cannot or will not express themselves for all sorts of reasons.

Exploring how other writers use narrative theory in ways that affirm human security is also instructive. Kay Schaffer and Sidone Smith (2004) write of narratives of human rights abuses that demand attention to lives that are very different from our own. Schaffer and Smith give a wide range of examples that testify to diverse narratives. They frame the bulk of their stories thematically, as narratives told in five circumstances: the South African TRC, indigenous Australians who were part of the stolen generations taken from their families, grandmothers telling of forced sexual slavery in World War II, US prisoners who identify as victims, and stories from 1989 post-Tiananmen China. The stories they tell are of terrible degradation of human dignity. They write that storytelling in public plays a strong role in human rights activism, "contesting social norms, exposing the fictions of official history, and prompting resistance beyond the provenance of the story within and beyond the borders of the nation" (2004: 4). Sometimes the controversy of a story depends on the context in which it is told. It might be in a formal truth commission, tribunal, or hearing. Other times it can be part of media accounts, with tiny snatches of the story excluded that change the narra-

tor's entire rationale for relating the experience. Other times, the dia-
logic nature of the storytelling creates a different dynamic, particularly
when there are unequal power relations and the storyteller feels as
though he or she has had to suppress meaningful elements or has been
undermined in the process of telling the story.

Emotions accompany the telling and receiving of stories. Schaffer
and Smith list sensations such as "embodied pain, shame, distress,
anguish, humiliation, anger, rage, fear, and terror" and claim that emotive
stories "can activate interest, excitement, vicarious enjoyment, shock,
distress, and shame" (2004: 6–7). They offer a useful definition of "life
narrative," understood broadly "as an umbrella term that encompasses
the extensive array and diverse modes of personal story-telling that takes
experiential history as its starting point" (2004: 7). What they include as
life narrative is extensive and consistent with the narrative statements and
interpretations of the stories appearing in subsequent chapters.

Taking war narratives seriously as the first point of analysis
requires changes in intellectual approach. Judith Butler (2009) draws
attention to two aspects of this concept. First, there is an epistemological problem in the framing of lives. "The frames through which we
apprehend or, indeed, fail to apprehend the lives of others as lost or
injured are politically saturated" (2009: 1). Butler's viewpoint is that
how the effects of war are framed or outlined has political dimensions.
Second, there is an ontological problem about determining the value of
life as part of the framing. Who is framed, and why are they framed?
Her argument is that, prior to making social and political claims about
the need for protection and entitlements to conditions through which
humans flourish, "a new bodily ontology" (2009: 2) is required. She
suggests that this "implies the rethinking of precariousness, vulnerability, injurability, interdependency, exposure, bodily persistence, desire,
work, and the claims of language and social belonging" (2009: 2). Such
ontology is comprehensive. Her argument is that our bodily beings are
influenced by the historical and social contexts that "maximize precariousness for some and minimize precariousness for others" (2009: 2–3).
As a consequence, some lives are framed as valuable and others as
expendable. Those lives deemed valuable are protected, while those not
are dismissed cruelly as collateral damage. Butler defends the normative
need for a more inclusive, equal recognition of precariousness as a common state of human life. This recognition is more than saying that we
are all vulnerable and death is certain; it is also saying that we all
should be valued and thus require adequate welfare, broadly construed,
to be sustained and to enable our capacities to flourish.

The way that Roméo Dallaire, commander of the UN Assistance Mission for Rwanda (July 1993 to September 1994), frames his "story of betrayal, failure, naiveté, indifference, hatred, genocide, war, inhumanity, and evil" (2004: xvii) draws deeply on his point of view as an insider to the conflict. His account of the decisions and failings of the UN is vivid, and his story is framed within the inflexibility of the UN security mandate and the indifference of the world community to a country with no strategic value to any world power. As he puts it starkly, "Instead, we watched as the devil took control of paradise on earth and fed on the blood of the people we were supposed to protect" (2004: 7). He writes that on April 12, 1994, the sixth day of the slaughter, "The swift evacuation of the foreign nationals was the signal for the génocidaires to move toward the apocalypse," and Dallaire "didn't sleep at all for guilt" (2004: 291). Days later, walking around a makeshift hospital, he struggled with composure when really he just "wanted to scream, to vomit, to hit something, to break free of my body, to end this terrible scene" (2004: 303). Ultimately, this story is of the failure of humanity to respond to a call for help from fellow humans. Narrative theory illuminates the framing of multiple versions of the story, with Dallaire's rendering representing a strong personal account.

Truth commissions, to be examined more fully in Chapter 4, are an obvious example of the importance of human narratives. Teresa Godwin Phelps analyzes the potential merit of the storytelling intrinsic to truth commissions as a way to throw light on justice. She identifies seven aspects to this point. First, "Making stories of our lives is what we humans *do*" (Phelps 2004: 55). Storytelling is a human act, and through it we strive to make sense of our lives and our connections with others. While many stories speak of atrocities, they are part of life's vivid and often painful tapestry, and telling them helps to give order and meaning to everyday life. Second, she confirms that telling one's story goes some way to balance the harm done. Usually there is some therapeutic or cathartic dimension to telling the story of loss, fear, shame, or being a wounded soul. Third, such stories uncover and correct truths, although the truths may be disputed. Fourth, "Stories can communicate the experience of pain and suffering between people who normally cannot understand each other" (2004: 55) or who have no reason to communicate with each other. Fifth, storytelling has the capacity to restore the dignity of victim-survivors who are being listened to as equals. Sixth, the telling of stories can restore shattered selves, families, and societies, and creating a responsive community is part of justice-seeking processes. The final aspect highlights the way the collective narrative becomes part of history, even if it remains contested. I am arguing that stories understood within narrative frameworks contain enormous potential to illuminate what peace, justice, and reconciliation really mean to people.

Women's Security Narratives

I continue my case for the importance of understanding war narratives by considering their significance specifically to women. As mentioned earlier, feminist theorizing begins from women's experiences of everyday life. Accordingly, certain feminist scholars of security studies, peace and conflict studies, and transitional justice use differing versions of narrative theory. A feminist approach to security narratives differs from traditional international relations approaches. Traditional security narratives revolve around the state, the protection of territory, and sovereignty. These narratives were crucial to Cold War thinking in that "we behaved as though there were a war between East and West, acted out through war games, exercises, military plans, hostile rhetoric, espionage, and counter-espionage" (Kaldor 1991: 321). In challenging orthodox security narratives, and in particular their often taken-for-granted nature, feminist and other human security approaches seek to humanize security narratives by honing in on the experiential nature of insecurity and injustice. In doing so, gender-appropriate responses can be made to improve security and justice.

An early feminist theorist to draw on the personal in this way was Carolyn Nordstrom. In writing of her experiences in war-torn countries, she saw how the realities of war shape the context in which identities form. In investigating the impact of war on people on the front lines, Nordstrom writes that the local Mozambique people "insisted that I understand the nature and culture of violence, not as it was fictionally portrayed in media and literary accounts but as they experienced it" (1997: 4). Violence is experienced as a profoundly personal event, affecting the body, mind, self-identity, and personhood. Violent turmoil unsettles identities, particularly for those who are displaced, seeking asylum, are in exile, or have experienced violent abuse. Schaffer and Smith (2004: 18) explain,

> Such dislocations of identity unsettle psychically experienced understandings of time (the before, the now, the possible future), space (the old place, the new place), subjectivity (the me I used to be and the me I am becoming), and community (the ones to which I used to belong and the ones of which I am now a member).

Storytelling enables people with complex and often confused identities to make sense of their lives, both past and present, although it is not a panacea that assists all war-traumatized people. However, for many, telling stories assists in formulating a narrative coherence. The arguments developed in this book highlight how to foster the conditions needed to move beyond dislocated, traumatized selves toward healed selves rooted in peaceful communities.

This goal is similar to that of Hilde Nelson, who argues that "because narratives are narratively constituted and narratively damaged, they can be narratively repaired" (2001: xii). She suggests that "identity-constituting counterstories" (2001: xii) can resist the harm of belittled moral agency by replacing degrading stories with ones that value lived experiences. Counterstories permit a retelling of a story in such a way that they reveal the extent to which an individual is a moral agent, worthy of respect. Typically, they are told in a community of choice as stories of self-definition. The purpose of these counterstories is to repair identities damaged by oppression and violence. In pulling apart the narratives that construct a damaged identity—and these can be stereotypes, sectarian stories, or myths about the other—and by "replacing them with a more credible, less morally degrading narrative" (2001: 186), damaged identities can be repaired through the freedom of agent self-expression. Nelson describes four key questions that anyone who adopts a narrative approach to selfhood and ethics must answer. First is a question about the narrative act and what is done with the story. Second is the genre and determining the kind of story being told. Third is a question about the narrative agent and discerning what they do with the story. Fourth, the important question is why the story needs to be told, to explore the moral purpose of the story. For example, a woman who has had a baby through war rape and who has been ostracized by her community for bearing a child of a mixed ethnicity can, in telling her counterstory of her curious affection for her child, be restored as a woman of worth. Of course, she may still be ostracized from the community, but her counterstory might give her the courage to care for her child and seek support. A combatant who has only been known as an aggressive fighter can start telling a different story about him- or herself, a story about someone craving education and a different way of life. This person needs to demonstrate personal change for the counterstory to be credible. This narrative approach situates people as active agents who rely on other moral agents to contribute to restoring their identity process.

Storytelling is a culturally familiar tool for men and women, but it seems to provide a space particularly for women who have experienced violations against themselves during and after war to express their feelings openly and share their traumatic experiences. Women are subjected to specific acts of violence during conflict, and when subjected to the same violence as men, women are affected differently due to the preexisting social, economic, and cultural meanings surrounding gender. Nancy Apiyo (2012), working with the Justice and Reconciliation Project's Gender Justice Department, explains how storytelling has been pursued in Uganda as a means of encouraging women to speak out. Courage is important; many women from all war zones stay silent due to the difficulties and fear in discussing sexual violence. Storytelling provides an important platform for women seeking reparations. When asked what kind of reparations they desire, most women ask first for basic needs for people close to them, and only second for redress for themselves. Many women who have suffered continue to put the needs of family members ahead of their own needs. Similarly, many women's stories talk about the experiences of their male relatives or children, rather than their direct and indirect suffering during conflict. I consider in other chapters the reasons for this recurring tendency.

To overcome any aversion to sharing personal stories, a body-mapping exercise was conducted in Uganda, whereby violated women put marks on a drawing of a woman's body in the places where they were physically, psychologically, mentally, spiritually, or socially hurt during conflict. This process allowed the women to discuss the sources of their pain. Storytelling permitted the women to discuss openly being subjected to forced marriages with older men, giving birth to children whom they raise without support, sexual crimes perpetrated against them, rapes, beatings, and difficult childbirth. The women also spoke of the trauma they faced upon returning home after being displaced by war or returning as former combatants. Storytelling gives women the confidence and courage to open up about their experiences, empowering many despite the atrocities they have faced. It provides opportunities to present counterstories that often defy culturally gendered expectations. During storytelling, women in Uganda expressed the desire for reparations to include the payment of their children's school fees, compensation for the physical ailments they suffer, and compensation for the time wasted while they were displaced. The women also want the truth about the war, acknowledgment from the government about their experiences, and an apology from the government for not protecting them during the conflict. For these women, reparations are an important mechanism for healing, reconciliation, and obtaining justice. One Ugandan woman expressed her desire for monetary reparations in an interesting fashion when she suggested that the government should pay her for the "time that was wasted that led to our being illiterate" (in Apiyo 2012).

Here I seek to show, as Annick Wibben also expresses it, that "narratives are essential because they are the primary way in which we make sense of the world around us, produce meanings, articulate intentions, and legitimize actions. . . . As such, both the *content* and the *form* of a narrative are crucial" (2011: 2). The storyteller reveals a lot about the content and form of the individual, society, and culture. Stories are always told in a context. Wibben calls on Hans-Georg Gadamer's (1976) idea of the hermeneutic problem: How do we interpret meaning? The task of philosophical hermeneutics is ontological, throwing light on the conditions that underlie self-understanding and interpretation. As Gadamer puts it, "Only the support of familiar and common understanding makes possible the venture into the alien, the lifting up of something out of the alien, and thus the broadening and enrichment of our own experience of the world" (1976: 15). In the process of questioning and answering, new meanings are articulated. Questions about narratives are always contextual and contested, and the answers are open to different cultural and philosophical interpretations. The written narrative shapes an understanding of the spoken question and answer.

Having established the importance of a narrative approach to human security, we turn now to some further examples of lived narratives.

What Are Lived Narratives?

This chapter asks the following question: Why are war narratives important? A good way to answer is to pursue a further question: What is the nature of the lived experience of war narratives? That is, what story do people tell about their experiences of war? Albie Sachs, who was placed in solitary confinement for his work in the South African freedom movement, lost an eye and an arm from a bomb placed in his car by South African security forces. He went on to become a judge in the South African Constitutional Court. In referring to the South African TRC, he writes,

> It was seeing the faces, hearing the voices, noting the tears of the victims, and also the crying of the perpetrators as they acknowledged, at least to some degree, their brutal conduct, and now sought amnesty. It was real. . . . It was Sergeant So-and-so. It was Mrs. So-and-so, speak-

ing about her son who had come home with his hair falling out, his
poisoned body dying. (Sachs 2009: 24)

The point Sachs makes here is that the TRC, in paying attention to
accounts of activity and suffering, raised the question of "how can people do these things to other people" (2009: 25). Arendt, writing in an
earlier and different context, asks a similar question: "Should human
beings be so shabby that they are incapable of acting humanly unless
spurred and as it were compelled by their own pain when they see others suffering" (1973: 23)? These poignant questions underlie the rationale for the somewhat unorthodox methodological approach I adopt in
this book. I place high priority on the importance of stories told about
war narratives from diverse contexts to illuminate varying understandings of peace, justice, and reconciliation. In drawing attention to the
lived experiences of those affected by violence, loss, and grievances, I
flesh out why an understanding of healing, sustainable peace, meaningful justice, and reconciliation is so vital. To give language to pain
"remains the task, always, of human rights narrative and discourse"
(Baxi 1999: 126). Upendra Baxi draws attention to three Hegelian
moments: the abstract universality that accepts the dignity of all human
beings; the abstract particularity necessary to differentiate from the
abstract notion of the human, such as women's rights as human rights,
rights of indigenous peoples, and the rights of children and migrants;
and the concrete universality where rights are embodied in individual,
culturally differentiated human experiences.

As I have stated already, stories of war pain undoubtedly raise emotions. It is hard to respond to such stories without feeling anger at injustices, grief at conspicuous loss, terror of the unknown, fear of violence,
and deep pity, sympathy, empathy, and compassion toward human suffering. For example, in reflecting on wars in Mozambique, Sri Lanka,
and Somalia in 1988, where Nordstrom's friends were killed, strangers
were massacred, and villagers obliterated, she writes that "the words
and the emotions of the survivors flowed through me like a river that
never seemed to end, flooding with new violences upon old" (1997:
xvii). Responding to such emotions is fundamental to empathetically
listening to stories—listening not just to the factual details of what has
occurred but to the underlying nuances, variable tones, confusing ambiguities, and contextual particularities. When Desmond Tutu was asked
what kind of people he would like as truth commissioners, he replied,
"People who once were victims. The most forgiving people I have ever
come across are people who have suffered—it is as if suffering has

ripped them open into empathy. I am talking about wounded healers" (in Krog 1999: 17). We cannot generalize from Tutu's statement. As Chapter 6 shows, many people who suffer war trauma cannot forgive those who abused them. Tutu's point is that careful listening needs sensitivity to human suffering.

Many stories give accounts of experiencing the horrors and traumas of war. However, other stories reflect the ability to overcome the agonies of violent affliction so as to progress toward a new future. Memory takes a significant role in such progress. For some victims, "Memory is a means for sustaining the quest for justice," but perpetrators of abuse often use memory "as a tool of justification" to rationalize further barbarous actions (Amstutz 2005: ix). Jean Bethke Elshtain usefully discusses a concept of "knowing forgetting," which is a coping mechanism, "a way to release present-day actors from the full burden of the past in order that they not be weighed down by it utterly" (1998: 42). One example is Des O'Hagan, who, as an academic in Northern Ireland in 1971, was interned for a year and a day in Long Kesh under the Special Powers Act. He wrote from prison, "There is to my mind a warmth of spirit which is a necessary part of being human; it can lead to appalling acts, and those who commit them know and regret it" (2012: 42). He did not shirk the consequences when he wrote the following:

> But in as much as the men of Long Kesh are for so many the heart of the present agonizing destructive situation it is surely worth saying that for us, as far as we can learn, the awful guilt for every death must be borne by those who seem to balance Parliamentary votes against a search for justice. (O'Hagan 2012: 43)

In trying to understand the meanings inherent in the lived experience of narratives, we learn much about the human condition, not only to endure suffering, but also to rise above the draining impact of war in order to create new visions of hope and peace.

Speaking and Listening to Narratives

Given the horrors of war, how then does one speak the unspeakable? How significant is the narrative voice? Also, how does one "tell the story of historical trauma when so much of what must be spoken lies with the dead, when speaking for those who cannot speak entails an ethical burden uneasily discharged" (Gilmore 2005: 99)? Further, "How do people express and then heal from violations that so destroy the essence of innocence, decency, and life itself that the very experience penetrates beyond comprehension and words" (Lederach and Lederach 2010: 1–2)? These questions are massive, given that violence typically crushes self-dignity. Indeed, for many, it erases voice, so that locating one's voice again is crucial in order to invoke change. Certainly, this finding of voice features strongly in truth commissions where testimony particularizes violence; that is, it gives "not only a human face and form, but a voice" (Gilmore 2005: 100). In doing so, the process of giving space to voice is an attempt to gain further influence on recovering the category of the human from histories of violence. As Arendt put it, "We humanize what is going on in the world and in ourselves only by speaking of it, and in the course of speaking of it we learn to be human" (1973: 32). Similarly, when victims are asked about their need for reparations, or their priorities in local postconflict reconstruction activities, there is an affirmation of selfhood in realizing that one's voice is being heard, and that some redress is being considered. This affirmation is critical, given that war trauma shatters the self with a crushing of personhood, home, family, and cultural traditions.

Some individuals manage to resist being crushed and find a courageous voice. Hanabeth Luke was in the Sari Club in Bali on October 12, 2002, when a bomb exploded, killing 202 people, including her boyfriend.[7] Her photo was featured in Australian newspapers as she assisted dying or suffering victims. She had the opportunity to speak directly with then prime minister Tony Blair prior to the UK entering the war in Iraq. Looking into his eyes in a British television studio, she said,

> I assure you, Mr. Blair, that had you seen the pain, death, and destruction that I have seen from just one bomb, you would be doing everything in your power to ensure that not one more bomb was let loose on human life. An eye for an eye and the whole world goes blind. (Luke 2012: 220)

Luke continues to speak out as a peace activist. Not everyone wants to remember the intensity of suffering; forgetting for some is part of survival and coping with trauma. War narratives show great diversity of the complex nature of humanity.

I look in more detail in Chapter 4 at the role of listening to stories. Some examples demonstrate survival skills geared toward facing tomorrow. As an example of the narrative transformation possible even in ethnic conflicts, Cobb tells of a women's cooperative of Rwandan Hutu and Tutsi widows called Dusohenye (Mourning Together). In this group the women ritualize their sharing of suffering. "They adopted positions as narrators, telling their stories; as listeners, as others told of suffering; and as characters, in the reciprocal stories that were told about community life, before and after the genocide" (Cobb 2003: 297). The genocide affected every widow in this cooperative, so the stories play out diverse meanings that destabilize dominant ethnic narratives.

Other examples show the complexities of listening to narratives. Catherine Bolten conducted one-on-one life history interviews with residents from the town of Makeni, Sierra Leone, during 2004–2005. In talking with soldiers, rebels, students, traders, politicians, evangelists, and parents, she gave the survivors "space to narrate their memories," and she claims that "what they narrate is *truth*" (2012: xi); that is, she accepts it as such. Narrative accounts of survival reflect how people remember their experiences so that, in the telling, the past comes to life but may be different with each recall and retelling. As we see in subsequent chapters, this acceptance of the stories' validity is significant because truth is an important yet not straightforward part of transitional justice. It might be valuable for one person to tell a story to a particular listener, while telling it to another listener may be less necessary.

Bolten confirms how crucial it is to people that their story is heard and thus validated. Any narrative of the present always comes through an interpretation of the past. In talking with a young rebel in Sierra Leone named Noah, who referred affectionately to the movement's leader, Bolten asks, "Was he immoral? Brainwashed? Evil" (2012: 2)? When Noah replied that he was not, her interest was not in judging him but in trying to work out how people make the sorts of choices they do during war and how they come to narrate these choices afterward. In conversation with another ex-combatant from the Revolutionary United Front, whom she calls David, she shows how "the purpose of his narrative was to distance himself from the brutality" of the rebel movement (2012: 85). He lamented the sense of loss of destroyed family relationships and that he could not care for his family. Bolten interprets this as an emphasis on the centrality of relationships in his narrative. When she followed up her interviews in 2010, she found that her "narrators emphasized qualities that resonated with their ideas of a functioning social world: love for family, sacrifice for others, one's own survival always dependent on relationships, whether with God, rebels, or terrified civilians" (2012: 245). Speaking one's narrative and listening to a narrative affirm the integrity of voice and sustain personal meaning. Keep in mind that not all victims can express their stories for shame, fear, or uncertainty of their stories' effects.

How are speaking and listening to narratives possible in times of violent conflict? To answer tangentially, Lederach (2008) reflects on the question of whether peace negotiations can be pursued while fierce conflict is raging. His answer adopts a cultivation metaphor—a farmer nourishing the soil and planting seeds. In doing so he emphasizes the connections between context, the developing of relationships, and a dedication to process over time. Thus, a relationship-centric orientation that is intrinsic to human security keeps the focus on people, their histories, and their narratives in working to move beyond the impasse of deadly conflict, and thus is fundamental to the arguments developed in the forthcoming chapters. Of course, seeds can wither and die. Sometimes, however, new shoots break surprisingly through rocky soil.

What Is Narrative Agency?

So far in this chapter, I have established the importance of attending to human security within the lived experiences of war narratives. I have built a case for why a narrative approach to understanding peace, justice, and reconciliation is useful in illuminating the importance of stories. To conclude this chapter I ask this question: What is narrative agency? This question is important because violence destroys people's sense of self-dignity and their capacity to make meaningful life choices. Rediscovering narrative agency is thus a fundamental part of redefining one's position in a transitional justice context.

What do I mean when I talk about agency? *Agency* refers to the self-awareness of making self-chosen choices and being responsible for their consequences. As moral agents, some individuals choose to engage in aggressive conflict, provoke antagonism, incite violence, and foster sectarianism. Other individuals decide to coexist, act harmoniously, cooperate peacefully, or actively seek reconciliation. Expressed starkly, agency is reduced to a simplistic dichotomy between evil and good. How and why people make choices in conflict zones are far more complex issues, with lots of messy, gray, in-between options. Undoubtedly, the nature of these choices is not always straightforward. Some individuals are coerced into thinking they have made the choice, or because they only have limited options, it seems the only choice possible. For example, child soldiers are often dragged into warring factions, or frustrated youth may see few opportunities other than to join guerrilla or paramilitary movements. How meaningful are these choices?

Meaningful agency is often lost in times of conflict. Rather than being able to tell one's story as, for example, a victim, a survivor, someone willing to confront the enemy, or someone responding humanely to the loss of others, during conflicts and even in a postconflict stage the capacity for action is constrained by structural and physical violence. Where the longevity of decades of violence means that patterns of bitter hatred are perpetuated, the possibility of challenging these patterns is not always obvious. The way that identities emerge in social relationships affects any challenge. When people have witnessed traumatic events, particularly attacks carried out by people who once were neighbors or friends, identities are shattered and agency crumbles. Yet there are always amazing exceptions to the norm. Judy El-Bushra, writing specifically about women in Northern Uganda, Somalia and Somaliland, and Rwanda, reminds us that even when women lack formal power, many "women exercise agency in the pursuit of self-identified goals" (2000: 80), demonstrating the resilience of their capabilities. Agency for women and men "describes the strategies used by individuals to create a viable and satisfying life for themselves in the context of, or in spite of, these identities" (El-Bushra 2000: 67). Empowered agents can make informed decisions about matters that affect them. Agency, understood as the capability to make deliberate choices and be responsible for their consequences, is complex.

Differing degrees of opportunities exist to enjoy the full range of capabilities that human agents possess, an idea that Martha Nussbaum advances (2011; 2000; 1999). She explains that the "capabilities approach" starts with straightforward questions: "What are people actually able to do and to be? What real opportunities are available to them?" (2011: x). While these questions appear to be simple, she points out their complexity in responding to what humans strive for. The capabilities approach is about improving the quality of life, creating a life that is truly worthy of human dignity. The focus of this approach is on choices and opportunities that people have to enjoy what Amartya Sen (1999) calls "substantial freedoms." Nussbaum's capabilities approach "focuses on the protection of areas of freedom so central that their removal makes a life not worthy of human dignity" (2011: 31). She lists her ten central capabilities as life; bodily health; bodily integrity; senses, imagination, and thought; emotions; practical reason; affiliation; other species; play; and control over one's environment (2011: 33–34). To use her language, in "thinking about capability security" (2011: 43) we need to think about how violence and conflict disrupt the opportunity for people to make choices about these central capabilities in their everyday lives. Not all choices made are preferred options. The availability of life options is narrowed during war, and information on making informed decisions is limited. Choices made may be the best of a bad range of alternatives, the lesser of two evils. Further, the degree of culpability of cruel choices varies. Certainly, people who give orders to commit horrible acts of violence are more morally responsible for such evils than those who carry out the commands, particularly when many perpetrators are co-opted into these acts as minors, but the respondents still carry moral weight on their shoulders. The memory of their actions often haunts combatants for their entire lives, blurring the lines between perpetrator and victim.

Agency is complex, and our lives are tricky, never more so than in divided societies. So, what is the type of agency I use in this book? I adopt a social ontology of what Carol Gould calls "socially understood *individuals-in-relations*" (2004: 4). Such a moral orientation assumes that human flourishing occurs through social interaction. In this concept of agency, men and women are empowered to make informed decisions about matters that affect them. Many emotions come into play in making these decisions, because emotions are central to ethical life, profoundly influencing agency. In conflict contexts, I maintain, victims are moral agents whose agency is hampered by gross abuses and injustices. The course of action that victims take to become survivors is a crucial part of their postwar narrative. This concept of agency is pivotal to my argument that, despite widespread conflict, many individuals make creative, courageous choices to overcome the terrible traumas suffered in war or develop resilience to cope with the ongoing suffering. Important also is the idea of degrees of moral responsibility. For example, as mentioned already, children coerced to join rebel groups and forced to engage in violent activities cannot be held to account to the degree of those who gave the orders. In knowing someone's narrative, this distinction can be made.

To summarize, in bringing together narrative and agency, I develop a narrative construction of subjectivity with a relational view of agency. Ontologically, relational theory accepts that the self exists in relation to others and develops through relationships. This idea of the self meshes with Seyla Benhabib's (1992) idea that communicative practice materializes with the concrete other—a person with a particular history, a narrative that establishes the speaker as having spoken. "It is the being heard that is critical to relational agency, to the production of the concrete other" (Cobb 2013: 153). Narrative agency thus is "the capacity to develop a story about self in which one is an agent" (2013: 159).

What is critical to narrative agency "is that the lives of persons cannot be thought of as a series of discrete, disconnected experiences or events. Rather, to be a person is to exercise narrative capacities for self-interpretation that unify our lives over time" (Mackenzie 2008b: 11). That is, we deploy interpretive constructions of practical reasoning in order to make sense of personal experiences. Sometimes this reasoning occurs as a solitary endeavor; mainly it occurs in conversations with others. Our narratives change; they are dynamic, as even patterns of coherence can shift. In conflict zones, trauma disrupts narrative consistency, undermining self-integrity, which is why I contend that understanding war narratives reveals a wealth of knowledge about lived experiences.

Narrative agency is enacted through everyday occurrences, all the small, ordinary events that make up our daily lives. During violent conflict, the ease with which people go about ordinary activities is hampered severely, so that every part of individual, communal, and national narratives is significant in understanding disrupted narratives and how to secure a sustainable peace. The point of using war narratives is to contextualize agency, thereby demonstrating the range of motivations and practices behind complicated acts of contrition, responses to revenge, struggles with forgiveness, or difficulties in building trust with former enemies. Social and cultural narratives are passed from one generation to the next through anecdotes told in families, media, and school, and through the creative arts. For example, Antoine Rutayisire, vice chairman (2002–2008) of the Rwandan National Unity and Reconciliation Commission, recalls a primary school incident where the Hutus were asked to stand, then the Tutsis were asked to stand, and the one girl who was a Twa was humiliated. Only as an adult working on healing destructive social and ethnic narratives did Rutayisire come to understand the effects of rejection. He writes, "When a social group has been despised for a period long enough to get to a point of believing the lie, their spirit becomes like a broken spring that will not bounce when pushed down" (2010: 174).

Continuing this theme of generational narrative, Ani Kalayjian writes as a child of survivors of the Ottoman-Turkish genocide. Both of her parents' families survived the forced deportation march from Asia Minor into Syria. She heard of the hardships that led to the substantial death of a large majority of the Armenian population in Asia Minor and writes, "I was traumatized by learning the tragic stories of the genocide of the Armenians" (2010: 244). She talks of the "pain and suffering collectively contained in my community" and that the denial of the genocide by the Turkish government caused her "tremendous psychic pain and feelings of helplessness" (2010: 245). Kalayjian began to use education and dialogue as ways to transcend hatred, not only in her own community, but elsewhere. In dealing with the collective impact of mass trauma in cycles of violence, she conducted mental health outreach projects in Armenia, Bosnia, Lebanon, and Syria. In 2007 in Lebanon, her team was training psychologists and mental health practitioners. They observed how difficult it was for their trainees to practice empathy and concluded that the practitioners themselves had endured suffering for so long that there was a "generational transmission of trauma" (2010: 247), with traumatized groups inflicting pain on others. As I explain more fully in subsequent chapters, often only a thin line exists between a victim who feels pain and a perpetrator of pain.

In the following chapters I highlight narratives that demonstrate the human capacity to transcend the dark potential of humanity's worst inclinations. The approach taken is not to be naïve and deny the depravity of war; it is rather to highlight positive accounts of narrative agency, and also to reveal ways of working toward reconciliatory spaces. As I outline more fully in the final chapter, these spaces occur on the grass; under a tree; in a hut; around a kitchen table; walking bombed streets; in a workshop, pub, or cemetery; around negotiation tables; or within the walls of new political assemblies or houses of Parliament. Spaces are multiple. Sometimes spaces merge. Other times they disappear as people move into them and crawl out, discouraged, embittered, or confused. Visualizing these spaces and naming them humanizes them, reminding us of the narrative story occupying these spaces, often with several agents involved—some able to talk, others trapped in trauma. Multiple spaces are messy. Within these variable spaces, agents agonize, deliberate, argue, disagree, dispute, sometimes agree, apologize, forgive, show compassion, build trust, confess, divulge new truths, and build new relationships that show the healing power of reconciliation. In reconciliatory spaces, agents' narratives are fascinatingly diverse.

* * *

In this chapter I have outlined a narrative approach to agency and given particular attention to the agency of victims in conflict and postconflict contexts. In situating the discussion within a human security framework, I have highlighted the importance of giving attention to people's particular plights. I argue that the stories of victims who have war narratives reveal deep subjective meanings that contribute to their life narratives and expose deep understandings of how peace, justice, and reconciliation affect people's everyday lives. Narrative agency permits the unfolding of stories about the self that demonstrate deliberate choices. Being creative in extending the spaces for narrative agents to come together enlarges the possibility of opening meaningful reconciliatory spaces, the focus of Chapter 8.

Notes

1. A book by Gabrielle Rifkind and Giandomenico Picco (2014) was released as I was completing this manuscript. I have not included its materials. The book argues that a new approach recognizing geopolitical complexities, but also understanding how people think, is urgently needed to try to understand the mind of one's opponents and to break cycles of violence.

2. The coalition formed in 1996 and dissolved in 2006.

3. Leymah Gbowee won the Nobel Peace Prize in 2011, along with Liberian Ellen Johnson Sirleaf and Tawakkul Karman from Yemen.

4. In particular, narrative is strong in communication studies, cultural studies, discourse analysis, ethnography, media studies, sociology, and psychology.

5. Outstanding students who were employed as research assistants included Zöe Darling, Elise Fantin, Phoebe Haymes, and Shari Reid. They assisted me in finding some of the relevant narratives. I acknowledge a small research grant from the University of South Australia's Division of Education, Arts, and Social Sciences that permitted me to employ these excellent students. There is nothing methodologically scientific in the selection of these firsthand accounts of everyday life. We simply tried to be representative across a wide range of conflict zones, seeking stories from women and men, and selecting stories that indicate hope for change.

6. See Cobb (2013: 22) for theorists who confirm ways in which narrative is foundational to individuals, communities, and also to international relations.

7. Hanabeth Luke was taking my course "Peace, War, and International Politics" at this time at Southern Cross University in Australia.

3

How Does War Damage Humanity?

As flesh-and-blood mortal beings, we are all prone to some suffering or pain in our lives. This ordinary suffering is part of being human. As humans, we attach symbolic meanings to our experiences of suffering as a way of dealing with the cruelty or randomness of the pain we endure. In reading stories of the suffering that occurs in war, it is easy to feel a range of emotions. Prime emotions include sadness, empathy, anger, deep repulsion, or even disbelief that one human being can inflict such harm on a fellow human being. My main task in this chapter is to explore the principal question: How does war damage humanity? The purpose of asking this question is to set the groundwork for knowing what the harms of war are and how we should respond to them. As preparation, I need to show that the evil of war creates massive human suffering. This point is obvious, but the unique approach here is to draw on personal war narratives of suffering to explain four points.

First, I explore the evil of war and situate it as an unbearable harm that affects personhood, dignity, and self-respect. The reason for making these connections is to highlight the consequences of war on people's lives and their agency, as explained in the previous chapter. Armed violence affects people deeply, not simply in obvious physical ways, but in intensely emotional ways that shape self-understanding. Second, I explore the nature of crimes against humanity, providing examples of genocide and war rape to show how such acts of evil obliterate human dignity. This exploration leads readily to the chapter's third main point, which is to highlight the features of victimhood. Understanding more about the shame and guilt that emanate from being a victim of crimes against humanity is important because it illuminates the human dynamics that underlie the reactions of those who suffer from the consequences of evil acts, and to some extent those who commit the acts. Grasping these dynamics is not easy; it requires trying to understand the motives behind morally abhorrent acts from a morally worthy position of defending the importance of human dignity. The potential contradictions of this position are striking, but they are fundamental to my overall argument that evil causes intense suffering that requires careful responses to restore broken dignity. I explore the question of what is involved in asking who is a victim, the answer that is very important when reparations are at stake. Understanding victimhood is also significant because it can enable people to move beyond a helpless state to a new identity as a survivor. My final point begins the discussion of what is needed to respond to suffering through adopting the principles of a responsibility to protect. I outline my fuller argument on our obligations to strangers and duties of care in Chapter 7. This chapter firmly establishes why such obligations are needed. In doing so, we see how war damages humanity in deeply severe ways. I argue that underlying the answers to the questions raised in this chapter is the urgent need to determine how we should prevent the injustice and harm of suffering inflicted by another human.[1]

Exploring these questions and gaining further understanding on narratives of peace, justice, and reconciliation requires delving into the pitches of darkness to see how people scramble into the light. I have already noted that violence triggers narratives of suffering that intensify the conditions that lead to further violence. How then can people speak about such violence when recalling how this suffering contributes to their violation? Many do speak about being violated, and for some comes a partial emotional release of grief. Those who listen to accounts of suffering are in an informed position to support the localized social, cultural, and political changes needed to reduce violence. At the base of conflicts are stories of exclusion, pain, and suffering. Many find it easier to talk about physical wounds than inner hurt. Deep emotional pain resists language. Feelings often overwhelm articulation. There frequently is resistance to expressing deeply suffered pain, sometimes because of social barriers to revealing emotional pain. People may be discouraged from expressing pain, or victims may find it just too difficult to talk about their feelings. For others, their lives or their family's lives are at risk if they speak out. Suppression of deeply felt emotions is oppressive when people cannot speak of their pain and thus cannot be heard.

Redressing this type of oppression involves finding ways to ensure that people can speak and are heard and thus legitimized. María Pía Lara, in discussing the moral wrongs of human cruelty, describes the reflective judgments that permit us to "find the connection between a specific violation to the integrity of a human being and a powerful way of describing it through disclosive (expressive) means" (2007: 10). These judgments enable us to describe atrocities as evil and to talk about normative concepts like humanity. She reminds us how human cruelty is thematized in stories by revealing the space of moral responsibility and choice. As she puts it beautifully, "Indeed, it is the privilege of a well-told story to be able to disclose aspects of the human condition that would seem impossible to translate into pure philosophical concepts" (2007: 14). She writes that, in narrating stories of cruelty, often the "moral imperative is directed at making others understand that what happened did not need to happen" (2007: 14). This goal places a high value on storytelling as a medium that helps us learn about evil acts, a way not merely to reflect on the past but to imagine a distinctive appreciation of the need for practical justice in the present.

Writing of Holocaust testimonies, Lawrence Langer (1991) explains how violence disrupts narratives in that it is difficult to make sense of what has happened. As a result, people step back from their pain, cut off from their self-identity and everyday lives. They walk, as Cobb puts it, "in a zone of half-alive, alive, but dead" (2013: 26). Institutionalized violence is where suffering is built into the ordinariness of life. In such contexts, suffering is so much part of the everyday that it seems normal, fitting into Galtung's definition of "structural violence" (1964)—the inequalities and injustices that come with poverty, discrimination, illiteracy, and other layers of violence structured into a society, such as sexual and gender-based violence. What happens then is that institutionalized violence "creates the living dead—persons so outside the realm of agency as to be objects" (Cobb 2013: 26) of the brutal system. In this context of narrative violence, people are cut off from reflective processes, so that they are able to relate episodes of events as part of their story, but they are unable to tie it into a meaningful narrative. This inability is significant because "it is narrative, not story, that is the threshold for humanity, for being human" (2013: 27). With narrative violence, something or someone on the "other" side succeeds in breaking someone's command of language to effectively deny their humanity. In this state, moral agency, defined as the "capacity of persons to narrate themselves as having the capacity to be moral actors" (2013: 29) is denied. As outlined in the previous chapter, all persons intrinsically possess the capability for moral agency, but narrative violence greatly reduces the capacity to express or narrate such agency. Part of the reason is that, despite speaking, when voice falls on deaf ears or does not matter to the other who caused the suffering, victimization continues. Great nonviolent leaders like Mahatma Gandhi, Martin Luther King Jr., and Nelson Mandela were able to narrate the violence and pain of colonialism, racist discrimination, and apartheid while refusing to participate in cycles of violence. Their agency and strength in stating a commitment to nonviolence and peace were evident politically. In this chapter I examine the effects of evil in rendering people voiceless.

What Is Evil?

What is evil, and why does it occur? "That humans are capable of harming other humans, and are choosing to do so, is still one of the most puzzling questions—dramas—that we must still confront" (Pía Lara 2007: 25). Pía Lara uses the term "evil" as "a paradigm that encompasses all our historical experiences in which human cruelty against other humans has been the defining experience of a specific type of act" (2007: 25). Humans willingly participate in these acts. Claudia Card defines "evils as reasonably foreseeable intolerable harms produced by culpable wrongdoing" (2004: 216). The "reasonably foreseeable" part of this definition is not easy to grasp. Certainly some horrible acts can be predicted in contexts of repressive, dictatorial, or violent regimes, but other violent acts are difficult to anticipate. The seemingly random nature of terrorist acts has removed the ability to predict acts of violence, but they are foreseeable from the perspective of those committing the acts. The "intolerable harms" and "culpable wrongdoing" of evil are incontestable. Card calls these atrocities "particularly gross evils" (2004: 217). She defines "intolerable harm" as "deprivation of the basics ordinarily necessary to make a life tolerable and decent" (2004: 218). Card explains that one of the challenges is to respond to evils without actually committing evil acts. That is, frequently as a response to acts of terrorism, bombings, killings, and all forms of violent conflict, some acts of retaliation, revenge, or retribution are as harmful and as wrong as the acts that prompt them. Using the term "evil" quite deliberately reveals the immoral nature of atrocities of violence that harm people's sense of self-integrity.

In uncomfortable discussions of evil, it is easy to distance ourselves from the idea that we could commit such horrors. Antjie Krog, South

African poet and journalist, discusses the need to claim responsibility for participating in acts of evil as integral to the process of reconciliation after the South African TRC, when she writes that "reconciliation will only be possible if whites say: 'Apartheid was evil and we were responsible for it'" (1999: 58). She explains further that this acknowledgment requires white people to feel offended by racism and not just to feel sorry for black people. As Desmond Tutu listened to the stories of perpetrators talk about their violations, he realized "how each of us has this capacity for the most awful evil—all of us. None of us could predict that if we had been subjected to the same influences, the same conditioning, we would not have turned out as these perpetrators" (1999: 76). Trudy Govier writes in a similar vein of how "an awareness of the vulnerability of ordinary people to the persuasive power of certain situations argues against a rigid notion of the evil perpetrator" (2006: 39). I showed in the previous chapter how even choices to become involved in armed conflict are at times murky. Instead, Govier suggests that there is a humbling reminder that "if I were placed in the same situation, with the same set of social identities, it could have been me" (2006: 39). The thought is a sobering one, and in Chapter 7 I discuss the related emotions of empathy and what is involved in imagining how different our reactions might be if we were in different positions and subject to varying types of atrocities.

For now, we delve further into the dark recesses of the human mind to explore what evil is. Gareth Evans was foreign minister of Australia from 1988 to 1996 and president of the International Crisis Group from 2000 to 2009. He tells a story of how, as a young Australian making his first trip to Europe to study at Oxford in 1968, he did what many students do and traveled. In the years that followed, he came across many people he had met on this trip—from India, Indonesia, Malaysia, Pakistan, Singapore, Thailand, and Vietnam. However, in later years he never met the students he had befriended from Cambodia. He muses about the reason, concluding that every one of them died under Pol Pot's genocidal regime, as intellectual enemies of the state or from starvation and disease. Evans writes that "the knowledge, and the memory, of what must have happened to those young men and women is something that haunts me to this day" (2008: 1–2). He states further that few contemporary events have seared the conscience of people around the globe as much as Rwanda in 1994, where about eight hundred thousand men, women, and children were slaughtered over a few short weeks while the world's policymakers found reasons to do nothing; also, in Srebrenica in Bosnia in 1995, eight thousand young and old men were massacred within a few days, taken from the so-called safe haven of UN troops deployed to protect them, but given their mandate, the Dutch peacekeepers had to stand and watch. How could we have said "never again" with so much conviction and confidence after the Holocaust of World War II and then the horror of Cambodia, where up to two million died in four years of tyrannical Khmer Rouge rule from 1975 to 1979? The Khmer Rouge's decision to evict Phnom Penh's twenty thousand hospital patients from their beds and force them on a death march out of the city had terrible consequences. Catholic priest François Ponchaud reflects on this decision: "I shall never forget one cripple who had neither hands nor feet, writhing along the ground like a severed worm" (in Maguire 2005: 37). No human should have to suffer such humiliation.

On media outlets and through so much availability of accurate information, there is increasing exposure of evils such as human trafficking, sexual slavery, war rape, torture, and worker exploitation, all rightly named as evils. However, the talk of evil in international politics has become more convoluted since the US-provoked "axis of evil" debates after 9/11. Stephen Chan reflects on the nature of good and evil and the presumption that "the US, in waging war on evil, is doing good in the world" (2005: 121). Further, this presumption can only be accurate "if the US first defeats evil and delivers the good" (2005: 121). This ambition is massive and groundless. States that affirm their intention to do good can and do instigate actions that lead to intolerable harms. No state has a monopoly on goodness or is incapable of practicing evil. Indeed, there is a triple level of accountability: individual perpetrators who commit abuses, the society that gives tacit endorsement to violence, and the state that sanctions the practices. Such accountability highlights the agency involved in individual, social, and state relationships. In relation to these triple levels, Jelena Subotic argues that the societal responsibility is the most significant because "it is only through a societal reckoning with the criminal past that the hateful ideologies that led to atrocity could be delegitimized" (2011: 161). The perpetrator society needs to come to an understanding that the past wrongs should not occur in a decent society. Social norms, values, beliefs, and practices take generations to change, and I believe the change needs to occur at all levels because they all affect each other.

As Hannah Arendt pointed out, life stories play an important role because, even in the bleakest times, they illustrate aspects of being human that theories cannot show; they provide insight "from the uncertain, flickering, and often weak light that some men and women, in their lives and their works, will kindle under almost all circumstances" (Arendt 1973: ix). As Pía Lara explains, according to Arendt's concept of storytelling, human understanding depends on giving meaning to our actions, showing that these actions are significant. Through such action, a disclosure of the self occurs. Arendt is saying that narratives are always open to reinterpretations, and that by retelling them to new audiences we pave the way for possible new meanings. Since narratives are open to additional interpretations, they are never definitive judgments. There is always a different way to describe the same action with another perspective. Sometimes the differences are so enormous that they remain a significant reason for the continuation of violence. All narratives, even those of people who have committed gross evils, sit inside a multifaceted web of human connections. Untangling the web exposes threads of harm and can also set a pattern that attempts to redress the harm. I am arguing that the more we understand the motives of evil acts of war and their consequences, the more careful we can be in responding appropriately to the harms that violent conflict cause. This understanding increasingly is pertinent for counterterrorist strategies as well as for conflict transformation. It should prompt strategies to prevent harms from occurring.

What Are Crimes Against Humanity?

Crimes against humanity are evils that produce intolerable harms and violate fundamental human rights. The UN Charter uses strong moral language to affirm human rights, the dignity and worth of the human person, equal gender rights, justice obligations, tolerance, and the need to live in peace. Whether it is Auschwitz, Baghdad, Coventry, Darfur, Dresden, Free Town, Hiroshima, Kabul, Kigali, Phnom Penh, Pristina, Sarajevo, Soweto, or the West Bank, some horrific occurrences make us wonder how it is possible for humans to commit such evil acts of torture, rape, violent assault, maiming, and killing. The term "crimes against humanity" is significant. The phrase was first used to describe Belgian atrocities against Congolese in the late nineteenth century. Crimes against humanity are defined in Article 7 of the Rome Statute of the International Criminal Court (ICC). It is a comprehensive statute that includes acts "committed as part of a widespread or systematic attack directed against any civilian population, with knowledge of the attack" and includes murder, extermination, enslavement, forcible transfer of population, deprivation of physical liberty, torture, rape, sexual slavery, enforced prostitution, forced pregnancy, enforced sterilization, grave sexual violence, persecution, enforced disappearance, apartheid, and inhumane acts that intentionally cause great suffering (UN Office of Legal Affairs 1998). Such crimes have their "origins in the denial of the full humanity of the stranger, the nonrecognition of the other as a human being" (Rigby 2001: 190). In the light of such crimes, how is it possible to embrace the humanity of the seemingly inhumane?

As an example of someone who was able to do so, Cynthia Ngewu—mother of Christopher Piet, who was murdered brutally by the apartheid police—in testifying in the South African TRC said,

> This thing called reconciliation . . . if I am understanding it correctly . . . if it means this perpetrator, this man who has killed Christopher Piet, if it means he becomes human again, this man, so that I, so that all of us, gets our humanity back . . . then I agree, then I support it all. (in Krog 1999: 109)

This statement demonstrates the enormous potential of certain humans to grasp that, despite being a victim of a terrible act—in this case, a mother losing her son as part of a widespread, systematic apartheid campaign—remaining a victim provides no release from the terrible negative emotions associated with bitterness and deep trauma. Without release, the agency needed to move forward is hampered. Being able to move forward differs for different people and types of violations but never occurs properly without dealing with the past. What constitutes "dealing with the past" is the subject of transitional justice, and it varies for different people also. Some individuals struggle and cannot find the release possible. They remain stuck in the past. In the context of violent conflict, persons often accentuate the outcome of a story—that is, their personal wound—whether loss of loved ones, physical maiming, nightmares, getting HIV/AIDS through war rape, having an unwanted child as a consequence of the rape, or suffering the poverty or displacement that accompanies long-term destruction of the means to sustain subsistence agriculture. When people are stuck in the past, their account of violence and the specific violation is told as a story about events, "rather than a narrative that contextualizes those events" (Cobb 2013: 26).

Part of dealing with the past and contextualizing the war narrative lies in considering the role of the perpetrator of violence in a victim's life, an immense challenge. Given incredible inhuman acts, those named as crimes against humanity, often it is virtually impossible to see perpetrators of violence as human. Yet the inhuman acts "illustrate our very capacity to do evil" (Pía Lara 2007: 37). Trying to see perpetrators of evil acts as human, as Ngewu above was able to do, is a crucial idea behind that of "humanizing the enemy," which is an exceedingly tough but integral part of reconciliation, an idea I return to in other chapters. My argument here is that even evil needs to be seen as part of agency, in the sense that humans can choose to do or not do an act of evil. Understanding these choices helps us to see that history could have been different, and finding this critical space is part of the process of creating a moral imagination to transform the evil of inhumanity to the release of liberated humanity.

Genocide

The traumatic nature of crimes against humanity makes dealing with the past supremely difficult. Genocide is an extreme example of evil. Genocide was used to describe Nazi atrocities against the Jews in the first half of the twentieth century. In 1946 political philosopher Arendt wrote to her former professor Karl Jaspers of Heidelberg University, questioning how one could comprehend what the Nazis had done within the existing criminal law. Arendt, in remarking on the Nazi crimes, wrote that they "explode the limits of the law; and that is precisely what constitutes their monstrousness. We're simply not equipped to deal on a human, political level, with a guilt that is beyond crime and an innocence that is beyond goodness or virtue" (in Thakur 2008: 117–118).

Ordinary humans commit extraordinary crimes. Strict definitions are given in the Convention on the Prevention and Punishment of the Crime of Genocide, and also in the Rome Statute of the ICC, where "genocide" in Article 6

> means any of the following acts committed with intent to destroy, in whole or in part, a national, ethnic, racial or religious group: killing members of the group; causing serious bodily or mental harm to members of the group; deliberately inflicting on the group conditions of life calculated to bring about its physical destruction in whole or in part; imposing measures intended to prevent births within the group; and forcibly transferring children of the group to another group. (UN Office of Legal Affairs 1998)

The naming of a genocide as a genocide is important, because with it goes the international responsibility to intervene. Who does the naming? Definitions in the above convention and statute relating to genocide mean that the Cambodian slaughter, which was directed at those of the same nationality, would not be classified as genocide. Frequently, meaningful initiatives like formulating new statutes only occur after horrible acts have been committed, like the atrocities in Rwanda and the systematic sexual violence in the former Yugoslavia.

Since 1955, twenty-nine countries have experienced episodes of genocide or politicide that tries to annihilate a group with a particular political belief, or attempts to remove politicized ethnic groups, with drastic statistics of losses in Afghanistan in 1978–1992, Cambodia in 1975–1979, Indonesia in 1965–1966, Pakistan in 1971, and Rwanda in 1994 (Marshall and Gurr 2005: 58). Genocide has an intense impact on memory, like an ongoing nightmare. Witnessing massacres, systematic rapes, and tortures leads to memories that constitute an intolerable harm.[2] Camila Omanovic, a Muslim woman, was herded away with other women and children after their husbands, fathers, sons, and brothers were taken from Srebrenica on July 12, 1995. In her voice, she told how "it was the sounds that haunted her. Screams suddenly filled the night. . . . It was the fear that didn't let her sleep. A fear more intense than anything she had ever felt. A fear that changed her forever" (in Crocker 2003: 44). The haunting memories linger.

Risk factors that leave countries susceptible to further genocide include a prior history of genocide; previous upheavals; a minority elite, such as Tutsi domination in Burundi and Rwanda and Tigreans dominant in Ethiopia; or an exclusionary ideology such as Islamists in Sudan, Hutu militants in Burundi and Rwanda, the Taliban in Afghanistan, Marxists in China, Maoists in Nepal, Tamil separatists in Sri Lanka, Sunni Islamists in Iraq, or conflict between secular nationalists and Islamists in Algeria (Marshall and Gurr 2005: 60). The human consequence of genocide is unspeakably horrific. Not only are there massacres, systematic rapes, and tortures, but there is a "destruction of the remembrance of individuals as well as their lives and dignity" (Minow 1998: 1). Yet Martha Minow reminds us that, despite these massacres, change can occur; democratic regimes emerged in Argentina, Brazil, the reunified Germany, and South Africa.

Another dimension to crimes against humanity is the resemblance between genocide and "ethnic cleansing," a term used to describe atrocities such as occurred in Bosnia and Herzegovina, atrocities that suggest "purification, homogenization, elimination, expulsion, and ritual violence" (Humphrey 2002: 77). Stefan Wolff defines the basis of these ethnic conflicts "in which the primary fault line of confrontation is one of ethnic distinctions" (2006: 2). The examples he draws upon include Cyprus, the Israeli-Palestinian dispute, Kashmir, Kosovo, Northern Ireland, and Sri Lanka as ethnic conflicts with violent manifestations. Not all have led to ethnic cleansing. "Ethnic conflicts are stories about deliberate choices made by human beings about action or inaction. Above all, however, they are stories of human suffering" (Wolff 2006: 24). In Chapter 5 I deal in more depth with the way that extremist ethnic conflict is an obstacle to building trust. Here I note that the atrocities of ethnic cleansing are genocidal in nature.

War Rape

A terrible example of human suffering is war rape. Rape destroys the soul, with shame overwhelming the victim's dignity and, for women in particular, their standing in the community. There were no rape charges at the Nuremberg tribunal of prominent Nazis after World War II. The Tokyo tribunal did not deal with the enslavement of Korean women who were forced to serve as sex slaves for Japanese soldiers.[3] Truth matters. The silence about rape in war can no longer continue. The stories of these rapes are disturbing; the realities of the trauma are horrifying. Men and boys are raped during war, often as part of torture, but typically more women and girls are raped systematically as a routine part of war. Historically war rape was categorized as a crime against the honor and property of men, rather than a crime of violence against women. There have been two notable international war crimes prosecutions on rape of women and girls that altered this historical basis.

First, in the International Criminal Tribunal for Rwanda (ICTR), "Rape formed no part of the first series of ICTR indictments" (Copelon 2000: 224). Women did not talk about rape. This silence changed when Judge Navanethem Pillay from South Africa, the only woman judge on the tribunal trial chamber, was hearing a case and pursued her inquiry with two women who were called to testify to other crimes. A witness's testimony linked Jean-Paul Akayesu, a Rwandan politician, to rapes. The Akayesu case was a landmark. It signaled the first international conviction for genocide with recognition that rape and sexual violence are "constitutive acts of genocide aimed at destroying a group," and it advanced "a broad definition of rape as a physical invasion of a sexual nature" (Copelon 2000: 227). This landmark case emphasized the ethnic targeting of Tutsi women as part of the genocide.[4] The international women's human rights movement had mobilized to support the election of women judges and prevent harassment of witnesses.

Second, the Kunarac case in the International Criminal Tribunal for the former Yugoslavia (ICTY) is also significant. Again, in the ICTY, evidence of sexual violence was not treated as seriously as other crimes until the female member of the trial chamber, Judge Odio Benito from Costa Rica, challenged the prosecutor. Again, she had been encouraged to do so after submissions from women's organizations. In the Kunarac case, rape was defined as a violation of sexual autonomy and an element of torture. The case offered the first indictment in which the crime of sexual enslavement was charged as enslavement—that is, either a war crime, a form of torture, or a crime against humanity, and not just an attack on the honor of women. The indictment expanded the definition of rape to encompass all situations in which consent is not freely and voluntarily given (UNRISD 2005: 246).

The Foča judgment set the second precedent in international criminal law in prosecuting rape as a crime against humanity. The trial shed light on the large-scale, systematic sexualized assault on Muslim women and on the role this violence played in the war in Bosnia and Herzegovina. There is evidence that a campaign of mass atrocities perpetrated primarily by the Serbian forces moved from "spontaneous and individualized rape as a spoil of war to a strategic policy of forced abduction and systematic gang rape of Bosnian women for reasons of humiliation, ethnic impregnation, and destruction of Muslim family structures" (Lopez 2009: 98). Uncertainties linger as to how it was possible that ordinary men who had been neighbors, relatives, teachers, shopkeepers, waiters, or policemen could turn into torturers. It is apt to recall Tutu's quotation that "each of us has this capacity for the most awful evil" (1999: 76). I add that each of us also has the capacity for profound good. Recall Arendt's notion of the banality of evil, that usually it is mediocre, ordinary men and women who commit crimes against humanity, with many using the excuse that they simply were following orders. The ICC marks a new era of international justice and accountability for women. The statute of the ICC represents another landmark, codifying crimes of sexual and gender-based violence as part of the jurisdiction of the court. Fionnuala Ní Aoláin reminds us that, while the "definitional advances" of these tribunals are significant, they "may speak little to the perceived impact of transitional justice for women as they experience the reality of inequality, exclusion, and ongoing vulnerability to violence" (2012: 213). War rape causes unspeakable degrees of damage.

For example, from 1999 to 2001 Bina D'Costa sought to talk to survivors of gender-based violence of the 1971 independence war of Bangladesh. Survivors were reluctant to speak with her for fear of being ostracized by their community. As a consequence, D'Costa needed to listen not merely to what the women said but also to "those pregnant pauses during the conversations" (2006: 148). In the next chapter we see how some silences are due to fear of speaking out, and some silences are deliberate, for reasons of protection for either themselves or others. In a different location, Binaifer Nowrojee has been talking with Rwandan rape victims since 1996. In 2003 she interviewed some victims on their perceptions of the ICTR. Nowrojee summarizes what the women wanted as "public acknowledgment" of the crimes and also the importance of a fair process of justice (2008: 112). These women wanted information on how to make an informed decision on whether to testify and what to expect, whether the courts would be an enabling environment, and whether there would be protection from reprisals following testimony. Many women in conflict zones have never told the story of their rape prior to giving testimony. A motivation for the Rwandan and Sierra Leonean women to tell their stories lay in wanting access to the AIDS medications that were provided to the defendants in custody. Nowrojee suggests that punishment and vengeance were the least frequently articulated reasons for why women wanted prosecutions of rape, despite the fact that, with prosecutions and convictions of sexual violence crimes, acknowledgment of the crime committed against the victim is a crucial dimension to healing—part of restoring a victim's sense of humanity and value. I contend that this restoration of dignity is a crucial part of the answer to the questions this chapter is exploring: How does war damage humanity? What are the harms of war? How should we respond to the suffering caused by war to damaged humanity?

With regard to law and prosecution, Julie Mertus offers a useful analysis on the legal system as being "counter-narrative," by which she means that "it opens and closes, letting in only enough information to prove the issue at hand" (2000: 144). A crime might be named as rape, torture, or murder, but as Mertus puts it, the "language of law transmutes individual experiences into a categorically neat something else" (2000: 150). In doing so, the pain and hurt suffered are lost or often not even properly recognized. "There is no crime of destruction of souls, deprivation of childhood, erasure of dreams . . . no crime of being forced to watch helplessly while one's loved one suffers" (2000: 150). Formal legal procedures of prosecution are a crucial part of addressing crimes, in this case of war rape. Informal advice, counsel, and ongoing support also are essential for those who have suffered this intolerable harm. After reliving the story event of rape, support is needed to assist women and men in rebuilding a livable narrative. Accounts of men's war rape are scarce, although more men are likely to come forth if, in doing so, they are granted victim reparations.

Victimization does not cease with the establishment of a peace agreement. Too many cases demonstrate that sexual abuse often continues with the appearance of peacekeepers. Peacekeepers come with money and create artificial economies that become ripe for sexual exploitation of local women and girls, particularly in a crisis like that in the Democratic Republic of Congo (DRC), with the age of consent for girls at fourteen and men at eighteen (US Department of State 2012: 32). Sexual violence against women is a constant feature in the DRC (US Department of State 2012: 27–29). In Algeria, armed Islamist groups treated women who lived in villages that opposed their rule as spoils of war, raping about five thousand women between 1995 and 1998, and abducting and killing many (Porter 2007a: 120). In East Timor, pro-Indonesian militia and Indonesian soldiers raped many women in the lead-up to the 1999 referendum on East Timorese independence (Porter 2012a).[5] Taliban members in Afghanistan abducted and raped Hazara and Tajik women (Brown and Bokhari 2001: 8). Even in postconflict settings such as in Kosovo, women suffered a rise in domestic violence, rape, trafficking, and abductions following the war. Rape is an important issue to highlight as part of the harms of war because women are reluctant to claim victimhood, and men's war rape rarely is documented.

For women who have endured other types of harms, Lisa Schirch (2012: 53–54) provides a useful analytical framework for examining the different forms of violence against women. She distinguishes between public and private, and direct and structural violence over phases of life. As direct violence she includes domestic violence, female genital mutilation, rape, torture, and injury due to landmines, which often strike more women and girls as they gather firewood or collect water. As structural violence, Schirch includes gender roles; sexual harassment; the providing of more food, education, and opportunities to boys; feminization of poverty; inadequate health care; unequal pay; and limited opportunities for female leadership. She quotes a victim of psychological violence, who said, "The body mends soon enough. Only the scars remain, but the wounds inflicted upon the soul take much longer to heal. And each time I relive these moments, they start bleeding all over again. The broken spirit has taken the longest to mend" (in Schirch 2012: 56).

The harm of war rape for men and boys, women and girls comes with the terrible undermining of self-dignity and the immense difficulty of living with the knowledge of the violation as part of one's narrative. This is another example where the capacity to make meaningful choice is undermined, because you cannot choose to delete the memory, and moving from the past into the present in anticipation of the hope of a transformed tomorrow can be a slow process, needing time and resources.

Who Is a Victim?

In painting a picture of the harm of evil, I have mentioned the perpetrator as an agent, choosing immoral acts that are evil in the harm they inflict. Now I must give priority to the victim whose humanity is damaged. Kai Ambos states clearly that victims have rights to truth, justice, and reparation (2010: 34–39). Before elaborating on these rights, we should understand more of what being a victim means. There are different degrees of suffering and vulnerability. The nature of victimhood created by violent conflict varies. It includes those who are bereaved, maimed, scarred, injured, tortured, intimidated, humiliated, raped, and silenced, and those who suffer from the loss of home, land, property, loved ones, status, and dignity. Other victims suffer because of the sights they witnessed while hiding and frequently feel guilty about being alive. One cannot measure the loss of a spouse, a child, or a loved one through war. A new spouse or a new baby never replaces the lost ones. Grief and loss continue in differing measures. Michael Humphrey suggests that "the politics of atrocity selects its victims, who then bear the legacy of suffering as trauma, a memory of pain in the body" (2002: 8). The selection may be random, accidental, or deliberate. All victims suffer trauma. The Greek origin of the word "trauma" is wound, so trauma is a "wound to the soul" (Kleck 2006: 344). Monika Kleck, in her work with traumatized women in Bosnia and Herzegovina, writes that "traumatic experiences often cause the survivor to question their view of reality, robbing them of their sense of integrity and wholeness and leading to the loss of self-esteem" (2006: 345). She is right to suggest that the key criterion when planning appropriate measures to rebuild war-torn societies is "not statistical benchmarks" that tick measurable boxes, but rather the rebuilding of human dignity (2006: 345), which is less tangible. Much of a victim's sense of damaged selfhood is suppressed, denied, or too hard to cope with. War damages the ability to give an account of its horror.

Curiously, disputes sometimes arise over who actually is a victim, particularly where cultural attitudes encourage victims to cling to feelings of grievance so that they view their narratives as a series of stories about victimhood. In Northern Ireland both sides of the conflict have used their status as victims (or perceived victims) of terrorism, British imperialism, sectarianism, or nationalist terror to justify their recourse to armed conflict and victimhood status. Given its all-pervading nature, "The status of victim becomes an institutionalized way of escaping guilt, shame, or responsibility" (Smyth 2003: 127). From a group of Catholics and Protestants, one interviewee claimed, "Everyone who lives in this whole city are victims no matter what side they are on. They all fear the same and have been affected and so on. There is no such thing as a non-victim" (in Ferguson, Burgess, and Hollywood 2010: 870). Another interviewee who had been involved in violence and now realized he had done wrong told the researchers, "I'm a victim of my environment, and I don't want that as an excuse, but it's fact, I did what I had to do in the circumstances that prevailed" (in Ferguson et al. 2010: 871). Another interviewee, acknowledging the common humanity of suffering, said that "the tears of a Protestant mother and tears of a Catholic mother meet in the same river of grief and that is the reality of life, the reality of humanity" (in Ferguson et al. 2010: 868). Victims share a common sense of woundedness.

In the South African Truth and Reconciliation Act of 1995, the definition of "victim" included relatives and dependents of victims. This expansive notion of victimhood is important, because in addition to male victims, "it locates wives, mothers, and children in center stage as having suffered 'the gross violations of human rights'" (Goldblatt and Meintjes 1998: 34). This broadened definition is important in a context where being a widow can mean the loss of status in the community. This extension of who constitutes a victim also occurred in Timor-Leste, where widows of resistance fighters could claim victim status and thus their right to reparations. The UN policy Basic Principles and Guidelines on the Right to a Remedy and Reparation for Victims of Gross Violations of Human Rights Law and Serious Violations of International Humanitarian Law (UN Office of the High Commissioner for Human Rights 2005) honors victims' right to benefit from reparation. Reparations, according to UN principles, include restitution, compensation, rehabilitation, satisfaction (recognition of the truth), and guarantees of nonrepetition (UN Office of the High Commissioner for Human Rights 2005).

Another group of victims are refugees and displaced persons. According to the UN High Commissioner for Refugees, at the start of 2008 there were 16 million refugees and roughly 51 million internally displaced persons (25 million of these are displaced by natural disasters and about 26 million as a result of armed conflict; in Kegley and Blanton 2010: 237). Many refugees and displaced people flee their homelands after being subject to war, human rights violations, ethnic conflict, and the full range of conflict-induced atrocities. In asylum, many seeking official refugee status in a host country are subject to racism or detention, despite it being unlawful in international law.

Any crude distinction between "victims" and "perpetrators" misses much of the complexity of the aftermath of political conflict. Often people are simplistically labeled as combatant, ex-combatant, ex-prisoner, murderer, offender, perpetrator, or terrorist, and these labels fail to grasp that some agents do change and some individuals "are both victims and perpetrators" (Govier and Verwoerd 2004: 371). Child soldiers who may never have had schooling but know all about guns provide an obvious example. People can go through profound changes—some through education while being imprisoned; others through the assistance of the international community, in refugee or reintegration camps; and others through independently realizing that violence will not prompt a move toward a sustainable peace. Too often, there is a failure to understand the nuance of identities and the importance of reintegrating former combatants into some semblance of normal life. Also, the reintegration requirements might differ for men and women, boys and girls, and older and younger combatants. Someone committing an act of violence takes "on the role of being an agent of violence," yet the person is not just a violent agent but "a human being with many other qualities and capacities" (Govier 2006: 28) which are suppressed by the act of violence. The underlying philosophy to this point is a commitment to the norms of human dignity, which has to allow for contingency, the accident of birthplace, and possible changes in humans' attitudes and practices. Someone who served many years in prison in Northern Ireland for a politically motivated killing introduced himself in a meeting: "Hi, I am John. I am a loyalist ex-prisoner . . . but I am also an ex-baby, an ex–shipyard worker, an ex-footballer, and an ex-husband" (in Govier 2006: 28). It is important to at least ask whether some perpetrators may also be considered as victims, and if so, what does this mean? Alex Boraine's view is that they can—in, for example, cases where police or soldiers have their conscience deadened by propaganda. His view does not condone abusive actions, but "it is simply to try to understand something of the ambiguity, the contradictions, of war, of conflict, of prejudice" (2000: 128). In a similar fashion, Govier explains that perpetrators "are victims in the sense that they have been harmed by the wrongful acts of others, and they are perpetrators in the sense that they have committed wrongs themselves" (2009: 41). I want to keep stressing that perpetrators of violence choose to be violent, and only a few acknowledge the harm that they have done, but their narratives reveal that their choices may have layers of complexity, particularly when people are deprived of meaningful opportunities to choose how they live their lives.

A visible example of the refusal to live with revenge or to be known as a victim is Father Michael Lapsley, who laid responsibility for the bomb that caused his hands to be amputated and an eye to be lost on F. W. de Klerk.[6] Lapsley has metal hooks in place of hands. A witness to Lapsley's testimony at the South African TRC writes, "Several times the pincers move towards his face in a reflex action—as if he wants to cover his face with his hands—and every movement flashes the inhumanity of South Africa's past into the hall . . . hard, shiny, and sterile" (Krog 1999: 133). Yet somehow Lapsley could say, "I do not see myself as a victim, but as a survivor of apartheid" (in Krog 1999: 133). Pumla Gobodo-Madikizela, a psychologist on the staff of the South African TRC, describes the victim's resolve: "'I cannot and will not return the evil you inflicted on me' not only as 'the victim's triumph' but as 'a kind of revenge'" (2003: 117). This is a powerful, active agency. Someone like Lapsley cringes at the idea of being called a victim, preferring to be seen by others as "survivors of apartheid or more importantly, victors over apartheid" (Lapsley 1998: 744; 2012: 21).

Similar examples highlight the strength of victims' resilience. Leymah Gbowee, in her 2011 Nobel Peace Prize lecture, explains how in 2003 seven Liberian women met to discuss the rapid advance of the civil war on the capital, Monrovia. These women had seen the effects of violence and, despite the suffering, "used our pains, broken bodies, and scattered emotions to confront the injustices and terror of our nation" (Gbowee 2011). Gbowee's use of language is strong, indicating the extent of embodied pain. The women's mass action campaign spread to over fifty communities across Liberia, where women dressed in white demonstrated in the streets, "daily confronting warlords, meeting with dictators, and refusing to be silenced" in the face of weapons (Gbowee 2011). Coming from different educational, class, and faith backgrounds, they focused on a common agenda. Despite the daily fear, they refused to be identified as victims. Gbowee (2011) states,

> We succeeded when no one thought we would, we were the conscience of the ones who'd lost their consciences in the quest for power and political positions. We represented the soul of the nation. . . . When confronting warlords we did so because we felt it was a moral duty to stand as mothers.

She affirms that the prestigious prize came "at a time when ordinary mothers are no longer baking for peace, but demanding peace, justice, equality, and inclusion in political decision-making" (Gbowee 2011). Victims who become survivors are often influential agents of change, able to respond to war's harm in brave, creative ways.

In a different context, Sumona DasGupta and Meenakshi Gopinath write about an initiative of the Women in Security, Conflict Management, and Peace (WISCOMP) group called Athwaas, which is a Kashmiri word that implies a warm handshake. In 2000 WISCOMP organized a roundtable for Kashmiri women from diverse backgrounds to share their stories. A group of Muslims, Hindus, and Sikhs decided to visit each other's realities, to "record women's voices, and build bridges of trust" (DasGupta and Gopinath 2005: 112). During 2001–2003 a group visited remote villages in North and South Kashmir and then migrant camps in Jammu. The women kept diaries and shared with the group their testimonies of horror, custodial deaths, torture, flight, escape, exile, and exploitation. The group reflected diverse experiences, ideologies, and views on the causes of the conflict. "The realities they encountered and the firsthand testimonies they heard shook some of these beliefs and perceptions to the core" (2005: 113–114). As I explain in Chapter 4, there is not a singular truth about reasons for violent conflict. Yet a common thread bound these women together. One part of the fabric of the story tells of shared "pain, loss, and suffering"; the other part tells of "courage and determination in the face of adversity" (2005: 114). This example demonstrates how many women in particular manage to negotiate the space between victimhood and agency, and the boundaries between these stages of one's narrative often blur. Only in taking into account a person's narrative does the complexity of this space come fully into the light.

The issue of memory recurs in the following chapters, so it is worth reflecting deeper on how memory affects victims. Some want to forget the harms endured but cannot because war damages humanity so deeply. Others never want to forget their suffering and remain tormented. Only a few live easily with the memories. Susanne Buckley-Zistal (2006) conducted interviews in Kinyarwanda from 2003 to 2004 in Nyamata district in Kigali Ngali province and in Gikongoro province in Rwanda. These sites were chosen due to their proximity to mass graves and memorial sites. The interviewees were chosen specifically for particular backgrounds, including details like relatives of people accused of participating in the genocide, individuals who have been released from prison, Tutsi returnees who were brought up in the diaspora, survivors working in survivor organizations or at genocide sites, and individuals seeking to contribute to the reconciliation process (2006: 132). Buckley-Zistal (2006: 136) notes that clarifying the exact role of the interviewees in the genocide is difficult; thus she acknowledges that many of the interviews are generalizations that simply homogenize the diverse experiences of war and genocide. The particularity of interviewees is important because attention to specific stories begins the process of further understanding the way that narratives can reveal hidden features about the cruelty inflicted on humans during war.

What Buckley-Zistal witnessed throughout the interviews was a "chosen amnesia" (2006: 133). Although remembering the genocide as important, certain aspects of the past were notably omitted from the interviews. Many interviewees expressed the view that, despite public sentiments of reconciliation, they felt differently in their hearts. Some interviewees also cautioned Buckley-Zistal that, although an impression of peaceful coexistence may appear, many people hide their true feelings, particularly from outsiders. The notion of "chosen amnesia" implies that a person does not choose to access a particular memory that is stored in one's mind. Buckley-Zistal acknowledges that the inability to remember seemed deliberate among many Rwandans because they did not want to recall events of the past. Many interviewees stated that they could not recall what triggered the genocide. Buckley-Zistal suggests that this effect is positive because it may serve a particular function deriving from a particular need of the present. This amnesia is chosen as opposed to coerced, since it does not represent a public denial of events, but rather a coping mechanism that enables those involved to live peacefully. Buckley-Zistal writes that "remembering to forget is thus essential for local coexistence" (2006: 134). One survivor told her that when prisoners were released into the neighborhood, there was an understandable anxiety because, while they see each other every day, they never talk. An elderly man told her, "It is important not to forget the past so that we can prevent the future. . . . Nobody has won this war; everybody has lost at least one family member" (2006: 137). Choosing to remember or forget is the victim-survivor's prerogative. The choice is an agential coping mechanism in dealing with war's damage to self-identity.

Shame and Guilt

Memories can torment traumatized victims when they are troubled by emotions of shame and guilt. Fear, silencing, and being silenced, as well as shame and guilt, freeze emotions, trapping the traumatized in inertia. As a consequence, the ability to make everyday decisions is difficult. The memory is the story, so the narrative is stuck in a rut. Nomfundo Walaza, a clinical psychologist, discusses some important differences between guilt and shame as she discerned them in the South African TRC. She suggests,

> Guilt is such a useless thing. Guilt immobilizes you. . . . Feelings of guilt are also open to abuse by those who suffered. . . . I prefer shame. Because when you feel shame about something you really want to change it, because it's not comfortable to sit with shame. (in Krog 1999: 161)

Yet I think that shame can also immobilize, particularly when the horrors of abuse debilitate the human spirit. Some victims remain trapped in shame; others seek to break free. Rose Marie Mukanwiza is a Tutsi from Huye, Rwanda. Her husband, five children, mother, father, six brothers, three sisters, and all of their children were killed during the 1994 genocide. When fifty-nine years old, she recounted the story that Gakuba raped her. Gakuba wrote to her from prison in 2007 asking for forgiveness, and she testified at his *gacaca* trial. She said, "I'm a living shame, but I know the cause of my shame is *theirs, the rapists,* and I would like to see him *to make him really think about what he did*" (in Totten and Ubaldo 2011: 32). This confirms Walaza's position above that shame can prompt some people to instigate change. As we see in the next chapter, providing space for survivors of violence to tell their story and be heard is an important step in psychological healing of the wounds of trauma.

Shame comes in different forms. Sekai Nzenza, a Zimbabwean international development consultant, writes of her "African grief" as she went from Australia to Rwanda to conduct her first interview with two widows who were survivors of the genocide. She knew that these women lost many relatives. The point of the interview was to assess how international aid can help with reconciliation. She felt tense and uncomfortable with their abrupt responses. She suspected they would be more comfortable with a white woman, but as a black woman she concluded that "working for a western NGO did not give me the right to intrude into these women's lives" (2006: 148). She felt excluded from even understanding the women's pain and grief. Her emotions changed when, on the next day, fifteen-year-old Claudine, head of a family of five siblings, asked her to visit her two-room house. Nzenza asked Claudine where her father was buried, and Claudine stood up, collected something, and emptied the contents of an old brown sack. With great shock Nzenza saw the contents: human bones, the bones of Claudine's father and aunt. The women helped each other return the bones to the sack. Nzenza went outside to pray to God and her ancestors and writes, "I spoke the way my grandmother used to speak—a mixture of fear, anger, and forgiveness" (2006: 151). She had understood something of what it means to "make the pain of strangers our own" (2006: 152). In Chapter 7 I argue that empathy and compassion are crucial qualities needed in order to connect to people with troubled narratives whose humanity has been damaged in war.

How Should We Respond to Suffering?

What, then, is involved in responding to victimhood, pain, shame, guilt, and suffering? How can moral agents of good find those multiple spaces that are sufficiently flexible to overcome the terrible harms that the evil of war create? Further, how can agents of good assist in nonpatronizing ways? By agents of good, I simply mean anyone who is actively trying to alleviate the harms of war and lessen the damage caused. A fuller response to these questions unfolds in Chapter 7 in a discussion on compassion. Here I examine briefly what is involved in the principles underlying the responsibility to protect those who are suffering because of ongoing war. I argue that there is an obligation to assist in the healing process of the traumatized, but the fulfillment of this obligation needs to be shared across a range of support services.

Responsibility to Protect

The Peace of Westphalia in 1648 set the foundations for the modern system of sovereign states that would not intervene in each other's affairs. Sovereignty implies immunity from outside scrutiny or sanction. The Realpolitik of Bosnia, Burundi, Darfur, Kosovo, Rwanda, and Somalia exposed the urgencies of intervention on humanitarian grounds. In the 1990s, seventy-nine of the eighty-two intrastate conflicts were on the African continent (Sarkin 2009: 2). The Responsibility to Protect (R2P) principles were formally embraced by the UN General Assembly at the 2005 World Summit and accepted by the UN Security Council in 2006. Before explaining these principles, it is interesting to recall how Gareth Evans, the primary architect of these international norms, reflects on his personal journey that contributed to their genesis. I told his story above in the section on evil, how in 1968 he travelled through Asia, Africa, and the Middle East. Later, he met again many of the friends he made on his travels, except he did not meet one Cambodian friend. This grave knowledge haunted him and underlies his contribution to developing the R2P principles.

These principles of R2P accept that "state sovereignty implies responsibility, and the primary responsibility for the protection of its people lies with the state itself" (Evans 2008: 40). Thus, "Where a population is suffering serious harm, as a result of internal war, insurgency, repression or state failure, and the state in question is unwilling or unable to halt or avert it, the principle of non-intervention yields to the international responsibility to protect" (2008: 40). Three responsibilities are central. The "responsibility to prevent" addresses "both the root causes and direct causes of internal conflict and other . . . crises putting populations at risk" (2008: 41). Second, the "responsibility to react" requires the need "to respond to situations of compelling human need with appropriate measures, which may include coercive measures like sanctions and international prosecution, and in extreme cases military intervention" (2008: 41). Third, the "responsibility to rebuild" is "to provide, particularly after a military intervention, full assistance with recovery, reconstruction, and reconciliation, addressing the causes of the harm the intervention was designed to halt or avert" (2008: 41). The priority of R2P is clear: *"Prevention is the single most important dimension of the responsibility to protect"* (2008: 41). Other components of R2P include: "instilling and installing democracy, human rights promotion and protection, good governance, the rule of law and anti-corruption strategies" (Sarkin 2009: 11). The linking of protection with prevention is fundamental; it is a felt imperative to act.

Again, stories relating to these principles help to capture their application. Lieutenant General Roméo Dallaire, as force commander of the UN Assistance Mission to Rwanda, wrote,

> At its heart the Rwandan story is the failure of humanity to heed a call for help from an endangered people. . . . While most nations agreed something should be done, they all had an excuse why they should not be the ones to do it. As a result, the UN was denied the political will and material means to prevent the tragedy. (2004: 516)

In response to humanitarian crises and the promise of R2P, Evans reflects with hope "a belief that even the most horrible and intractable problems are soluble; that rational solutions for which there are good, principled arguments do eventually prevail; and that good people, good governments, and good governance will eventually prevail over bad" (2008: 7).

In addition to the responsibility to protect and to prevent violence, there is an obligation for local and international communities to assist the healing process for those who have been traumatized by violence. As noted, the reasons for victim trauma are multiple and include injury, loss, bereavement, humiliation, pain, and nightmares. Perpetrators of abuse can also experience trauma, reliving the horrors of acts they have committed. Trauma manifests itself in multiple ways, through emotions of anger, distrust, fear, hatred, helplessness, shame, and vengefulness. Some traumatized people withdraw, unable to socialize and interact. Their humanity has been so severely damaged. Others lash out in frustration and bitterness. Still others are overwhelmed by the poverty and material deprivation that accompany violent conflict. Hence, "Healing must take a holistic approach" that aims "to rebuild the whole or complete person" (Clark 2008a: 200). What individuals require for this healing differs according to individual identities, gender, types of victimhood, or violence committed. "Thus, healing requires rehumanizing survivors and perpetrators to overcome the negative identities that they assumed during conflict" (Clark 2008a: 201). This type of healing is crucial for reconciliation.

Gaining justice can advance healing for those who suffer lingering injustices. Assisting the process of furthering justice is part of the responsibility to protect victims, and it can go a long way to fulfilling the obligation to aid healing. Naomi Cahn, Dina Haynes, and Fionnuala Ní Aoláin posit a comprehensive concept of "social services justice," which "requires a multi-sectoral approach that involves the community as well as health, legal, security, and the social services actors" (2010: 357). This practical justice orientation can respond to specific needs for healing injustice because it is grounded in lived experiences. One example these authors give of a gender-specific approach to responding to postconflict needs is the cookstove project in Darfur. When it became clear that women and girls were often sexually assaulted when venturing out of refugee camps to collect firewood, engineers talked with women about alternatives for developing fuel-effective stoves. Practical engagement with people to discern their needs is crucial in responding to long legacies of deprivation and injustice.

To conclude, to say that suffering is part of the human condition, according to Elizabeth Spelman (1997), suggests at least three implications. First, to take suffering earnestly is to take the humanity of the sufferer seriously. Second, in acknowledging the humanity of others and in taking their suffering sincerely, there needs to be "the willingness to consider their view of what that suffering means" (Spelman 1997: 168). Listening and seeking to understand a narrative necessitate stepping outside of one's comfort zone. In this listening zone, there is no place for reproach, hasty judgment, or criticism. For many of us, this space is awkward because it goes against the natural grain of our tendencies to react. Third, when we listen to the voices of suffering, differences between humans are articulated. Types of suffering vary; thus, responses must differ. We can never fully restore the brokenness that occurs when people are harmed during wars' torment, because the harm is part of the life narrative. We are who we are because of life's experiences. To apply a phrase Govier uses, in "righting wrongs" (2006: 178) there are a range of options—from compensations to redress, rehabilitation, remedy, repair, reparations, or restoration. Through listening to stories told by someone who has suffered under extreme cruelty, we provide for that story to cease to overshadow the life narrative. In responding this way, hope is instilled for a transformed future.

* * *

In this chapter I have explored the overarching question of what considerations are needed in knowing how to respond to the harms of war, and particularly the way these harms damage the humanity of victims. The focus was on three central issues: the profound effect of evil in causing suffering, the extreme harm of crimes against humanity, and the long-term loss of dignity in being a victim of violent conflict. My central argument is that, in the light of deep suffering caused by the evil of war, a fourth key issue comes to the fore: the responsibility to respond to alleviate anguish where and when it is possible. These responses should be differentiated according to lived experiences and the specific needs of differing genders, ages, families, communities, and cultural norms. However, far preferable is the prevention of violence.

Notes

1. I do not refer to the suffering that occurs through natural disasters.

2. In teaching courses on these topics in Australian universities, refugee students, particularly African students, tell me how incredibly difficult it is for them to read, study, think, discuss, and write on these issues. When they feel ready, some come to tell me parts of their story or share parts of it in class. Memories linger. Many have told me that, after overcoming initial difficulties

in reliving the past, they are grateful to have the opportunity to reveal aspects of their story and reflect on their war-influenced narratives, discovering that they are not alone.

3. For a discussion of the Nuremberg and Tokyo tribunals, see Kaufman (2010).

4. The most powerful female member of the pregenocide Rwandan government, Pauline Nyiramasuhuko, the national minister of Family and Women's Affairs, in 1994 ordered civilian death squads to rape Tutsi women. She is the first woman to be charged with rape as a crime against humanity.

5. I use "East Timor" prior to independence and "Timor-Leste" after 2002.

6. De Klerk was the last president of apartheid-era South Africa and helped to broker the end of the era.

4

Do Truth Commissions Work?

What happens when we tell the truth? The role of truth telling in transitional justice settings is crucial. The reason is that without knowing the truth about history, it is too easy to be stuck in the past, and thus ignorant about the range of truths. Also, not knowing the truth about how your loved ones die or where their bones lie can haunt one to mental distraction. In examining the powerful consequences of telling the truth, we need to understand the central place of narratives told in truth commissions in transitional justice processes. Before examining some of these narratives, we must explore some of the major obstacles to acknowledging the truth or engaging in the truth-telling process. Truth is not straightforward. There are different types of truths to examine. After establishing this groundwork on the complexity of truths, my emphasis is on exploring the stories of those who give accounts of the truth. While I give some attention to perpetrators' accounts of their crimes, more attention is given to the emotional impact on victim-survivors who publicly acknowledge their truth stories. I assess the significance of a public platform for victims in being both witnesses to the truth and testifiers of the truth.

The purpose of this chapter is twofold: to investigate the differing weight that different narrative voices give to the importance of telling the truth, particularly in the context of a truth commission, and, to a lesser extent, to gain a better understanding of whether this truth heals some of the damage discussed in the previous chapter. The prime question I am exploring is: Do truth commissions work? Prior to answering this, we need to explore: Does telling the truth work? With "work," my intent is to query how effective the truth told in formal and informal transitional justice contexts is in furthering a just peace. That is, does telling the truth about violence committed or suffering experienced, and uttering the truth or knowing the truth, further peace? If it does, then is truth a form of justice? If so, then does truth telling move people closer to reconciliation? The focus is primarily on truth told in a formal commission and to a lesser degree in informal and traditional postconflict contexts. I argue that there are notable exceptions where withholding the full truth is necessary to protect lives or personal dignity, or to maintain the momentum of a peace process. However, in the main, I believe that truth telling works—that is, it is effective in collecting the truth of a nation's narrative, acknowledging victims' stories, and bearing witness to the extent of human suffering.

What Are the Obstacles to Truth?

Before looking at the positive dimensions of truth telling, it is important to clear the path and examine what obstacles block truth. In particular, there often is a refusal to state the truth, and so it is worth trying to understand some of the reasons why people or states hide the truth, suppress it, or lie. Obstacles to truth at high levels are significant. Desmond Tutu asks a pertinent question: "If leaders may lie, then who should tell the truth?" (2012: 31). Days before US president George W. Bush and UK prime minister Tony Blair ordered the invasion of Iraq in 2003, Tutu contacted the White House to urge that UN weapons inspectors be given more time to confirm or deny the existence of weapons of mass destruction. Since the invasion, enormous numbers of Iraqis have died or been wounded along with soldiers from the "coalition of the willing."[1] Tutu asks questions about the relationship between leadership and morality and what messages are sent out "if it is acceptable for leaders to take drastic action on the basis of a lie, without an acknowledgment or an apology when they are found out" (2012: 31). Within international relations, decisions are based on a combination of moral principles, pragmatism, and international law in order to make sound judgments that are protective of citizens and states. Lies defy good ethics.

However, politicians often conclude that telling the full truth is not always prudent. For example, when a senior politician is arrested for questioning on allegations of murders that happened decades ago, such an act to gain the truth may jeopardize a peace process.[2] As we see later when analyzing victims' stories, truth telling can lead to all sorts of anticipated or unexpected implications. There are limitations on what truth actually achieves. Juliane Okot Bitek witnessed the effects of the war in northern Uganda between rebel groups, particularly between the Lord's Resistance Army and the government of Uganda. She writes as an Acholi woman who lives in the diaspora, but identifies with a home situated in a war zone. She calls truth and reconciliation "warring siblings" and warns that "they can be harmful to the process of attaining healing" (2012: 394). She suggests that any notion of "the whole truth and nothing but the truth" should be limited to courts, because, "like remembering and forgetting, truth must be taken in with restraint and respect, just enough to propel us forward towards healing" (2012: 394). We have different capacities for taking in the details about the horrors of the past. Sometimes a sketch of what has happened will suffice. For others, the full picture is needed, even when it is dark and gloomy.

So often, truth is seen as integral to transitional justice processes because of the assumption that truth decreases the desire for vengeance. Karen Brounéus conducted a large random survey of twelve hundred Rwandans from four provinces who were witnesses to the gacaca village tribunals after the 1994 genocide. Her research questions led her to challenge whether truth telling necessarily is cathartic. In her study on truth telling and psychological health, she speaks of her results as disconcerting in that "witnesses in *gacaca* reported higher levels of depression and post-traumatic stress disorder than non-witnesses" (2010: 409). Later, I explain more fully how witnessing to the stark reality of horrible truths can retraumatize victims. Yet some people achieve an emotional release in learning about others' stories, despite the trauma of hearing the truth. The point here is to note some limitations to the value of the truth-telling process. Telling and hearing the truth are important to most people, but how the truth is learned—and what support there is after telling the truth or learning about the truth—is crucial. Appropriate support is particularly essential for women and girls who tell the truth about being sexually abused, because it takes courage to do so. Possible obstacles of partial truths, varying values to truth, or the range of retraumatization in truth telling need to be considered in assessing whether telling the truth works to further peace, justice, and reconciliation.

A further possible limitation in the truth-telling process relates to amnesties, which frequently are offered as part of truth commissions. They are pardons given in advance of the promise of telling the truth about crimes committed that had a political motivation. Someone who receives amnesty cannot be prosecuted in court for the political act. The reasons for granting amnesties are complex. Sometimes the intent is to seek to get a fuller historical record than would be possible if the chief perpetrators of abuses were not included. In cases of peace negotiations, without the presence of leaders of conflict groups and reformed high-profile perpetrators, there cannot be fair interaction between opposing groups that are vying for power. Other times, the reason for amnesty is more pragmatic; there may be many perpetrators of violence, as in the Rwandan genocide, so some form of pardon or adaptive judicial process is warranted.

Sometimes amnesties act as obstacles to truth because victims and survivors of abuses feel that justice is compromised and the full truth is never discovered in the interests of the political pardon for perpetrators. While amnesties frequently are an important compromise in messy transitional justice processes, and all sorts of compromises are accepted to get truth-telling processes moving, should truth be prioritized over justice?

Certainly, amnesties can help truth commissions increase the numbers of people who are able to testify and thus broaden the scope of the truth told. Ironically, this approach can be seen as both enlarging the scope of justice (in allowing perpetrators to tell their stories) and undermining justice (in considering truth, pardon, and forgiveness from victims to be more important than prosecution of perpetrators). Amnesties also can limit the type of truth that perpetrators are willing to provide when they know they have been given some political pardon in exchange for telling the truth. When truth commissions hide the identification of perpetrators of abuses, they deprive "victims and their families of one of the most important forms of redress—the public naming and shaming of those directly responsible for their injuries, pain, and loss" (Rigby 2001: 89). Andrew Rigby suggests that there was a weakness with the Latin American model of truth commissions in Argentina, Chile, and Uruguay, where the mandates were limited to investigating disappearances and unlawful killings, which meant there was "too little justice, too little truth, and hence, although social peace was maintained, there was no solid foundation for reconciliation" (Rigby 2001: 126). In contrast, in the South African TRC, amnesty was offered in return for truth.

If one was to think of justice solely in retributive terms, one would never contemplate amnesty. Otherwise, amnesty simply compromises justice to gain limited truth. A conditional amnesty "makes the benefit of an amnesty conditional on certain acts or concessions by the benefited person(s)" (Ambos 2010: 62). Immunity from prosecution is exchanged for the details of testimony. However, an empirical study of South Africa shows that among white South Africans, accepting the truth did seem to contribute to reconciliation, but among black South Africans, this did not occur to the same degree (Gibson 2004).[3] Not all truth telling in societies undergoing transitional justice processes, particularly in truth commissions, has reconciliation as its prime goal, but increasingly there is a strong orientation for it to be so. However, amnesties, while often essential in order to hear the stories from more groups, often continue to block the chance of reconciliation because victims retain a sense of injustice with perpetrator pardons.

Take, for example, Uganda's Amnesty Act of 2000, which granted amnesty to anyone engaged in armed rebellion; all ex-combatants who denounced rebellion were given pardons and could not be prosecuted. Recognizing the absence of grassroots responses to the act—in particular, those of women's voices—the Justice and Reconciliation Project carried out consultations in 2012 in northern Uganda to discern the views both of those impacted by and benefitting from the act. A male respondent told the researchers that what he hated about the Amnesty Commission was "that they forgive the perpetrators, but they don't look at the survivors. It makes people think that you first have to join the rebel group, then you come out to gain from government" (Justice and Reconciliation Project 2012: 4). A female respondent felt that "the Amnesty Act has left out the victims. . . . We're seeing that the perpetrators are enjoying life, while we're suffering" (Justice and Reconciliation Project 2012: 4). Another female respondent expressed dismay that, from the time of the massacre in 2004, people came to seek their views on amnesty. She said that, repeatedly, "We told them that we have chosen to forgive. But from that time up to now, we have not received any report from the people we forgave saying that they have also forgiven us" (Justice and Reconciliation Project 2012: 5). The consultations showed that there was an acceptance that amnesty brings some benefits, but it has limitations in meeting the needs of those who have been through deep trauma during the conflict. Each story of amnesty brings a similar seemingly contradictory conclusion: that amnesty expands the potential scope of truth told, and there will always be victims who feel a sense of injustice that perpetrators of violence gain political pardon and go unpunished.

Why Are Truth Commissions Important?

Taking into account some of these obstacles and limitations to truth, I turn now to examine the more encouraging narrative dimensions of truth telling, testifying, and witnessing, as they are manifest in truth commissions. To clarify, I do not provide here an in-depth account of truth commissions. Rather, I seek to unpack the fundamental value of telling the truth in a truth commission.

Truth is complex. There are degrees of truth. There are whispers of truth, partial truths, half-truths, hearsay, and discrepancies with different versions of truth. Even within one so-called truth narrative there can be great variance in the interpretation of a story. In this chapter, "'Truth narratives' are stories about people's lives as they understand them" (Porter 2007b: 21), while accepting that others may interpret the narratives differently. Such an open understanding differs from claims to exclusive truth, where anybody else's versions of truth are seen as heretical; that is, all contrasting versions are considered to be wrong. This exclusivity of truth is a dominant stance in divided societies. It is unyielding.

There are important questions to ask—for example, whose version of truth is reliable and to be trusted? When there are a range of stories about the same event, how do we assess what is true and worthy of consideration and what is simply stated for expediency, pragmatism, or convenience, or to receive some type of amnesty or pardon? John Paul Lederach cites an example from Tajikistan where philosopher Professor Abdul told Lederach his story about negotiations with a warlord and how the meeting took a long time because "you have to circle into truth through stories" (2005: 18). Such circling may involve movement in and out of the truth, always getting closer, but not quite reaching the nub. In this chapter I concentrate on precisely these connections between the complexity of truth telling, the layers of the story, and the role of the story within someone's life narrative. In discussing complexity, layers, and a holistic approach, the rich humanity of multifaceted narratives and the variations in meanings of truth come to the fore.

Before contextualizing truth within commissions, let's be clear that in some circumstances truth commissions might not be appropriate, such as when there is fear of ongoing or renewed violence, lack of political interest, insufficient capacity or resources, alternative preferences, or other urgent priorities (Freeman and Hayner 2003: 127). Also, as already mentioned, a truth commission may actually cause more harm than good if it comes too late—that is, if former supporters of armed violence have been part of peace negotiations and have adapted to peaceful democratic politics. Being forced to tell their stories about the past in a formal truth commission would disrupt the ongoing peace process and possibly incite a return to violence.

There are also different ways to look at the potential benefits of truth for a truth commission. Some of these benefits include establishing the truth about the past, promoting the accountability of perpetrators of human rights violations, providing a public platform for victims, informing public debate, recommending victim reparation, recommending legal reforms, promoting social reconciliation, and consolidating a democratic transition (Freeman and Hayner 2003: 125). The focus of a truth commission decidedly is on the victims rather than the perpetrators of violence.

The prime purpose of a truth commission is to uncover the truths that have been either suppressed or are in dispute between individuals, warring rebels, separatist movements, and paramilitary groups, or between the state and citizens. Priscilla Hayner's definition is widely accepted:

> A truth commission (1) is focused on past, rather than ongoing, events; (2) investigates the pattern of events that took place over a period of time; (3) engages directly and broadly with the affected population, capturing information on their experiences; (4) is a temporary body, with the aim of concluding with the final report; and (5) is officially authorized or empowered by the state under review. (Hayner 2011: 11–12)

Note that there is no reference to reconciliation or healing in this definition, yet the terms "truth" and "reconciliation" are often placed together. Hayner rightly cautions that "the central aim of a truth commission is not therapy," and further, "a one-time catharsis" is inadequate for meaningful healing (2011: 151). Yet, as I demonstrate, many truth commissions have the working assumption that public testimony by both victims and perpetrators "affords opportunities for individuals and the nation as a whole to heal" (Minow 1998: 61). I return later to this issue of healing.

In taking into account the experiences from diverse truth commissions, Kai Ambos (2010) suggests that best practices from truth commissions can be summarized as guidelines for further commissions. To summarize Ambos, they include commissioners appointed from all social groups as part of an open process, a contact person for victims and witnesses, adequate resources and independence from the state, a mandate that sheds light on the causes of conflict, follow-up processes, victim reparations, cooperation with state authorities, suspected perpetrators giving evidence with victims present, conditional amnesties, a public report, and a monitoring body to assist with implementation of the recommendations (2010: 46–47).

To date, there have been thirty-three truth commissions and twelve commissions of inquiry.[4] Hayner suggests that the five strongest truth commissions in terms of constructive outcomes occurred in South Africa, Guatemala, Peru, Timor-Leste, and Morocco (2011: xv).[5] Hayner (2011: 235–236) contends that the role of the commissions is changing. Early ones in Argentina, Chile, El Salvador, Guatemala, Sri Lanka, and Uganda focused on what happened and why it happened. Then in South Africa, Sierra Leone, and Timor-Leste came a push for reconciliation. A focus on perpetrators emerged in Ghana, Nigeria, and Liberia, and a deeper analysis of historical facts in Peru and Guatemala. An emphasis on prosecutions and reparations was pronounced in Morocco and Peru, with economic crimes part of the Kenyan commission. The mandate of the commission needs to reflect the nation's history and context. The mandate also provides scope to evaluate the extent to which the outcomes of the commission are fruitful, as a means to assess whether a truth commission is worthwhile and furthers sustainable peace.

Types of Truth

Before examining truth telling in truth commissions and its healing potential, we should clarify different types of truth. Alex Boraine (2005) posits four aspects of truth evident in the South African TRC, and it is reasonable to generalize about these types of truth in other commissions. First, there is objective, factual, or forensic truth, for which there is evidence to establish what has happened—for example, the apartheid state substantiating torture by its security forces. Second, there are personal narrative dimensions of truth told in the stories by victims and perpetrators. These forms of truths arise from being a witness to the experiences of personal suffering and victimization, and also of being a victim with firsthand knowledge of suffering. These subjective truths are based on personal perceptions and memories. Third, there is a dialogical truth that can emerge through social interaction, transparency, and mutual respect. Fourth, a healing comes with restorative truth when knowledge is "accompanied by acknowledgment and acceptance of accountability" (Boraine 2005: 329). As Trudy Govier puts it, truth "is irrelevant unless it is both known and *acknowledged* by the people involved" (2006: 14). She explains further that this acknowledgment should involve a public expression of the truth. Ambos discusses additional types of truths, including global truth, macro-truth, moral truth, overall truth, objective truth, and historical truth, not merely judicial or factual truth (2010: 41). To clarify, in this chapter I concentrate on three types of truths: narratives, dialogical truth, and healing truth. However, I do not always narrowly clarify the distinctions between the types of truths because they are so interrelated.

Having said that, it is useful to explain healing truth. Healing truth usually accompanies commissions that have mandates for reconciliation in addition to truth. The idea is that, in securing a full public version of the truth, more chance exists for healing the nation. Healing truth should come with the production of a collective narrative of a nation's story that includes the voices of those who previously had been deprived of a space to express their stories. It is easy to understand why. When stories are suppressed, the underlying reasons for ongoing hostilities and alienation are not exposed. Truth underlies reconciliation. However, to go beyond a mere cliché, what it really means needs to be spelled out. Lederach reflects on the way that, in postaccord processes, many people repeat to him that they have no voice in decisions that affect them, and here he defines voice as "meaningful conversation and power" (2005: 56). He elaborates further, "*Meaningful conversation* suggests mutuality, understanding, and accessibility. *Power* suggests that the conversation makes a difference: Our voices are heard and have some impact on the direction of the process and the decisions made" (2005: 56). In such a meaningful conversation, agency is realized. Juan Méndez, a survivor of torture by the Argentinean military dictatorship, suggests that truth commissions "work best when conceived as a key component in a holistic process of truth-telling, justice, reparations, and eventual reconciliation" (2001: 29). Certainly truth must be exposed for justice to be realized and for reconciliation processes to be launched, when the groundwork for healing has begun.

We return now to the point that different people experience different truths. Even the interpretation of one particular historical act can have multiple versions of the truth. For example, in Bosnia and Herzegovina, among Bosnian Serbs, Bosnian Muslims, and Bosnian Croats, there are at least "three ethnic versions of truth" on issues such as "who were the aggressors and on who were the principal victims" (Clark 2011: 248). While tribunals and truth commissions can establish facts, communities interpret these details differently and develop different communal and national narratives accordingly. Sometimes the narratives energize a nation; other times only particular groups experience some healing of wounds.

South African Truth and Reconciliation Commission

The South African TRC played such an important role in establishing fundamental guidelines on what can be achieved in a commission that it is worth paying it particular attention, not solely in this section, but throughout the rest of the chapter. Alex Boraine, deputy chair of the South African TRC, wrote his "insider's story" from a personal vantage point influenced by "experiences, observations, participation, feelings, prejudices, biases, and the like" (2000: 1). He describes the TRC as arising "out of the white heat of traumatic and often heart-wrenching disclosures from victims, survivors, and perpetrators alike" (2000: 1). He stresses the anecdotal, personal interpretations, and that we have a lot to glean from them. Boraine summarizes it this way: "The story I have tried to tell, therefore, is a personal account of hope breaking the bonds of hopelessness and goodness triumphing over evil, through truth-telling and accountability" (2000: 3). There is honesty in admitting that the TRC affected people differently. For some, it ended their night-mares; others felt relief at hearing the truth, despite the accompanying and continuing pain. Yet for others, truth did not bring closure.

The aims of the TRC had a focus on victims' civil and human rights with the hope that recording the truth would help restore the moral order. In listening to the stories, many of the commissioners absorbed much of the grief of the victims' trauma. Boraine writes of the story told by Nomonde Calata, widow of one of the Cradock Four murdered in 1984. In giving evidence, "She broke down and the primeval and spon-taneous wail from the depths of her soul was carried live on radio and television" (2000: 102). Boraine explains how that soul cry symbolized the dark horrors of the apartheid years, capturing "the collective horror of the thousands of people who had been trapped in racism and oppres-sion for so long" (2000: 102). He tells another story of Beth Savage, a white woman who carries shrapnel in her body from a hand grenade attack at a golf club. In her account she confirmed that she wanted to meet the man who threw the grenade in order to forgive him and hope that he could forgive her. Boraine felt that her sentiments "acknowl-edged the responsibility of the beneficiaries of apartheid for some of the horror and tragedy of the conflict" (2000: 104). Boraine underlines that the stories told in the TRC were heart wrenching. He writes that "to lis-ten to one man relate how his wife and baby were cruelly murdered is much more powerful and moving than statistics which describe a mas-sacre involving many victims" (2000: 290). Boraine's writings reinforce the prime purpose of this book in showing that the human face of these narratives is painfully real.

Within the TRC, the use of the traditional African concept of *ubuntu* helped to accentuate the human face. Tutu's explanation is helpful in explaining how ubuntu speaks to the essence of what it is to be human:

> It is to say, "My humanity is caught up, is inextricably bound up, in yours." . . . It says rather: "I am human because I belong. I participate, I share." A person with ubuntu is open and available to others, affirming of others, does not feel threatened that others are able and good, for he or she has a proper self-assurance that comes from knowing that he or she belongs in a greater whole and is diminished when others are humiliated or diminished. (Tutu 1999: 35)

This concept is rich in significance in implying that relationships that are in disrepair jeopardize one's humanity. It underlies the basis to narrative agency outlined in Chapter 2 where our narratives influence and are influenced by networks of relationships. Truth commissions are important in bringing to the fore this narrative complexity and telling the truth about the violent past.

Can Victims Be Storytellers and Witnesses?

I now turn to those whose humanity has been deeply jeopardized: the victims. As I discussed in the previous chapter, even the notion of who is a victim can be controversial. In this context, anyone who self-identifies as victim is of concern. Central to truth commissions are individual victims' testimonies of suffering. They are storytellers. Their stories are tragic, but most need to be told. There are always exceptions, where solid reasons for untold stories are apparent. Witnessing to these stories "is an integral part of the dialogical process of establishing social recognition and meaning" (Humphrey 2002: 114), because, as Martha Minow puts it, truth telling has a restorative power. By this she means that "when the work of knowing and telling the story has come to an end, the trauma then belongs to the past, the survivor can face the work of building a future" (1998: 67). However, her qualification about what is involved in knowing about the story is important. She reminds us that the commissioners and staff in truth commissions must attend to the importance of the personal narrative, which is always going to be emotional because it evokes traumatic memories. Knowing how to respond to the telling of a story requires great sensitivity. The hope is that, through the process of telling one's story and in being listened to, survivors of trauma become subjects again, able to reclaim their individual and group identities. The opportunity to express one's voice should stimulate hope for a transformed future. My point here is that storytelling and witnessing are connected.

Pumla Gobodo-Madikizela addresses three levels of witnessing in narratives that deal with traumatic pasts. First, "witnessing through language" involves the words told in retelling a story to an audience (2008b: 176). Second, there is the witnessing of trauma that is carried internally, often at an unconscious level. Third, another layer of witnessing happens, typically at truth commissions or trials, where perpetrators of abuse are present, particularly those who feel some remorse. In these situations, Gobodo-Madikizela writes that "victims find their voice to speak the unspeakable," and perpetrators "confront the consequences of their actions in public" (2008b: 176). In poetic terms, she calls this the "witnessing dance," where both victim and perpetrator speak to each other and also bear witness to the stories they bring. Through doing so, perpetrators rehumanize the victims and reclaim their own sense of humanity. The possibility of this happening must be qualified. This "witnessing dance" can only happen when the perpetrator is remorseful and the victim is willing to confront the perpetrator. In this sense, victims can be both storytellers and witnesses.

What are some examples of victim storytellers? Before the Guatemalan Historical Clarification Commission began, many journalists and human rights workers reported the population's strong desire to share their stories and tell truths. A Guatemalan forensic anthropology group that exhumes bones from massacre sites held a public meeting on April 18, 1996, in an area known for political violence. They were releasing a report and expected fewer than one hundred people to attend. Instead, more than five hundred people came to the meeting, which speedily turned into a series of testimonials about their experiences. In a subsequent interview, Fernando Moscoso and Juan Alberto Chamale Gómez from the Guatemalan Forensic Anthropology Team discussed this need to share stories and acknowledge truth. Many victims wanted to relate their story, despite not knowing who was listening or who might "report back to the military about who was saying what" (in Hayner 2011: 148). The urgency for many to tell their story compels truth telling. These stories are not idle gossip; rather they are stories that touch the deepest part of a dehumanized soul and sit within a range of individual and communal narratives of loss, pain, and despair.

The examples, unfortunately, are manifold. In South Africa, Sylvia Dlomo-Jele's teenage son was killed in 1988, and she went to the TRC to tell her story. She later told Hayner that giving testimony differs for everyone. This woman knew a woman who told her, "I don't want to talk about it; my son won't come back" (in Hayner 2011: 150). But for Dlomo-Jele, her testimony at the public hearing was the first time she had told what had happened to her since the death of her son. She said,

> Not talking about it . . . was killing me inside. . . . Giving testimony, telling the whole world what happened to me. . . . It was painful, but also a relief. The way they listened to me, the interest they showed in my story, that was good for me. (in Hayner 2011: 150)

Giving testimony in a truth commission involves having one's story acknowledged. Acknowledgment is a crucial part of recognition of the other; it helps to break down dualistic them-and-us mindsets, and in particular it affirms the person who has given testimony. Telling the truth in truth commissions works to improve greater acknowledgment of diverse stories.

In addition to the importance to individual victims of telling their stories and having their stories heard and their dignity even partially restored, truth telling in truth commissions is significant as part of redefining a nation's narrative.

> In the context of truth commissions, the commitment to narratability—to witness and confession—contributes to the mandated retelling of the nation's past, to establish an archive, opens the country to new narratives of identity, and legitimates the authority of the "new" state for all its citizens. (Schaffer and Smith 2004: 66)

The storytelling process of a truth commission can never capture the whole story of individuals, groups, and a nation, but it goes a long way to contributing toward a much broader, enriched story of a nation's history. There does seem to be a distinct need on the part of many victims to tell their stories and to be listened to, despite many knowing that unsympathetic perpetrators of their abuse live close to them, while others know that their violator has shown a degree of remorse.

Silence

To understand more about the significance of truth, curiously, we need to understand more about the withholding of truth, and here I refer particularly to deliberate, intentional silence. A Tutsi survivor of the 1994 Rwandan genocide declared that "the intimate truth of the genocide belongs to those who lived it and so does the right to withhold this truth, for it is not something to be shared with just anyone" (in Clark 2011: 250). This statement reinforces the need to claim personal power with regard to truth, so that telling one's story and withholding one's story can both be acts of agency. One of the starkest examples of this agency lay in the South African TRC, where special hearings on women were instituted because women were not testifying about themselves, but about their fathers, brothers, sons, nephews, and uncles. In these hearings,

> It was easier to keep silent. Female Premiers, Ministers, business women—kept silent. Some of them had been tortured, some of them raped. One of them gave birth in jail in front of a horde of laughing, jeering wardens. All of them are formidable women. Yet they did not come forward. They did not speak. (Krog 2001: 205)

Since being abused, these particular women had gained high-profile status in the community and understandably did not want to be reminded of the shame of their past or have anything jeopardize their prominent public positions.

Fiona Ross's account of bearing witness to the special hearings of women's experiences in the South African TRC is powerful. The basis of her analysis is that the "telling of pain is an act of intimacy" (2003: 6). In giving testimonies, individual experiences of violence were translated from narratives of pain into stories of human rights violations. To be a witness to such testimonies is to recognize and acknowledge suffering through attentive listening. Of course these were highly emotive accounts, and "the hearings were a public performance of memory, loss, and grief" (2003: 15). Such accounts give voice to pain through words and gestures, and sometimes through appropriate, intentional silence. The issue of silence is crucial. Ross stresses that women's deliberate silence should be recognized as meaningful—that is, as an act of agency. The only way to recognize silence as agency is to probe "the cadences of silences, the gaps between the fragile words, in order to hear what it is that women say" (Ross 2003: 50). Antiapartheid and liberation organizations state that testimony was different from those women who were not activists. "The activists tended to speak more directly of pain, its agents, and its consequences" (2003: 58). Giving voice to one's suffering, affirming one's agency as a speaking subject cannot be too rapidly equated with the healed subject. There is a diversity of efforts to cope with a vast range of different experiences of harm. Speaking might be a first step to all sorts of possibilities associated with personal recovery from trauma. Ross suggests that the "integrity of silence" needs to be respected, given the fragmented and often unfinished nature of emotional recovery (2003: 165).

In a later work, Ross (2010) continues her study on the complexities of silence and speech and what it means to give voice to experience. Reflecting further on the TRC, she draws attention to two underestimated features of violence. First, as mentioned, the commission did not adequately pick up differential gender implications of narratives of harm whereby "women experienced the violences of colonialism, capitalism, and apartheid in the aftermath differently from men" (Ross 2010: 74–75). Hayner, also stressing the need for a gender perspective on stories told in truth commissions, suggests that the question needs to be asked "of how, by whom, against whom, and in what context this sexual violence is taking place" (2011: 88)? These questions are directed toward gaining the full picture of war narratives. While typically these questions are relevant for women and girls, sometimes they are pertinent for men and boys also. Ross's second point here is that the TRC did not grasp the dangers to women of testifying in public mainly because "it read the absence of women's testimony of direct harm as silence caused by reticence, proprietary, or lack of education about rights" (2010: 75). This was not the case. As stated, for many, it was a self-chosen act of agency. Ross's argument is clear, that there are "positive effects of speaking about violence for those who receive adequate support" (2010: 75). However, the motivation behind the decision not to speak about such violence must be understood.

Support is more likely to be forthcoming when there are gender experts present in truth-telling contexts. Where trust and betrayal are entwined, socially sanctioned relations can conceal coercive violence. Thus, narratives of violence call for "trust in the capacity to attend to suffering" (Ross 2010: 79). This involves more than just listening to stories. Often women are blamed for sexual violations; hence their reluctance to speak about the offense is understandable. "It takes courage both to speak of harms done and to be silent in their face and aftermath" (2010: 81). By speaking, some women in the TRC believed they would betray fellow comrades in armed struggle; by keeping silent, many felt that they were resisting solidarity with other women's harms. Deep searching of conscience and personal and communal morality is at stake, and a feeling of being "caught between conflicting desires—to free oneself of a burden, to refuse to open wounds; to reveal, to conceal" (2010: 81) can be overwhelming. Ross acknowledges the weight of responsibility that can fall on some women's shoulders when they feel they should speak for those who are unable to do so. I endorse Ross's conclusion:

> Silence calls for empathic engagement and an assessment of the subtleties of the unspoken in everyday life. In other words, what appears to be silence or absence may actually indicate a failure of recognition and of empathy, and institutional incapacity to attend to suffering. (2010: 90)

Her argument of the requirement to link justice, attentiveness, and responsibility, and thereby to be aware of what happens when there is a failure of attention and responsibility, is one I fully endorse and is extended more fully in Chapter 7. Recognition of unique selfhood is a crucial aspect of healing, and many truth commissions are successful in providing this recognition for women and men.

Charles Taylor's (1992) scholarship places a high priority on the role of this acknowledgment in the mutual recognition of selves in the processes of intersubjectivity. The absence of recognition is a symptom of unrest, with people struggling for acknowledgment, land rights, self-determination, the vote, gender equality, justice in all of its variations, and a decent standard of living. In witnessing victims' stories, there is recognition of the humanity of the other. Often this humanity is affected by a range of factors such as age, disability, ethnicity, gender, religion, and sexual orientation (Ní Aoláin and Turner 2007: 245). Acknowledging such intersectionality of factors increases the chance of gaining a richer understanding of diversity in a narrative. The person's life can be understood more fully than before. Such narratives have greater significance and meaning, and "offer a more compelling story of its past" because they show the multiple ways in which women and men both "experience and articulate harms" (2007: 245). Recent truth commissions from Liberia, Timor-Leste, Peru, Sierra Leone, and Morocco have been more proactive in addressing significant gender challenges and including attention to gender-specific crimes and experiences of women (Hayner 2011: 89). Repeatedly, while men tend to tell their own stories, women tend to tell what happened to their male relatives. Gender responsiveness increases the likelihood of truth commissions fulfilling inclusive, meaningful outcomes.

Beyond the truth commission, sometimes there are legitimate reasons to keep deliberately silent; it is not necessarily a position of weakness or powerlessness. Yet sometimes it is, and the reasons for silence should be explored in truth commissions and other contexts where gaining truth about the past is imperative. Silence can make "us complicit bystanders to the perpetrators of yesterday" (Zorbas 2004: 30), when we do not speak up against the causes of violence and oppression people face and when we knowingly keep quiet. For others there may be a legitimate fear for one's safety or even life if one spoke the truth. This was certainly the case for Elena, the leader of a Mayan women's organization, who knew the danger in talking and thus "had to remain quiet. One could not say what one felt, what one thought, like one was sleeping. One's conscience was sleeping" (in Stern 2005: 92). For others, who may be survivors of gender-based violence, the shame may be more than psychological; it often means being ostracized from communities. As noted in the previous chapter when discussing shame, Bina D'Costa's work on survivors of gender-based violence during and after the independence war of Bangladesh shows the difficulty of finding survivors who are willing to speak of their humiliation. She "learned that the enduring reality of war and survival after the war was articulated not only in women's uttered words, but also in those pregnant pauses during the conversations" (D'Costa 2006: 148). To intuit accurately the potential meaning in such pauses requires empathy and wise judgment in knowing how to respond with attentive care.

Other writers throw further enlightenment on the intrinsic virtue of self-chosen silence in diverse contexts. It is not restricted to women's experience. Cobb describes conversations she had with Hussein, who, after the violence of 1991 in Somalia, fled on a boat that capsized, forcing a swim through shark-infested waters alongside fellow Somalians who did not make it to shore; walking for days; and finding a refugee camp before being granted political asylum in the United States. Hussein explained to Cobb that within the Somalian diaspora the violence experienced and the trauma that resulted were not topics of conversation. When she asked why people did not discuss it, "He explained that they were ashamed and fearful" (Cobb 2013: 169). For some, this shame was caused by realizing their failure to challenge the impunity of perpetrators, others contested accusations of complicity in participating in the violence, and some carried "survivor's guilt" (2013: 170). Hussein had never talked about the violence to anyone previously. Hussein's story is replicated over and over again with people from all conflict zones. Cobb argues that the West's diagnosis of post-traumatic stress disorder is an inadequate description of people's war torment in that "it falls far short of a rich description of their suffering and how it disrupts and harms their lives today" (2013: 170). If people cannot talk about their past for whatever reason, peace negotiations, processes of justice that account for the past, and reconciliation are all stymied. Cobb argues that a particular type of storytelling is needed, one that "demands a kind of witnessing that can generate the conditions for healing and learning at local levels" (2013: 172). These conditions vary across different cultures.

In some cultures, silence is accepted as the way to deal with pain. Marita Eastmond and Johanna Mannergren Selimovic write of how "social strategies of silencing may reveal the interdependency between people in many communities and the need to maintain and nurture social relations and reciprocal arrangements, sometimes as a means of survival" (2012: 504). That is, in "cultures of silence," such as when the reintegration of former Khmer Rouge soldiers into Cambodian villages depended on their showing regret rather than telling truth, or when former refugees of Timor-Leste accepted culpability, "Silence may hold important meanings and carry agency in making and upholding vital relationships" (2012: 505). When these authors write on local communities in Bosnia and Herzegovina, particularly Foča and Sarajevo, they suggest that silence can be understood in pragmatic ways as a strategy for coexistence. Within the Bosnian context, coexistence "refers to the culturally acquired knowledge of how to live with difference" (2012: 508). Their research shows that silence protects social relations, thereby affirming normal life. They concentrated on listening to informal conversations, as well as narratives and semistructured interviews. They found that choices about speaking or being silent are deliberate. A Bosniak man in his seventies who had suffered severely during the war said that his emotions were still too raw, so "it is better to 'keep the peace.' . . . The only civilized way is to forget it and continue living" (2012: 512). These authors stress that this sort of silence does not erase emotions or knowledge of the past. This is not the deliberate amnesia discussed in the previous chapter. A teacher from Foča who had been involved in rebuilding social trust "contended that the possibility of acknowledging the pain of the other is dependent on keeping the silence on central contentious issues" (2012: 514). That is, choosing silence as a conscious way to build peace is a strategy to promote civility. It is also a sign of respect to those who had lost loved ones. One old man, trying not to talk about the war, said, "So if I talk about the war to one who lost a close relative, I will make him remember all of those things" (2012: 515).

Loss for some becomes a family secret, with the details kept tightly within clan groups. Children grow up with stories about their mother's and grandmother's lives or their father's and grandfather's lives and claim this as their private family history. Secrets often remain as secrets, part of the narrative that is a parent's or a grandparent's nostalgia that may or may not resemble actual truth. What I think this reveals is a space for multiple narratives of violence, of understanding the past, and of the courage or reticence to speak the truth. Truth in silence plays very different roles for different people. Overall, in this Bosnian case, these authors conclude "that silences are a consensual and tacitly agreed-upon means of avoiding the personally painful and the socially disruptive when it comes to violence committed during the war" (2012: 521). Silence is both "part of the struggle to normalize life and in itself a normalizing discourse" (2012: 522). Hence, in this context, silence is curiously a crucial part of agency and civility in the difficult postwar period.

Other forms of silencing can occur in a devious fashion. This might happen when the listener frames the speaker as an agent in the conflict. When speakers do not perceive of themselves in this way, powerlessness to be a self-defined agent is debilitating; it damages identity. This is particularly influential when the person doing the misframing is in a powerful position, as often is the case in gendered relationships. The damage comes about because personhood depends on the capacity to speak and be heard with legitimacy. Persons might speak, but when their voices are not validated it is as if they are not speaking at all. The legitimization issue is crucial. Group narratives can delegitimize the other when all the well-used accusations and counteraccusations arise. Where there is no space given for speakers to elaborate the foundation of their narrative core, their central values and plot episodes are spurned. Hence, "The life-world, the lived experience of the speakers, is denied and cancelled; their subjectivity is never materialized, and thus they never can constitute themselves as speaking subjects" (Cobb 2013: 95). When words cease to be a resource, the space in which language matters is emptied of meaning, and the coherence of narrative lives is diminished.

When Malalai Joya was the youngest member of the Afghan Parliament (2005–2007), her microphone was cut off, and she was banished from her seat and threatened with death because of her outspoken words on the inappropriateness of warlords working in elected positions in the government. Joya wrote, "I refuse to compromise my position to the warlords and fundamentalists or soften my speeches denouncing them" (2009: 3). Her statements are strong. She writes that

> telling the truth was not a choice. . . . I had to speak out. It is my duty and my responsibility to the people who voted for me, who gave me

their trust. I had promised them that I would never compromise with
the enemies of human rights. (2009: 89)

A commitment to truth in telling one's story does not always work
in someone's favor. The consequence of this risky stance for Joya is that
she has to live a semisecretive life, always on the move, disguising her
partner's and family's identities. Another instance of the personal costs
of telling the truth lies in Olivera Simić's story. Her parents are Orthodox Serbs, and she identifies as a Yugoslavian and Bosnian with "no
homeland" (Simić 2014: 5). She is a survivor of the Bosnian war who
writes "because of feelings of moral responsibility and shame for injustices and terrible acts committed" by what she calls "my clan" (2014:
20). She faces intense personal tension from her family and friends in
telling the truth as she sees it in her book *Surviving Peace*.

What Is the Power in Truth Telling?

Having examined silence and silencing, within and beyond truth commissions, it is prudent now to examine testimony and the role it plays.
Kelly Oliver (2001) maintains that in the process of giving testimony,
where people are offering a personal account of their experience, they
develop some relationship with the violence they lived through, which
enables them to subdue the violence through storytelling. This idea is
fascinating: that a victim can, in a partial way, potentially come to grips
with the devastating effect of violence through recounting what happened. Just as the instance of suppressed voice can humiliate, debilitate,
and destroy dignity, so in contrast the act of giving voice to one's story
has great potential power to reinstate self-confidence and restore self-
dignity. The idea of subduing violence is deep in symbolism. It can
pacify, moderate, tame extreme emotions, and soothe. What is unique
about giving testimony is "that no other person can give testimony for
someone else" (Cobb 2013: 180). In the performance of testimony given
in a truth commission, there is a bringing of the "silences and blind-
nesses, inherent in the event" (Oliver 2001: 86) to the seemingly impossible: articulating the inarticulable. By witnessing testimony from individuals and groups who have a damaged sense of self, the struggle to
make sense of reality comes alive. In this space where people frame
their suffering, witnesses to the testimony observe a narrative performance that often is at the outer fringes of the ordinary. This is to be
expected, given the types of stories being told. Witnessing to stories of

suffering can lead to the emotional release of the teller and the witness. Strong emotions of anger, bitterness, torment, and grief are expressed. I like Cobb's expression that "bearing witness is the process of pushing narratives toward that edge where meaning is born, where new ways of knowing Self and Other are called forth" (2013: 183). Hovering close to that edge is a transformative space where new narratives are forged with fresh possibilities for improved relationships. Does telling the truth work? Yes, telling the truth works where these spaces emerge because reconciliation becomes possible.

As noted, giving testimony and hearing stories narrated are complex, given the confusions that memories can establish. "Narratives of personal remembering become sites for knowing the past differently in the present" (Schaffer and Smith 2004: 26). Further, deliberate forgetting may be an important part of memory, the only way some people can cope. Not everyone wants to give testimony of their pain or feels relief in doing so. While often the distinction between victim and perpetrator is simplistic—reduced to the sufferer and the oppressor—in terms of memory it may be relevant. Memory may be important for many victims to sustain a quest for justice, or they might just want to forget; yet for perpetrators, historical memory may act to justify further violence, or with remorse, it might prompt a turning away from violent actions. Further, memory does not always limit the story to the past. Memories are relayed to others through stories, particularly in families and close-knit communities, and the narrator may then relate multiple versions of stories. Each version may be adapted even slightly—sometimes intentionally, other times inadvertently tweaked a little, often to an individual's own point of view—or exaggerated for effect. "Hence memory (and thus remembered stories) are as much a part of the present as they are part of the past. They are also shaped by expectations for the future" (Stern 2005: 62). Acknowledgment of the role of pain in forming narratives grants recognition to the bodily, psychological, and spiritual components to suffering.

What then is the power of truth telling? The answer has to be that it is contradictory. On the positive side, there is liberation in being able to tell one's story, particularly if it has been suppressed or one has not before had the courage to tell it. As I have already explained, for many, telling the truth is a massive relief, an unburdening of one's soul. "Those once reduced to screams or paralyzing fear now may share a personal narrative" (Crocker 2003: 47). Once-humiliated victims can regain respect as persons with dignity, which is empowering. On the negative side, telling one's story can be traumatic, in exposing old wounds and in reliving long-forgotten or desperately desired-to-be-forgotten memories. Also, for those who tell their story in the presence of their perpetrators, this moment can be cathartic for some, or it can be deeply difficult for others, particularly for rape victims and those who have lost loved ones. Some of the power of truth telling comes in the listening, when those unaccustomed to being in a "quiet" role have to step back from dominant positions to listen to the story they hear. It can be a reversal of typical power positions, but the strength is not in a new power relationship, but in the narrator's restoration of dignity that comes from being listened to and having one's story acknowledged. People struggling in contexts of deep violence and experiencing profound loss are in pain, feeling anxious, angry, and often fearful for their lives or the lives of their loved ones. Listening requires patience to really hear what is being said, given that words, images, and memories can blur the meanings being communicated. There is no clear prescriptive pattern of storytelling. Words blurt out. Listening thus is "the attending to a sharp sense of what things mean" (Lederach 2005: 70). Such listening has the potential to grant massive redeeming power to the storyteller whose narrative has some chance of being humanized. I discuss further this importance of listening in the next chapter.

* * *

In this chapter I have explored the question of whether truth telling, particularly in truth commissions, works to further a just peace. In the main, it does—in establishing a historical record, in hearing the accounts of violent acts committed and suffering experienced, both justice and the conditions for sustaining peace coincide. Sometimes truth telling is confrontational and provokes instability. Truth telling has its limitations as well as advantages. In exploring a little about the types of truth that emerge in truth commissions, I argue that the outcomes of commissions increasingly bear fruit in furthering not only peace but sometimes justice and reconciliation as well. This is particularly the case where attention is given to victims' needs for the truth and to tell their story, while acknowledging also the potential power of deliberately withholding the truth to maintain personal dignity. Long-term benefits of truth commissions are more likely to be realized when the reports' recommendations are carried out. Unfortunately, the recommendations are rarely sustained to the full, so skepticism as to their value creeps back.

Notes

1. The number of reported Iraqi civilian casualties varies in different reports. As of July 2013, the Brookings Institution (2013) reports between 113,925 and 118,861 civilian deaths in Iraq from 2003 to May 2013.

2. Gerry Adams was arrested in May 2014 amid talk of this threatening the progress of the peace process in Northern Ireland. He was not charged.

3. Caution is needed regarding differentiated generalizations.

4. See the US Institute of Peace's Truth Commission Digital Collection: http://www.usip.org/publications/truth-commission-digital-collection.

5. See Hayner (2011: 27–44) for a detailed account of these five commissions.

5

Can Trust Be Built
in Divided Societies?

Whom do you trust? This question can be challenging. I begin
this chapter by examining the reasons why trust between individuals
and groups who at some time have viewed themselves as enemies is so
difficult to achieve. I note demonstrable links between extremist nationalism, ethnic separatism, and fundamentalist religion that play a major
role in disrupting trust—or in preventing it from ever developing. These
links are manifest in interrelated negative practices of othering, sectarianism, scapegoating, and myths created about the enemy. These practices result in an undermining of human dignity. In this chapter I
explore how these harmful practices can be transformed so that trust can
be built, or in some cases rebuilt.

Indeed, what actually is involved in trust? After setting the context
for my discussion—namely, the obstacles to overcome in order to build
trust—I explore the fundamental question of this chapter: Can trust be
built in divided and conflict societies? I answer affirmatively and examine interrelated positive practices, specifically the importance of dialogue and listening; the need for a deliberate, positive recognition of
differences; and the difficult ideal of the embrace of the other. My argument in this chapter is an obvious one: that obstacles to trust in divided
societies are massive. What is not so apparent is that building trust is a
crucial first step in moving closer to reconciliation, a goal that I am
arguing is highly desirable. Trust takes time to build but is easily broken. Full embrace of the other, that person or group that once was considered an enemy, is rare. I argue that all steps toward meaningful trust
are to be welcomed.

What Are the Obstacles to Trust?

Extremism

The obstacles to trust in divided and conflict societies are enormous and need to be understood as root causes of violence. One of the key overarching obstacles lies in the strength of extremist forms of identity politics, where people's identities closely align with the divisive politics surrounding them. These forms of collective political expression are central to violent conflicts and usually are mixed with a nationalist identification with states, ethnicity, and religion. The expressions are manifest in many different ways, depending on the historical context. Sometimes they are expressed in provocatively flying flags, in wearing certain colors or symbols known to antagonize, and in songs and other cultural practices that deliberately mock others' cultural traditions. These artistic expressions of identity are not necessarily violent in themselves, but they often provoke responses that flare into antagonistic interactions that escalate into violence between opposing sides.

While generally ethnicity and religion overlap so tightly that it is hard to distinguish them, it is useful to begin to try. *Ethnicity* involves the shared set of cultural characteristics like language, religious beliefs, rituals, and practices of art that derive from membership of a particular national origin and includes a sense of belonging and identification. This sense of belonging is vital to most people and can be a very reassuring and positive aspect of identity. But when ethnicity is part of an exclusive identity politics, it has the potential to become dangerous. Ethnic extremism too often results in ethnic hatred of the "other." Such extremism is often connected with extremist versions of nationalism. The connection between nationalism as loyalty to a nation and war has a long history. Nationalism, like ethnicity, can be a positive force that binds people in common bonds, or it can be a destructive force that divides nation against nation. When combined, ethnic nationalism plays a powerful role in countries where ethnicity, religion, and politics define identities. Nationalism is ethnic-based when the nation is defined "in ethnic terms" and "anyone who is not a member of the same ethnic group" is excluded through disenfranchisement, ethnic cleansing, or genocide (Wolff 2006: 32). Extreme nationalism is to be feared because of its "deep connection between violence and belonging. The more strongly you feel the bonds of belonging to your own group, the more hostile, the more violent will your feelings be toward outsiders" (Ignatieff 1993: 188). Confrontational ethnic distinctions include disputes between Greek and Turkish Cypriots, and Israelis and Palestinians, as well as disputes in Kashmir and Sri Lanka, Kosovo, Northern Ireland, the civil war in the Democratic Republic of Congo, and the genocide in Rwanda.

Why does ethnic identification frequently lead to conflict? Stefan Wolff presents a powerful view on some people's willingness "to kill and to die because they see themselves as ethnically different from others" (2006: 23). There are always messy, ethically gray areas around judging killings in conflict. For example, one woman testified as follows to Amnesty International of her involvement in the Rwandan genocide:

> I killed three people, three men. I knew them, they were my neighbors. . . . I didn't have any alternative. When I refused to kill, the government soldiers banged a gun on my child's head and she died. She was six weeks old. (in Wolff 2006: 21)

Such a confessional statement is heartbreaking and reveals complex reasons underlying people's actions. This woman did not choose to kill her neighbors, but distraught over the murder of her baby in front of her eyes, she reacted to evil orders. What choice did she have? Agency often is limited by opportunities to express true desires. Ethnicity is sometimes a trap. Falling into the trap prevents personal preferences from being realized. For example, being a Hutu or a Tutsi was so significant to the 1994 Rwandan genocide that, afterward, a Hutu in Rwanda was "presumed to be a perpetrator" (Mamdani 2001: 266). Roméo Dallaire, in writing on "the toxic ethnic extremism that infected Rwanda," offers some reasons for the deep-rooted extremism, including "colonial discrimination and exclusion, personal vendettas, refugee life, envy, racism, power plays, *coup d'état*, and the deep rifts of civil war" (2004: 513).

Ethnic hatred is basically a fear of difference, particularly of the difference of "others"—other ethnic groups, racial groups, clans, or tribes—and often it parallels a fear of other sexualities, classes, and religious groups. Ethnic hatred evokes strong feelings with deep resentment toward others and leads to cycles of hatred that extend across generations. Angry victims of ethnic hatred can become perpetrators of ethnic animosity, and perpetrators then become victims, in ugly cycles of violence. Cycles of violence regularly are driven by almost primeval urges to reduce complicated histories into dualistic polarities that circumscribe reality in contrived ways. Lederach gives an example of the stance where such polarities lead:

> We are right. They are wrong. We were violated. They are the viola-
> tors. We are liberators. They are oppressors. Our intentions are good.
> Theirs are bad. History and the truth of history [are] most fully com-
> prehended by our view. Their view of history is biased, incomplete,
> maliciously untruthful, and ideologically driven. You are with us or
> against us. (Lederach 2005: 35)

Within such dualistic views, there is no respect for the value of difference in the complexity of human narratives. In theorizing about ethnic hatred, we should seek to avoid a detached, emotionally unaffected
position because of its harsh consequences on people's lives. The personally destructive nature of ethnic extremism becomes obvious when
we reflect on its effects on human narratives. Ethnic extremism prevents any bridging of differing narratives, because of the assumptions
that differences are to be opposed. Illan Pappe (2006) suggests that the
attempt to bridge narratives requires a willingness to consider reconciliation in recognizing the legitimacy of the weaker party's narrative, as
well as the incompleteness of one's own narrative. This suggestion is
important because it keeps a focus on the difficult process of building
reconciliation.

What makes this process even more difficult is the merging of
racism with ethnic extremism and nationalism. Zillah Eisenstein, in
writing about the "racializing of difference," explains how ethnic hatred
is written onto bodies that are beaten, castrated, decapitated, macheted,
raped, shackled, starved, tattooed, and tortured, and "bodies locate the
borders for hate while nations are reconfigured" (1996: 14). Such deep
hatred is subject to repetitious flare-ups and reopening of old wounds
every time triggers are fired. Her point is as follows:

> Hatred embodies a complex set of fears about difference and other-
> ness. It reveals what some people fear in themselves, their own "dif-
> ferences." Hatred forms around the unknown, the difference of "oth-
> ers." . . . Because people grow othered by their racialized, sexualized,
> and engendered bodies, bodies are important to the writing of hatred
> on history. (1996: 21)

This is a powerfully blunt statement that focuses attention on the
physical, bodily manifestations of violence that have a massive impact
on war narratives. The physical nature of this hatred is pertinent, particularly for all forms of sexual and gender-based violence, as well as for
torture and the physical maiming of people's limbs and bodies. Reading
the accounts of what occurs to human bodies during violent conflicts is

deeply disturbing; the accounts churn one's emotions. Christine Sylvester also stresses the need to write about the direct experiences of war, because "war is about human injury and human injury is experiential" (2013: 114). Further, this type of injury frequently occurs in the context of ethnic extremism.

In addition to ethnic extremism and the violence that accompanies racism, many of the world's violent outbursts are couched in religious terms. From the first-century Jewish-Roman war to the eleventh-century Crusades, to the seventeenth-century Thirty Years War, to recent violent conflicts in Bosnia, Chechnya, Darfur, Iraq, Israel, Palestine, Kashmir, Kosovo, Nigeria, Northern Ireland, and Sri Lanka, violence is presented as interreligious conflict. Terrorist attacks in Algiers, Bali, Colombo, Istanbul, London, Madrid, Mumbai, Moscow, and New York by organizations that claim religious motivations raise questions about religious attitudes toward violence. Yet death in war challenges the key religious proposition that life is given by God, and in the main, diverse religions oppose military means, as well as the hatred and violence that lead to the loss of lives. Indeed, many religious leaders have been or are well-known advocates of peaceful processes and reject war, including the Dalai Lama, Desmond Tutu, and Pope Francis. Religion does not always drive violence; increasingly, it is used in peacebuilding and reconciliation processes to bridge multifaith groups.

However, there is little doubt that we are more accustomed to seeing the worst excesses of religion in many conflicts. In rivalries between Christianity and Islam during the Crusades in the Middle Ages, or between the United States and other Western powers and al-Qaeda and other terrorist groups today, both sides see themselves as virtuous and demonize their adversary. When one party is certain of its rightness, it sees the enemy's responses as wrong, negative, and hostile. Not only does each side have different preferences for different outcomes to the conflict, each sees the issues differently. There is also a self-fulfilling prophecy that when one side expects the other to be hostile, it treats its opponent in ways that lead to a vicious cycle of deepening hostilities that reduce prospects for peace. Clearing up these misperceptions can help negotiations between hostile sides, when there is the realization that the person once thought of as an enemy is actually human, with shared feelings and goals. Here, I keep returning to the central argument of the importance of understanding complex narratives in transforming conflict and in moving closer to peace, justice, and reconciliation. Self-defined narratives develop over a long historical period. In a conflict, dominant narratives can delegitimize lesser-known narratives. Hence, from a narrative perspective, political negotiations constitute a puzzle in that they require each party to be willing to have their narrative laid bare and therefore also to be challenged. This involves more than just understanding the interests of the other, given the complexities of multiple stories, with variable characters and plots.

Consider one notion of radical disagreement from the Israeli-Palestinian conflict:

> For we Israelis our past lingers. We do not forget it. We are ultimately the most alone and historically insecure and persecuted people in this world. . . . We have been chased and murdered and hated and scapegoated, we are also here, in this our own land, in this our own birthright. . . . Jerusalem is our soul. (in Ramsbotham 2010: 3)

This position sits uncomfortably alongside a counter one:

> For we Palestinians, it is very clear, our dignity has been crushed; our ability to determine the fate of our future, to ensure that our children grow up with a sense of purpose and direction, not reactive and hostile but creative, has been undermined. . . . Jerusalem is the core of our cause, the core of ourselves. . . . We must rule ourselves here. And from Jerusalem the moral, cultural, and spiritual strength of our nation will grow. (in Ramsbotham 2010: 3)

Each position seems reasonable from its side of the conflict. Holding these disagreements closely, without permitting any space to try to understand the other's view, contributes to obstacles in resolving conflict and denying the opportunity to transform antagonistic relationships. Self-righteousness backed by an assumed religious or political justification contributes to dogmatic closed-mindedness. Where this occurs, there can be no development of trust, healing of wounded relationships, or reconciled communities. Within dogmatic communities, those who differ are branded as outsiders, intruders, or enemies. Those from within the community who dare to step out as dissidents, or sometimes as lovers, are estranged and alienated from their families.

Denial of the collective narrative or a consensual interpretation of the narrative is widespread among many conflicting groups, such as Bosnian Muslims, Croats, and Serbs; Protestant Loyalists and Catholic Republicans in Northern Ireland; whites and colored people in South Africa; Indonesians about Timor-Leste, and so forth. Trudy Govier suggests that there are different types of denial about the nature of conflict. Straight denial is where people say, "What you say happened did not happen at all" (Govier 2006: 62). An alternative interpretation says, "Something a little like this happened, but it wasn't what you think" (2006: 62). Then there is the preferred justification, which acknowledges wrong acts but seeks to justify them, given the context. Excuses also can be made that imply "our" actions were not as bad as "their" actions. Scapegoating tries to shift responsibility onto a few isolated individuals or groups.

To summarize this section, extremist ethnicity, nationalism, racism, and religious fervor contribute greatly to the process of conflict escalation. Understanding the historical reasons for the escalation is crucial in order to comprehend differing narrative interpretations. For example, with the Rwandan genocide, there are different explanations for its occurrence, such as colonialism that set Tutsi above Hutu, deprivation that marginalized Hutu, and the stories told on hate radio. Storylines can position one ethnic group as a dangerous threat that needs to be exterminated for the sake of ethnic survival. These narratives anchor fear, particularly when there are face-to-face encounters with those inciting violence. Cobb considers the nature of a "hardliner" who tells "a narrative that exhibits a very simple storyline" with a plot, subplots, characters, and themes (2013: 81). The hardliner narrative is based on simplistic binaries of good and bad, friend and enemy, which means that when hardliners approach potential or practiced perpetrators, the perpetrators feel that not to oblige puts them in the "bad" and "enemy" categories. They submit to the demand for violence to gain a sense of acceptance. Within a hardliner narrative, agency is questionable, but the narrative account explains more about the complexity of agential responsibility for actions, even evil ones. With hardliner narratives, the other's voice is silenced in fear of challenging the powerful. During the Arab Spring across the Middle East and North Africa in 2011, protestors tried to change the dominant state narrative, using social media as a new form of storytelling to break hardliner views. Extremism and hardliner positions are major obstacles to the building of trust in divided and conflict societies.

Othering

At the root of violent extremism is a negative notion of othering. Obviously, some form of "otherness" is integral to self-identity, recognizing that we are different from each other and that we have unique qualities. There is no harm in this understanding of otherness. However, where difference is seen as part of a dualistic outlook on life—an outlook that divides life into us and them, friends and enemies, superior and inferior, and citizen and foreigner—there is a terrible propensity to justify violence against different others. Harmful othering is based on dichotomies that are not simply statements of difference or even simple opposites, but they are starkly divided hierarchies that can mask the power of one side of the division to dominate the other. I have maintained elsewhere that "this form of 'othering' drives war rape, ethnic cleansing, and genocide where people are not treated as humans worthy of respectful dignity, but as conquests or beasts to be destroyed" (Porter 2007a: 48).

The creation of these dichotomies often occurs in a frenzy, built up by fanatical leaders, hardliners referred to above, or the media, with an approach that requires a "construction of the other as evil," as someone who exists only to be exterminated, crushed, contained, or converted (Galtung 2004: 2). This construction is stark, but being so vivid, it helps us to understand why so many people are dehumanized through the process of othering. Jill Steans explains how the nation-state functions as "a fundamental category for understanding relations between self (citizen) and other (foreigner), between inside (order) and outside (anarchy)" (1998: 7). She explains that the interpretation of the hostile other as being dangerously threatening is fundamental to the stories people tell and to the securing of national boundaries. Absolutist dichotomies are blind to the pain of those who are destroyed by the stereotypes that define who is included in or excluded from valued activities and positions. These dichotomies are divisive because they increase the vulnerability of the other, those who are in need of protection because the divisions put at risk an increasing number of people who simply look different, are born into a different ethnicity, hold a different faith, or have different political values and cultural practices. The sad fact is that much of the stereotyping and destructive othering occurs without face-to-face dialogue or understanding any of the narrative aspects related to these differences. Without such dialogue, misunderstanding of diverse narratives and mistrust continues.

This cultural construction of the other as an evil being can only be "accomplished through a fictitious conspiracy. It is under these conditions that ideologies are transformed into real weapons" (Pía Lara 2007: 146). In this process of dehumanization, language is a powerful political tool. People can be likened to parasites, excrement, filth, cockroaches, rats, and snakes. False narratives of othering dehumanize people and often pave the way for cruelty and a justification for extermination. This cruelty is done by the dominant group toward others, who are seen as a threat—a group that needs to be excluded or destroyed. It is easy to see how propaganda can be used in totalitarian regimes. "The construction of the other as having evil intentions leaves the speaker of that story with little option except to restrain or kill the other" (Cobb 2013: 96). Cobb expands on this point by explaining that once there is a social construction of the other as having "evil intent," this begins to function as a hardline narrative, as discussed in the previous section, so that any contestations risk relationships within and across the community where this narrative is told (Cobb 2013: 96). In such difficult situations, non-violence is a valuable way to materialize forbidden or suppressed narratives. For example, the protestors in the Arab Spring were portrayed clearly on global media as speaking, active subjects. I elaborate shortly on the critical role that speaking and being heard plays in developing relational history and changing mistrusting narratives. Often in an attempt to create community there is an emphasis on building consensus, but accord can obliterate crucial differences that must be incorporated into the community of narratives in order for shared narratives to be acceptable. Circumscribed sets of narratives where only certain roles, values, or moral frameworks occur cannot lead to inclusive types of speaking.

In treating someone as subhuman, all sorts of assumptions can be made: that this person does not really feel, hurt, or "bleed as we do," and thus "they can be killed and disposed of" (Boraine 2000: 129). How can the breaking down of othering translate in practice? Again, selective stories show different ways to answer this question. Lian Gogoli founded an institute in Poso, Central Sulawesi, called Mosintuwu, which means togetherness. Poso is a place where Muslims and Christians were engaging in brutal riots and violent attacks against each other. The media kept telling stories about violence. Gogoli writes that, when living with women and children in the refugee camps, she heard "different stories about how Muslims and Christians had helped and rescued each other during the conflict, at times even risking their own lives" (in Behuria and Williams 2012: 6). She gives a wonderful example of a story given to her by Christian women that when there was a search for Christians in a village, "The Muslim women let them hide in their houses and gave them headscarves to disguise them as Muslims" (2012: 6). These women were a fruitful resource for fashioning social harmony because they were willing to transcend destructive otherness. In teaching the importance of interfaith dialogue to prevent conflict, there was a positive impact on peaceful living and thus on economic and social development. This impact was put to the test in late 2012, when violence erupted again, and housewives made public speeches stressing the need to reject violence and to work together.

A further example shows ways to overcome othering. Siti Rohmanatin Fitriani is Javanese, and she was assigned to Papua for community development work. She felt that people defining and dividing themselves along ethnic, racial, religious, and gender lines caused widespread insecurity. She stated that she "realized that when one draws heavily on these cues, we 'other' those who are different" and thereby occupy a space between the stereotype of us and them "where suspicion and prejudice flourish" (in Behuria and Williams 2012: 18). Siti began to build a community of women willing to engage in peacebuilding efforts and in creating a narrative on peace with a group called Perempuan Bicara (Women Speak). These examples show that despite massive obstacles, trust between different groups can be built in conflict and divided societies.

As another example, Cynthia Cockburn, writing on the green line that acted as a partition between the Republic of Cyprus and the Turkish Republic of Northern Cyprus,[1] describes how differences are "the source of much pleasure and cultural richness in human life. . . . Yet, difference is often constructed as insurmountable otherness. We can hate for difference" (2004: 24). She asks her readers to contemplate what is implied when we draw lines between who is included or excluded, who is loved or hated. In her Hands across the Divide project, she found that "when a successful dialogue takes place across difficult differences it is because the participants have come to understand the plurality of truth" (2004: 39). Hence she encourages the notion of transversal politics, whereby groups seeking to avoid racism, fundamentalism, nationalism, and violence look for commonalities and affirm differences, while seeking not to let these differences be a stumbling block. Working alliances across differences requires an open capacity to see the world from the position of the other.

Neriman Cahit, a Turkish Cypriot, told Cockburn how she felt about being allocated an empty Greek Cypriot home. She told of houses where there were half-cut loaves of bread on the kitchen table. "When I was cooking, for example, I was always thinking: 'What was the other woman doing? Where was her table? Were they sitting like us? How many children did they have?' There's nobody to ask" (in Cockburn 2004: 83). This personal story of everyday musing exposes a sensitive response to the other, in this case a displaced woman whose kitchen Cahit was using. Across the ethnic and nationalist divide, women told Cockburn many stories of mutual aid, such as practical help given to each other in finding food and milk. These were "women who were capable of standing in the shoes of 'the other woman,' even while the fighting was going on" (2004: 87). As Sevin Uğural recalls hearing the jets overhead, she recounts her reflection, "One sound but two different responses. I feel relieved, she feels afraid" (in Cockburn 2004: 87). Othering is a powerful blockage to the building of trust, but these stories of assistance toward vastly different others generate hope. They stand out for this reason.

More typically, stories about the past account for the present and dictate the future as stories are embellished. Cobb explains the breeding ground of violence in which stories emerge. The origin of the violence "is never a function of the acts of the storyteller, the narrator, but always a result of the acts of the 'other'" (Cobb 2003: 295). Regardless of the little knowledge of each side's myths, the foundation myth of each side attributes the cause of the violence to the other. In other words, we are "actors in stories we did not make" (2003: 295). These narrative-origin myths form the basis for identity, particularly for collective identity; hence they are resistant to change. Indeed, particularly after ethnic cleansing or sectarian violence, an act of revenge lies in "creating myths about the eternal evil of the ethnic Other" (Borneman 2002: 288). Transforming narratives is thus core to transforming identities in ethnic conflict. As part of the change, a different story about the other must be told, which can only occur when a different story about one's self is cultivated as part of a narrative transformation.

Enemies

Many steps have to be taken before such a transformation that permits fruitful alliances can be built. Until so-called enemies are seen to possess humanity, identifying common ground of shared but different forms of grievances, or of hopes for the future, is not possible. Before agreeing on common goals and needs, the notions of "enemy" need to be broken down. If you are perceived to be an enemy, you are excluded from dominant prized activities. Exclusion is a root cause of violence because not feeling included or having a sense of belonging alienates and heightens feelings of insecurity. For example, Miroslav Volf writes about the elimination that is signified in a term such as "ethnic cleansing," where he describes exclusion as "barbarity *within* civilization, evil *among* the good, crime against the other *right within the walls of the self*" (1996: 60). As a response to this barbarity, Volf suggests that an adequate reflection on exclusion should satisfy two conditions. First, it should "name exclusion as evil . . . because it enables us to imagine non-exclusionary boundaries that map non-exclusionary identities," and second, "It must not dull our ability to detect exclusionary tendencies in our own judgments and practices" (1996: 64).

Again, an example of attempts to cross boundaries in this way helps to throw light on what is involved in overcoming perceptions of someone as enemy. Sixty-seven Palestinian students from Bethlehem and sixty-four Jewish-Israeli students took part in workshops over two days where they dealt with "social, cultural and political issues through sharing of personal narratives and through discussions of conflict" (Maoz 2000: 724). Dana, a Jewish female participant, said,

> I thought they were all against peace. This is what you see in television and at home, you grow in a society where they say that Palestinians are bad, that they are all the same. The media relayed to us only the negative things. Here, I saw that they are really similar to us, identical. The same dreams, only that they live like in jail. (in Maoz 2000: 728)

Breaking down notions of enmity requires understanding that inclusivity broadens the scope for creative relationships and can only happen when there are new practices of trust building.

How Does Dialogue Build Trust?

Having analyzed extremism and othering the enemy as chief obstacles that need to be overcome in order to build trust, my defense of the claim that trust can be built in divided and conflict societies needs further explanation. I turn now to some of the positive practices that facilitate the building of trust—in particular, dialogue and listening, recognition of differences and of common humanity, and overcoming fear of the other to contemplate an embrace of the other. Before doing so, I make a case for why trust is important between former adversaries and all those who practice peace, justice, and reconciliation. Many preparatory steps precede reaching trust. A typical starting point to build trust between adversaries is sharing stories about experiences of the conflict, violence, or war. This exchange typically includes stories of loss, pain, and fear. Realistically, this sharing can lead to blame and accusation rather than trust, but often it enables both sides to begin to realize that one common ground is the pain and suffering of the past as part of everyone's narrative.

What is trust? In a fascinating divergence from the norm, Selma Sevenhuijsen suggests that the opposite of trust is not "distrust or mistrust, but rather fear, or fear of the unknown" (1999: 211). This fear of the possible power of the other is not merely psychological but also discursive in that it is "an established mode of thinking that thrives on negative cultural and historical mythologies of Otherness" (1999: 211). Sevenhuijsen explains that trust involves "concrete, real life others, with whom the truster is engaged in networks of interaction" (1999: 214). Practically, such networks may not exist in divided societies. However, Sevenhuijsen suggests that "trust relations are relations in which persons are dependent on others, because they need their help in looking after things they value" (1999: 215). In the context of a divided or transitional society, things of value include health, education, jobs, water supply, infrastructure, equality laws, support to care for orphans, access to land ownership, sustainable economic well-being, justice, and fair representation of different groups in democratic institutions.

A narrative approach to conflict transformation renders vulnerability and the need for trusting relationships as everyday parts of human life. Certain contexts are more enabling of trust building and trust enhancing, such as where there is openness, where mistakes can be admitted without penalty, and where parties learn from each other. For those who live in protracted conflict with valid reasons for distrust, or where trust is fragmented readily, it is hard to grasp that trusting someone from the other side is possible. The starting point in building trust among enemies "is the assumption that distrust among enemies is inherent in the relationship" (Kelman 2005: 649). Distrust is reduced gradually once parties are persuaded that the situation is changing. Building trust is fundamental to overcoming personal and collective enmities in order to begin to form reconciled relationships.

Trust comes primarily through dialogue. Again, qualifiers are needed. Talking to the enemy can be seen as a cop-out, a weak compromise, unacceptable to the hard single-mindedness of the tough, uncompromising group—the hardliners referred to earlier. Realistically, in dialogue the powerful can and do dominate, so that parties are intimidated and little is achieved, particularly when root causes of conflict are not addressed. The challenge of creating dialogue across radical differences of view is enormous, given that deep mistrust has complex historical roots. The dialogue referred to here is one that validates "the legitimacy of the 'other' when recognition has been withheld as a bargaining chip" (Kaufman 2005: 475). Such dialogue can diminish long-held misperceptions, prejudices, and stereotypes. With this type of dialogue, even though it may be tentative initially, all sides can gradually come to understand each other's realities a little better, despite sometimes remaining unconvinced of the rightness of these differences. Seeking a wide variety of dialogue partners thus is ideal because more prejudices are likely to be broken down.

In violent contexts, dialogical deliberation offers hope for moving beyond violence because the goal of a civil, respectful conversation is to be free of fear, prejudice, and falsity, as this is the only way to resolve problems. If deliberation offers hope for conversations, on what basis is a dialogue that permits such deliberation built? Seyla Benhabib offers a sound response to this question:

> Universal respect means that we recognize the rights of all beings capable of speech and action to be participants in the moral conversation; the principle of egalitarian reciprocity . . . stipulates that in discourses each should have the same rights to various speech acts, to initiate new topics, and to ask for justification of the presuppositions of the conversations. (2005: 13)

Benhabib sets the deliberative task as mediation between moral universalism and the attachments that accompany ethical particularism. She suggests that "we can render the distinctions between 'citizens' and 'aliens,' 'us' and 'them,' fluid and negotiable through democratic iterations" (2005: 21). This willingness to accept life's fluidity requires a process where, beginning with the common human factors we share, people begin to discover what is unique and different about the other person or group with whom they are beginning a dialogue. Trust grows. Such a deliberative process sounds minimally problematic within a multicultural, pluralist society, whereas the first stages of deliberation in divided societies are always fraught with tensions, because an acceptance of reciprocity is considered to be impossible. Hence, a constructive approach to conflict works to develop shared spaces where respectful dialogue takes place. In these shared spaces, the human aspects of differences come to life. "Words—of an apology, recognition, or respect—aren't enough on their own, but they are the beginning; they are the things that just might make the other side willing to listen and calm the heat in their anger" (Atran 2010: 379).

Speaking and Listening

Words are one part of the story. Narrative storytelling is relational. As I have already stressed in earlier chapters, it involves speaking and listening. Spaces for conversations of trust require a listening engagement. This engagement is critical because without trying to understand another's position, gaining an awareness that might lead to respectful reciprocity is not possible. Listening necessarily is relational and thus opens politics to difference. Listening is not passive. It involves listening to views that annoy, frustrate, or anger, as well as those that resonate and invoke hope. Listening is a central component in dialogue. Where listening and speaking are shared equally, there is a movement backward and forward, equal participation in the process of trying to communicate complex notions of difference, while building varying degrees of trust. Without the equality of status as both listener and speaker, power plays block the process. Where this blockage exists, conflict continues because people speak but are not heard. As I have stressed repeatedly, telling one's story is a critical part of each stage of the deliberation, mediation, negotiation, peace settlement, and strategic planning of transitional justice processes, where myriad different viewpoints are expressed. Reflective listening is crucial.

Dialogue is a unique form of recognition. To listen intently to the voice of the other—to engage with its concerns and consider its viewpoints—is to recognize the other as an equal. During this *"respectful listening* we give the parties the opportunity to express their needs and communicate their perspectives" (Kelman 2010: 376). Mutual recognition as equals is incredibly important when giving voice to those who have been silenced. In this sense, "Voice represents acknowledgment, recognition, and participation in meaningful and accessible ways" (Lederach and Lederach 2010: 89). Given that violence destroys voice, and thus the dignity that accompanies equality, finding one's voice is a search for restoration of connections, and listening is an opening act of recognition and fundamental to trust. Where identities have been devalued and voices not heard, finding one's voice can be life changing. John Borneman stresses that to listen "always involves listening for" (2002: 293) something—that is, listening for the truth, degree of suffering, or divergent truths or falsehoods across contradictory narratives. In this sense, listening is both a practice and an art that some are better at than others, and it is "interactive, involving soliciting, questioning, and weighing competing accounts" (2002: 293). In many ways, "Healing ultimately is about restoration of voice, both for individuals and communities" (Lederach and Lederach 2010: 110).

An example of this healing through expression of listening to voice is evident in a Rwandan women's cooperative called Dusohenye (Mourning Together), where Hutu and Tutsi women, many of whom are widows, ritualize a shared sense of suffering. In this cooperative, discussed in a previous chapter, the women "adopted positions as narrators, telling their stories; as listeners, as others told of suffering; and as characters, in the reciprocal stories that were told about community life, before and after the genocide" (Cobb 2003: 296). Woven into these stories were accounts of fear and uncertainty, as well as acknowledgment of how much it is possible to learn simply by listening to others. Listening has the potential to open once-silent spaces. It breaks down fixed myths of ethnic identity and religious faiths. It exposes complex layers of meaning that are evident and latent in people's stories. This type of open listening builds trust, an important component to meaningful peace.

Another example of mutual recognition is the Seeds of Peace program, which is aimed at creating links between young people living in conflict zones. Since the program began, young people from different conflict zones have been brought together to meet their "enemy" for the first time; to live together for a short while in a camp setting in the United States; to negotiate, share, discuss, and generally break down barriers. After one of the group's Serbian participants had shared her feelings of oppression and fear of living in Kosovo, a Kosovar Albanian group member admitted,

> I cannot hear you, because when you share your story, the volume of my own story goes up in my head. I cannot imagine your fear because I am blinded by the images of my own story that play themselves out before my eyes when you start talking. (in van Woerkom 2004: 43)

This response is interesting because it shows the openness needed to hear others' stories without being overwhelmingly preoccupied with one's own narrative. On the other hand, great sensitivity to the enormity of trauma tempers theoretical prescriptiveness. The Kosovar Youth Council came into being after the 1999 bombings, embracing different ethnic groups. It began in the displaced persons camps and continued once people were resettled. The Women's Commission for Refugee Women and Children (1999–2000) interviewed youths as they were contemplating their return to Kosovo. When an Albanian Kosovar was asked whether she could live with Serbs, she answered, "Never!" (in Kurhasani 2005: 170). Another person reminded them how some Albanians had helped them get to safety, but another replied, "No, no, you can't trust any of them" (in Kurhasani 2005: 170). Another asked, "Why not? We were friends before. We could be friends again" (in Kurhasani 2005: 170). Another believed that youth would be the most likely to change attitudes toward each other. This belief cannot be taken for granted, but educating youth to develop trust for others plays a crucial role in breaking down entrenched stereotypes and creating the space where the possibility of reconciliation can be recognized.

I discuss empathy in detail in Chapter 7, but it is worth mentioning briefly here because of its connection with listening and openness. Christine Sylvester's (2002) idea of "empathetic cooperation" is useful in this discussion on trust. She describes it primarily as a "method for managing, working with, respecting, and surpassing rigid standpoints, positions, and issues without snuffing out difference" (2002: 244).[2] She refers to this process as "positional slippage" that occurs when one listens seriously, "taking on board rather than dismissing," finding the overlaps between others' concerns and one's own fears (2002: 247). Rina Kashyap writes similarly that "active listening, predicated on empathetic listening, establishes a potentially affirmative role for the bystander" (2009: 456). Active, empathetic listening requires engagement with the narrator and acknowledgment of the whole story being told, not selective bits. As is evident from the quotation by the Albanian Kosovar above, this activity is not easy when distrust remains, fears are deep, and worries are unresolved.

Another story brings these issues to the fore. Berak in Croatia is a small village that suffered extreme trauma during the 1991–1995 fighting. Between 1996 and 1998, displaced persons who were mainly Croats began to return to Berak with an expectation that the Serbs who had primarily stayed would inform them of the whereabouts of the bodies of their loved ones who had been killed.[3] The silence of the Serbs was unyielding. A multiethnic Peace Team from the Centre for Peace, Non-Violence, and Human Rights in Osijek came to the village to conduct a listening project. They went to the house of Dragica Aleksa, a Croatian returnee who was grateful for their listening, "given how terrible the lack of communication between people was. You have to know how dark our future seemed" (in Bloch 2005: 654). When her best friend, a Serb, asked her why she was not visiting her, she answered, "Because you didn't come with us either when we had to leave" (in Bloch 2005: 655). The listening project provided a space for people to express their feelings and the extent of their trauma, which gave them a chance to rebuild mutual trust and open a dialogue on a central, painful remaining problem, "the issue of missing persons and postwar justice" (Bloch 2005: 658). As a result, Serbs and Croats both engaged in the efforts to find the missing bodies. I am reinforcing the point made by Pumla Gobodo-Madikizela that "bringing victims, perpetrators, and beneficiaries of repressive regimes together for sustained dialogue about the past is the only action that holds promise for the repair of brokenness in post-conflict societies" (2008a: 335). She talks of this action as "empathetic repair" (2008a: 335), a concept that does not indicate any finality, but points to the possibilities that arise when there is an openness in the dialogue with one's former enemies. Dialogue and listening as practices of trust are reassuring in affirming humanity's ability to transform brokenness into healing. These practices are imperative in connecting peace with justice in moving closer to the possibility of reconciliation.

Why Is Recognition of Difference Important?

In identity-related conflicts, all types of differences must be handled carefully, because differences often are used to justify violence, such as occurred in the Balkans or Sri Lanka. However, granting too much weight to difference at the expense of searching for the commonality that might assist reconciliation can result in backlash, sectarianism, and civil war, such as in Rwanda. A fine balance is needed, because shifting too far to either side can have powerful implications for the possibilities of peace. The crux of being open to the other is recognition, which is an affirmative acknowledgment of the unique differences in others. Recognition and the affirmation of multiple identities help to include different groups in peacebuilding, thereby minimizing the chance that the negative feelings that arise through historical legacies of exclusion erupt into further violence. Recognizing different identities is a prerequisite to knowing how to attend to particular differences. There are many different ways to express the fundamental value of each person. The need for recognition of individual and shared identity "is one of the driving forces behind nationalist movements in politics" (Taylor 1992: 25). Charles Taylor's point is important: "Our identity is partly shaped by recognition or its absence, often by the *misrecognition* of others. . . . Nonrecognition or misrecognition can inflict harm" (1992: 25). International politics offers many examples of misrecognition, which underlies mistrust.

For example, writing on the "humiliation, disrespect, and social exclusion" that many women face, Fionnuala Ní Aoláin maintains that "recognition is therefore an essential component of redress" (2012: 226). She suggests that "advancing recognition of the individual female 'I' . . . demands attention to particularity, openness, and placement in particular and contextual settings" (2012: 226). Such attention includes gender- and culture-specific needs that everybody has. Vincent, a young Burundian man, said, "These ideas of differences are fixed inside people's heads today and we can't stop that. All the time, we categorize others. It's our habit. When someone passes by, we will categorize him. It's automatic. We can't stop ourselves" (in Mclean Hilker 2009: 84). It takes a long time to break down stereotypes that play a major role in conflict. Without breaking them, an underlying feeling remains of being threatened by differences, and the genuine need for differentiated responses to crises is not met.

How then does a positive notion of recognition of differences come about? As I have mentioned, recognition occurs in processes where dialogue is open, where patterns of social exclusion are challenged, where notions of identity are forged through negotiation, and where there is meaningful engagement between those seeking mutual recognition. These processes require parties to engage with each other's and their own differences, and a willingness to transform old notions of the other that harm particular groups. Through dialogue, fixed perceptions of identity can be dissolved as differences are encountered, and hopefully appreciated. The dialogical relationship broadens people's horizons with recognition of you and me, us and them, in ways that lose the antagonism typically associated with hostile views of differences. Where this relationship develops, the differences that have been the basis of conflict should become a productive resource, creating a shared space in which differences are suddenly valued for their uniqueness. Through these relational aspects of recognition, trust is built and meaningful peace can expand.

As an open-ended process, dialogue is dynamic, with an inherent plurality. Being surrounded by stories, "We narrativize ourselves as well, giving an account of ourselves in a story that is not finished till we die" (Cockburn 2004: 25). Dialogue presupposes a willingness to exchange ideas, but this does not always occur. While antagonism supposes that there can be no common ground between those who see themselves in terms of friends and enemies, agonism in contrast requires that one's opponents are constructed as legitimate adversaries, which presumes a "common symbolic space in which conflict takes place" (Mouffe 2005: 20). With agonism, "A collectivity sees dialogue and engagement with its 'different other' as necessary to its own fulfillment" (Cockburn 2004: 26). This is a fruitful way of thinking realistically about recognition between adversaries.

Where there are asymmetrical conflicts, where parties have different access to forums in which they can have their voices heard, is it possible to alter narratives? As I have already argued, for trust to develop there needs to be a legitimacy of the individual speaker as a moral agent and the legitimacy of parties involved. Cobb (2013) explains how in 2010 she drew on narrative theory to write a draft reconciliation plan for Somalis. In talking with Somali ministers, President Sheik Sharif Ahmed, and US State Department officials, she asked people about the story of Al Shabbab, an insurgent terrorist group. She had heard the stories about their attempt to destabilize, and their desire for control, power, and imposing their extremist Islamist beliefs. While not defending any notion that political leaders should normalize relations with terrorist groups, Cobb's point is that a typical narrative truncates the exchange—in this case, between a militant insurgent group and political leaders. Hence, the discourse of power prevails, mutual trust fails to form, and violence continues. Engagement with jihadist terrorist groups is rare. Obviously these relations are almost impossible to develop between political leaders and militant insurgents and seldom eventuate. Breaking down the legitimacy of leadership in a terrorist organization may lead to a group's dissolution. I extend this discussion on talking to terrorists below when we look at the nature of political compromise. The possibility of improved relationships that comes with reconciliation is remote without the mutual recognition that comes with open, dialogical relations.

There is a fundamental link between reconciliation and language in that, as Paul Komesaroff writes, "No matter how divergent the theoretical perspective there is always some possibility of translation, of the joint construction and sharing of meaning, even if it remains limited, imperfect, and partial" (2008: 4). Viewed in this light, he suggests that the project of reconciliation is about honoring the complexity of communication in ways that sustain the possibility of ongoing dialogue. Komesaroff stresses the realistic obstacles that culture, race, religion, and politics present to communication, but he suggests that, as long as there is a readiness to move beyond the oppression of violence and fear, some kind of dialogical contact is possible. Building up to the readiness takes time. Insurgent groups might never be willing or ready to do so. Despite the hurdles of contrasting narrative voices, effective communication can occur, if there is a readiness. Komesaroff summarizes five ways that dialogue is linked to reconciliation. First, reconciliation is concerned with "restoring fractured communication and enabling dialogue where it has encountered obstacles. . . . It seeks to break the silence, to speak the unspeakable" (2008: 10). Second, whatever the differences, some common meaning can be found. Third, personal stories and complex social relationships both must be taken into account. Fourth, reconciliation is realized through the sharing of meaning, which usually then generates new meanings. Fifth, reconciliation dialogues across cultural differences are imperfect. I elaborate on these themes on reconciliation in the final chapter. However, they are significant here because of their integral link to the trust that emanates when mutual recognition occurs as part of building peace.

Memory

Part of the recognition of difference and of developing trust includes appreciating that the past affects people differently. In previous chapters I have examined memory in relation to victims' stories. Here I explore how recall of memory is a crucial part of recognizing valid differences.

Memory is complex. We construct memory by selecting bits of information that make sense to us in terms of prior narratives and merging these with current beliefs about what we think is important. What makes sense to us today can change over time. Our memory of an event can differ from somebody else's recollections of the same event. Memory is subjective, often blurring the boundaries between fact and fiction. "Memories, intentions, beliefs, desires, mental and bodily dispositions are not discrete and singular but are only intelligible in the context of the complex networks of other memories . . . within which they are embedded" (Mackenzie 2008b: 8). Fear, desire, hope, and despair distort the accuracy of memories. "Blind spots, ethnic amnesia, denials of historical evidence operate to unmask unpalatable truths and magnify others out of proportion" (Lemarchand 2008: 66). As René Lemarchand points out, in Rwanda the official government view of memory contrasts with different ethnic views, so that "the clash of ethnic memories is an essential component of the process by which the legacy of genocide . . . is being perceived or fabricated by one community or the other" (2008: 67). In criticizing the government's position on a public ban on references to ethnicity, he suggests that this is an enforced memory that suppresses ethnic difference and thus "rules out 'recognition'" so that any search for a "critical memory" is likely to be denounced (2008: 75).[4]

Writing similarly on Rwanda, Susanne Buckley-Zistal (2008) explains how subjective experiences of suffering are deeply etched in memory and kept alive through the stories people narrate, often retaining the dichotomy of us and them, or friend and enemy. A narrative approach recognizes that stories are selective, and that they rearrange, redescribe, and simplify events. Portrayal of the past involves both the deliberate and the inadvertent inclusion and exclusion of information. The way that groups explain their past helps to establish collective identity. Buckley-Zistel talks about the fact that, while the deaths and destruction of the genocide constantly crop up in conversations, discussion about the causes of the tensions between Hutu and Tutsi is silenced. There is, she explains a "*chosen amnesia*, the deliberate loss of memory" (2008: 126) about what is not said or what one does not want to remember. This amnesia, discussed also in previous chapters, expresses agency because it "signifies the deliberate choice to not remember some aspects of the past" (2008: 130). The problem, though, is that there is no closure with this choice and it works against the building of trust. Survivors have one type of memory; the accused and their families have another. Choosing not to remember is a coping mechanism. A woman of mixed parentage who was married to a Tutsi and had lost all of her and most of her husband's family expressed her dependency. She said, "We live with a family who killed our relatives. We have to . . . pretend that there is peace" (in Bickley-Zistel 2008: 137). Buckley-Zistel found that many of her interviewees adopted this coping mechanism as the perceived only option in a context of mutual mistrust. What remain unresolved are the underlying ethnic identity tensions. These narratives of pretense expose the complexity surrounding agency. As I showed earlier, the actual choices made do not always reflect preferred choices. A façade of peace cannot herald a new era of trust.

Memory links the past and present, and influences the direction of the future. Martha Minow, writing on memory and hatred, suggests that a crucial part of mass violence is the dehumanization of people. She writes vividly in explaining what is involved with this dehumanization, as "the treatment of people marked by membership as subhuman, dirty, a cancer on the society, incompetent, immoral, unworthy, or excrement calling for immediate disposal" (2002: 32–33). Minow continues, saying that in such contexts it is possible to have "either too much memory or too much forgetting"; hence the question "is not whether to remember, but how" to do so (2002: 16). The answer to this question must include narrative connections between those who have been injured and those who use violence to respond to those injuries. Minow suggests that one understandable response to memory is vengeance. However, vengeance unleashes unreasonable, destructive responses, so that "by retaliating, you become what you hate" (2002: 17).

Minow also suggests that a second typical response is forgiveness, the focus of the next chapter. I mention this point briefly here because forgiving the wrongdoer can break the cycle of revenge. The person who forgives can escape from the self-destructive consequences of holding onto pain, grudges, and victimhood. In the act of forgiving, the offender and the victim can reconnect, and then establish or renew a trusting relationship. The downside means that forgiveness often forgoes rightful punishment, and hence a sense of injustice lingers, preventing mutual recognition of respect and continuing negative patterns of mistrust. Minow's search is thus for responses to collective violence that forge "a path between vengeance and forgiveness" (2002: 18). She provides an apt example: the story of a lawyer named Jadranka Cigelj, who had been raped repeatedly and confined to a detention camp in Bosnia. After her release, she began to talk with other survivors. She describes how she had been filled with hatred and the desire for revenge until she "met an eighty-six-year-old woman whose 14 family members had been murdered, and she had to bury them all with her bare hands" (in Minow 2002: 19). The old woman said to Cigelj, "How can you hate those who are so repulsive?" (in Minow 2002: 19). Cigelj then realized how exhausting hatred is and that it is better to "focus on prosecution, punishment, and documentation of victims' stories" (in Minow 2002: 19). The power of memory can be altered through listening to others' stories and embracing a new narrative.

Kris Brown, writing on Northern Ireland, discusses the way that communities foster their own narratives about the past. He says that these "everyday practices of memory making matter" (2012: 445) because they provide a critical lens to analyze transitional justice mechanisms. Local narratives are embedded deeply in everyday encounters, with many conflict fatalities in Northern Ireland occurring close to residences or villages, increasing the feeling that a whole community is under attack and intensifying mistrust of the other side. The irony is, as Brown suggests, that in some sections of east Belfast, "Irish Republican and working-class Unionist or Loyalist narratives have a similarity in that each community loads its narratives with a sense of grievance and persistent threat" (2012: 455). As a consequence, acts of political and personal remembering construct a siege mentality felt by both sides. Then there are power struggles over who is more a victim than the other. This situation is manifest explicitly in political murals where paramilitaries' images are conspicuously favored in commemorative spaces. Where colors, flags, and names identify individuals and groups immediately, the particularity of stories is pronounced, and the development of trust between differing groups is minimal. Recognition of differences is a powerful way to boost trust.

Is an Embrace of the Other Possible?

So far, we have looked at obstacles to building trust, defended the importance of dialogue and listening as crucial to building trust, and established that without recognition of differences the mythical perceptions of the "other" remain a blockage to the emergence of new trusting relationships. The bar can be raised. What would an embrace of the other look like, and is it worth the effort? Before answering this, I must delve further into the importance of overcoming fear of the other.

Overcoming Fear of the Other

In trying to understand the barriers to accepting the other as sharing fundamental features of common humanity, Michael Walzer's views on tolerance and difference are insightful. He suggests that toleration has five different degrees: a resigned acceptance of difference for the sake of peace; a benign indifference that it takes all sorts to make a diverse society; a moral stoicism that others have rights, even if the exercise of them is unattractive; an openness to the other—a curiosity, possible respect, and willingness to listen and learn; and an endorsement of differences (Walzer 1997: 10–11). Opening up the range of possible ways to understand toleration increases the chance that previously repressed voices might be heard. "Toleration makes difference possible; difference makes toleration necessary" (1997: xii). I argue that an important qualifier of difference is that we should value and respect those differences that respect human dignity and do not hurt others. "Openness to difference duly recognizes ethically legitimate differences, what I am calling *respectful differences* that do not harm others" (Porter 2000: 170). This qualifier is imperative because there are so many practices that undermine dignity and do harm. Many of the practices humiliate women and girls, including female genital mutilation, femocide, and prioritizing boys' education and nutrition needs over those of girls.

The choice between tolerating and respecting differences is crucial. Amy Gutmann suggests that, while toleration has broad connotations, "Respect is far more discriminating. Although we need not agree with the position to respect it, we must understand it as reflecting a moral point" (1992: 22). Within multicultural as well as conflict societies, a wide range of disagreements exist, although admittedly of a dissimilar nature and with vastly differing consequences, but the point is to seek to defend our views, listen to those with whom we disagree, and therefore learn from our differences. This is how trust develops. Within multicultural societies, we need to be willing to articulate disagreement and be open to the consideration of other views with regard to different faiths and different cultural values. Within conflict societies, such a view is relevant in relation to disputes over boundaries, territories, rights, scarce or lucrative natural resources, and decisions concerning power and peace processes. Yirmiyahu Yovel regards "tolerance as the capability to recognize humanness" (1998: 901). This recognition is stymied in conflict societies where others appear as a threat to one's identity, tribe, or nation. Yet this tolerance can also form the basis on which power-sharing arrangements between former enemies can begin.

> At the opposite end of the table, the other side acquires face, allowing for listening to take place, and for the development of an understanding of the motives and/or grievances of the other party. Even so-called enemies will be seen to possess humanity, making it possible to identify common ground. (Garcia 2004: 35)

The late Mo Mowlam, when UK secretary of state for Northern Ireland during the crucial years of peace talks, was highly critical of the dominant blame culture, where the reason given for violence was thrust on the "other side." She argued that you can only build trust and confidence when "you give people a sense of hope. Then the fear and distrust begin to decline. The aggression declines, too" (in Anderlini 2007: 80). During the peace negotiations, the Northern Ireland Women's Coalition considered that trust building was a priority that comes with a willingness to engage honestly, openly, and with all parties. The capability to recognize humanity in one's previous foes is a crucial step in overcoming fear of the other.

Political Compromise

Once fear of the other has started to diminish, the political compromise that is needed to move a peace process forward may become possible. "Parties cannot enter into a peace process without some degree of mutual trust, but they cannot build trust without entering into a peace process" (Kelman 2005: 641). Scott Atran is an anthropologist who has spent many years talking to terrorists in order to try to understand and mitigate the rise of religious violence. He gives the example of how in 2006 the Hamas leadership invited him for talks. Deputy Chairman Abu Musa Marzook explained to him that respect for Palestinians was fundamental to opening dialogue. Marzook told him, "For us, you see, there are values, and one value is *karama*, dignity, and an apology. An apology would be important to us, but words alone are not enough" (in Atran 2010: 368–369). In his research, Atran's Middle East team surveyed nearly four thousand Palestinians and Israelis between 2004 and 2008, asking citizens from across the political spectrum how they would respond to "compromises in which their side would be required to give away something it valued in return for lasting peace" (2010: 375). Their results imply that material offers and sweeteners to soften a compromise are often "interpreted as morally taboo and insulting (like accepting money to sell your child will sell out your country)" (2010: 377). Thus, a failure to compromise may be due not to mere obstinacy but rather because of a felt insult to a cause or belief that is a fundamental part of one's origin myth. Yet without some willingness to compromise on certain issues, dogmatism sets in, and political intransigence remains with no progress on negotiations for peace.

Often what is effective in breaking political deadlocks when there is an unwillingness to contemplate relating to others is a concerted engagement with community relations, which, when improved, might open doors for reasonable political negotiations. Mari Fitzduff (in Ramsbotham 2010: 75), writing on the Northern Irish context, suggests a range of options, including mutual understanding work, particularly in schools (to increase dialogue and reduce ignorance, suspicion, and prejudice); antisectarian and anti-intimidation work (to transfer improved understanding into structural changes); cultural traditions work (to affirm and develop cultural confidence that is not exclusive); and political options work (to facilitate political discussion within and between communities, including developing agreed principles of justice and rights). The view of compromise as a weakness in relating to the enemy can be broken down slowly, changing the reluctance of politicians, many of whom come from combatant, warlord, rebel leader, or paramilitary roots, to engage with the other with varying degrees of trust.

A constructive example of changing one's views of the enemy lies in Jamaa, a Burundian youth organization that promotes positive relationships between Hutu and Tutsi youth who had been involved in fighting former friends, neighbors, and sometimes relatives. Adrien Tuyaga, born to a Tutsi mother and a Hutu father, and his friend Abdoul Niyungeko began Jamaa (which means "friends" in Swahili) in 1994. Tuyaga writes that in a retreat with eighty leaders of youth militia, drawn particularly from rural areas, "Many of these youth could not have imagined the possibility of even sitting together, much less discussing a complete change of attitude toward each other," given that they had become so accustomed to acting as if "killing and maiming the 'other' was a most ordinary activity" (2005: 158). They pledged to turn from violence and played a soccer match. The mixed teams had members that included former killers from different ethnic groups playing together. This sport helped to break down fear and suspicion. Other games were organized as well as trauma counseling, and a network of former militia leaders and at-risk youth was formed to contact each other when new waves of violence appeared probable. Reflecting on the first decade of this organization, Tuyaga highlights "inclusiveness" as the essential quality of his organization, along with flexibility as a type of political compromise, as well as respect for human rights, whatever people's ethnicity. Political compromise is rarely possible without trust.

Embracing the Other

Obviously the obstacles to trust in divided societies are massive. However, building trust is a crucial first step toward forming the meaningful relationships that are necessary for recognizing differences and common humanity. Building trust takes time, and trust can easily be broken. Full embrace of the other is rare, standing as a normative ideal. However, it is possible to move beyond the seemingly irreconcilable options of them and us, or enemies and friends, toward valuing differences in inclusionary politics. Different responses help with this move.[5] First, humility is a rare trait in many politicians—and scarcer with warlords, tribal warriors, and rival ethnic groups—and between conflicting parties. With humility, there must be openness to learning from others' narratives. In doing so, and in recognizing the fresh understanding that we gain from others, we break down the distance between ourselves and the other and confirm others as important persons who are worthy of respect. Such esteem assists in the building of trust. Second, openness to the other enables all sorts of opportunities to be enlarged. Openness accepts questions, uncertainties, doubts, ambiguities, and gray middle positions that the dualism implicit in an "us and them" mentality disallows because it assumes a hierarchical superiority. This type of openness allocates space for deliberation, reflection, and the possibility of being persuaded to change one's view. An attitude or mindset of openness is vital in all forms of conflict transformation, mediation, negotiation, and peacebuilding, precisely because it allows new relational spaces to form.

Third, as discussed above, open dialogue is the avenue through which we listen to the voice of the other. Through listening and talking, the trust that strengthens relationships can build, albeit slowly and often haltingly. Indeed, in careful listening to others' narratives, the other becomes a subject, person, or agent capable of making crucial decisions and being accountable for them. Some of the historical myths that emerge through ignorance, misunderstandings, or total lack of contact with the "other side" cautiously dissipate. In beginning to trust those who have been feared, despised, or minimally tolerated, differences must be taken seriously and the possibility of common ground must be explored. "This is where creative moral imagination permits an empathetic crossing into unknown spaces, the unfamiliar territory of the world of others. Such creative imagining allows for a stutter and then a flow of alternative ideas and practices that dualism prevents" (Porter 2007a: 65). Potentially, this can be an enormously satisfying time for groups that have been kept apart through apartheid, ethnic segregation, racism, religious persecution, or sectarianism. The moment of illumination can occur when individuals and groups realize that what they share with those they had considered enemies may be greater than what divides them. Elements of a common narrative can form.

A reconciliation of differences challenges the dangers of exclusivism that undermine people's integrity. Such reconciliation is not about eliminating differences, but about some acceptance of them and thus not using differences to justify a resort to violence. The commitment to inclusivity entails the desire for healing divisions between conflicting groups through the protection of respectful differences. Elise Boulding describes "a mosaic of identities, attitudes, values, beliefs, and patterns that lead people to live nurturingly with one another" (2002: 8). This ontological argument is based on the idea of moral agency as being situated within relational contexts.

Finally, a full embrace of the other, including their differences, is rare. Miroslav Volf demonstrates how demanding such an embrace is, by maintaining that the will to embrace is unconditional; it presupposes truth and justice, and "embrace is the goal of the struggle for justice" (2000: 171). How does embrace refract given memories inflicted or experienced? Volf argues that the "will to embrace ought to govern the way we remember" (2014). Volf explains further that to remember rightly is to remember truthfully, because untruthful memories are unjust memories. Therefore "only truthful memories are just and are a stable foundation for embrace" (2014). His emphasis is that we do something with our memories. That is, we hope that with reflecting on the memories victims may heal, observers honor those who have suffered and try to prevent the suffering from happening again, and wrongdoers try to avoid guilt. Sometimes we remember in order to reconcile. While the embrace of the other is highly idealistic because its demands are great, and it tests the full parameters of the moral imagination, for trusting relationships to develop, the embrace stands as a worthwhile goal. For this embrace to occur, we need to create a space within our self to be open to others and to search for commonalities rather than disagreements, which requires that our boundaries be porous in order to be open to vulnerabilities.

* * *

In this chapter I set out to answer a tough question: Can trust be built in divided and conflict societies? In outlining the massive obstacles to trust that present in the forms of extremist nationalism, ethnicity, and religion, I noted how these stark forms of identity politics lead to othering, which cements the idea of an enemy. These obstacles ensure that trust does not develop. However, I then built a case to show how, through dialogue and listening, the recognition of other differences can be appreciated, and trust can haltingly be built, albeit with great difficulty. Once there is trust, fear of the other lessens, and political compromise can validate trust rather than be a weakness. I argue also that an embrace of the other is a major hurdle in building trust, but the goal is worthwhile, because it is a full expression of a trusting acceptance of differences.

Notes

1. Cockburn (2004) acknowledges that both of these nation names are contested terms.
2. Sylvester (2002) describes "empathic cooperation" as a feminist method, which I agree it is, but in the context of this chapter, other methodologies and practitioners intent on employing a similar framework use it as well.
3. Fifty-six people, about 10 percent of the village population, were killed (Bloch 2005: 655).
4. President Paul Kagame, in the preface to this edited collection, is critical of Lemarchand's contestation of ethnicity, suggesting that the colonial and postcolonial prejudices associated with Hutu and Tutsi were responsible for the genocide.
5. These responses are fully articulated in Porter (2007a).

6

What Can Apology and Forgiveness Achieve?

In this chapter, the complex issues of apologizing and forgiving unfold. Note their active nature. As we know so well, it takes effort to apologize and a different type of activity to forgive. Their complexity derives from their difficulty in being realized, as well as the way they are interconnected to issues already discussed, like truth telling, justice, trust, and the possibility of reconciliation. Apology and forgiveness are intensely subjective in that the need for them arises in response to acts of abuse that have seriously harmed people's sense of self. In accepting a narrative conception of the self that builds on the social foundations of trust, apology and forgiveness also are social in nature. Both are needed to reestablish the ethical foundations of a society. They build or restore moral relationships between former enemies or between a victim and wrongdoer. What I hope to draw out in this chapter is the way that when apology and forgiveness occur in public spaces—such as in truth commissions, tribunals, or community reconciliation practices—the act of apology takes on a political dimension, and the response of forgiveness becomes part of a social process that builds peace and sometimes leads to reconciliation.

We have seen in previous chapters how a legacy of memory, truth, and acknowledgment can awaken empathic bonds, the focus of the next chapter. A central purpose of this chapter is to explore the degree to which apology and forgiveness create the context in which these bonds can begin to form. I begin by looking at some obstacles to apologizing and forgiving, in particular the desire for revenge and the refusal to show remorse for misconduct. It is then important to try to understand what is involved in the giving and receiving of an apology in order to

133

answer the central question: What can apology and forgiveness achieve? Public, political apologies by political leaders or governments are relatively frequent now and play a meaningful symbolic role for those who are affected. These apologies should be accompanied by practical expressions of changed attitudes and practices that show the government's commitment not to repeat injustices or violations directed toward a group. However, these general political apologies are not the focus of this chapter. Rather, I explain why the narrative dimension of apology and forgiveness is important in the overall goal of repairing wronged relationships. I first scrutinize specific individual narratives to analyze the emotional intensity of apologies and the motivation for apologizing. I then seek to explain types of forgiveness and reasons for forgiving, concluding with the idea that ultimately forgiveness is a gift.

My overall argument has two dimensions. First, for there to be a foundation for strong reconciliation, a goal I am defending as a worthy ideal, acknowledgment of wrongdoing and of the suffering caused is the first step in a continuum of possible steps. I believe that where acknowledgment, apology, and forgiveness converge, there is the strongest likelihood that, with this type of narrative truth, reconciliation between former enemies might occur. The second dimension to my overall argument in this chapter is that an apology potentially is a powerful healing tool, but forgiveness can never be assumed, because it is a gift of generosity from a victim-survivor.

What Are the Obstacles to Apology and Forgiveness?

Apology and forgiveness do not come easily. The obstacles to these practices are formidable. In particular, the frenzied urge for revenge—that feeling that "you hurt me" so "I'm going to hurt you"—is primeval, and in the context of civil wars or postconflict settings these urges generally are spurred on by collective groups, bound together by exclusive notions of ethnic, religious, ideological, or cultural supremacy. In such contexts, revenge appears natural, the inevitable result of being harmed. The hardness of enmity presents as a stubborn blockage, where there is an "absolute refusal to concede anything" (Biggar 2011: 207). Breaking down such a mindset so that the individual or group involved accepts that some regret should be shown for harms inflicted is an enormous goal, so I begin by exposing some of the elements of revenge and a lack of remorse.

The desire for revenge is a powerful obstacle to even considering offering an apology. It can be unbridled, passionate, and devoid of proportionality, with an absolute belief in its rightness. Revenge is a powerful driver for many reasons. The harms committed in war are so horrific that revenge often seems to be the most natural response. Sometimes people "are 'wallowing' in a victim identity or consumed by anger, and anger sometimes leads to dehumanizing and heinous acts of excessive revenge" (Brudholm 2006: 11). One less expected reason is that it "reverses the roles of perpetrator and victim" (Minow 1998: 13). However, Martha Minow qualifies her point by saying that, while vengeance sounds derogatory, it can incorporate a moral response to wrongdoing. By this she means that vengeance can be a conduit to express basic self-respect because it animates justice as a form of recompense. She warns, however, that vengeance "can trap people in cycles of revenge, recrimination, and escalation of violence" (1998: 10). She distinguishes vengeance from retribution, which reflects a belief that wrongdoers deserve blame and punishment in direct proportion to the harm inflicted. Further, she suggests the need for constraints on retribution as well, ones that are tempered by "mercy and moral decency"; otherwise it threatens "bounds of proportionality and decency" (1998: 13) and loses any association with justice.

This argument is similar to that of Trudy Govier (2002), who distinguishes between vindictiveness and the desire for vindication: the former is objectionable, the latter understandable in restoring self-respect. She explains that when others hurt us we feel humiliation, suffering, and anger. We can feel a desire for revenge but not act on it. She defends her belief that revenge is immoral. Her argument is that, given that morality and the promotion of human well-being require the obligation to respect others, "to deliberately seek to bring suffering and harm to another person" violates fundamental principles of morality (Govier 2002: 12–13). Hence, Govier's objection to revenge is that it is founded on a morally evil aim of harming others. To provide an example of someone seeking vindication, not revenge, she discusses Samuel Pisar, one of the youngest survivors of Auschwitz, which he entered at twelve and emerged from at sixteen. As an adult he vindicated "himself in the sense of proving that he had deserved to survive the camps" (2002: 21) as a worthy human being through excelling in studying how international law can aid peace.

Thomas Brudholm also talks of how societies can "tire of the angry and accusing voices of survivors who cannot or will not forget and reconcile with the past. The rage, some may say, *was* legitimate, but it has had its time; now it is time to let go, true grief and anger have an end" (2006: 22). He clarifies how sometimes, after extreme atrocities, forgiveness can be refused and the resentment that remains has a moral justification. His view is similar to Minow's—that resentment is not just an emotional feeling, but it is distinguished by the way in which someone who has these feelings links them "to perceived injustice, injury, or violation" (Brudholm 2006: 15). He suggests that this is often the case, with examples apparent in Algeria, Armenia, Bosnia, Cambodia, Rwanda, and South Africa. In previous chapters I have emphasized the importance of listening in order to pick up the cues of what people need to assist their healing. Brudholm maintains that expressions of anger can be evidence that no one has listened to cries and moral norms have been breached. Reasons for anger, I suggest, must be noted. Hence, he concludes that in the aftermath of mass atrocity we should consider whether refusing to forgive could "be the reflex of moral protest" that might be as acceptable as the values that underlie "the willingness to forgive or reconcile" (2006: 23). He is suggesting that this outrage and bitterness are part of the struggle for accountability. These considerations are important, yet what is a victim to do with powerful negative feelings after years of oppression, domination, violence, exclusion, and suffering? As Judith Shklar expresses it, "No theory of either justice or injustice can be complete if it does not take account of the subjective sense of injustice and the sentiments that make us cry out for revenge" (1990: 49). I am suggesting that the instinct for revenge and vengeance can be understood in moral ways, but acting on these feelings needs to be curbed, for fear that the resultant acts will be just as immoral as the acts against which the revenge is directed. Some contemporary terrorism is motivated by anger at the West's imperialism, but the terrorist acts prevent any justification of legitimacy, given the harm they cause.

Narratives provide examples of how revenge translates. In 1996, months after the end of the war in Bosnia and Herzegovina, Savo Heleta encountered the man who tried to kill his family during the conflict. The Muslim man was driving a truck in a convoy going to the Bosnian capital of Sarajevo to get food for the city of Goražde when Heleta spotted him and stopped the truck he was driving to confront him. In his memoir, he recounts the words he said to the man: "I can get over starving, freezing, bleeding, losing my home and everything my family ever owned, but I can't get over what you did to us" (Heleta 2008: 3). The reasons for this are clear given that the depth of the scars defy healing. Consequently, Heleta writes, "I want you to be as frightened as I was when you came to my home. I want you to feel the fear I felt for so long. Your days of kicking people around are over" (2008: 4). As a victim of incredible cruelty, Heleta found comfort in the way that South Africa emerged from apartheid despite a brutal history. He traveled to South Africa and spoke with former Robben Island political prisoners. In response to their capacity to choose peace and reconciliation in spite of their suffering, Heleta writes,

> For a long time after the war, I considered reconciliation as a weakness. I saw revenge as the only way, the "manly" way to move on with my life. But with the help of my family, and after my life changed for the better and I got exposed to education and traveled all over the world, I realized that was wrong. I realized that only brave and strong people can put years of suffering behind them, reconcile with the past, and move on with life. I wanted to be one of them. (2008: 225)

When Heleta encountered the man who tortured and oppressed his family, he went to get a gun and readied himself to kill the man. But he recounted his father's words: "Be a good person and don't hate anyone. Let that be your revenge. Show them that they couldn't break you" (Heleta 2008: 203), which is what he eventually did. Resisting revenge is a significant act.

Hellen Lanyom Onguti's story differs. In 1991 Onguti was staying at her parents' farm in Uganda with all of the relatives who had gathered to help with the harvest. Each night the family slept in hiding places near the riverbank because they feared attacks from the Lord's Resistance Army. On the evening of October 4, rebels came onto the farmland and started hunting for targets. They tortured members of Onguti's family and beat them to death. Onguti's two brothers were serving in the military on the government force, and the rebels kept asking her where they were. The commander ordered for Onguti, her sister-in-law, and her niece to have their lips cut off so that when Onguti's brothers came home they would be able to see what the rebels, including child soldiers, had done to their family. In 2000 Onguti's husband was brutally captured and beaten with clubs and axes because he was riding a bicycle after the rebels declared it was illegal to do so. Onguti, when in her sixties, recounted her story of how when the rebel commanders were returning she went to see some of them. "When one of them saw me, he just started weeping and telling me sorry. He said, 'Mummy, forgive us. We did it against our will.' I told him, 'Don't fear me. I have no grudge against you'" (in Sara 2007: 23). This story of not giving in to revenge, when it would seem understandable to do so, highlights the strength of the human spirit in resilience and rising above cruelty and is repeated in every conflict zone, despite the fact that we hear more about the cruelty than the withholding of revenge.

The desire for revenge, the refusal to give in to it, and the refusal to show remorse all come with different emotional responses. Joni Hendrawan, known by his Indonesian name Idris, was a key logistics man behind the 2002 Bali bombing and convicted for his role in the 2003 Marriott Hotel bombing in Jakarta. He seemed to worry about his actions only in terms of his own salvation. While never happy about his actions, he said, "In my heart I keep hoping that what I did was right and that I will be rewarded. . . . However, I'm always worried that it was wrong and that Allah will punish me" (in Bachelard 2012). There is no remorse in this position, only a self-interest motivated by religious extremism. Elsewhere, in a quite different encounter—between an architect of apartheid killings and two African women whose husbands he had murdered—a man said, "First, to recognize another as a sufferer is to recognize that person as an emotional being. Second, to be capable of remorse is to experience oneself as morally human" (in Halpern and Weinstein 2004: 574). Keeping in mind these massive obstacles, I turn now to examples of those able to feel remorse and then to apologize.

How Significant Is an Apology?

Apology After Wrongdoing

How significant is a genuine apology? It is hugely significant. An apology acknowledges responsibility for wrongdoing. Apologies "acknowledge the facts of harms, accept some degree of responsibility, avow sincere regret, and promise not to repeat the offense" (Minow 1998: 112). Clearly, not all apologies fulfill these requirements. Some might accept a degree of responsibility and blame, but not be able to identify the harms committed. Discussing apology is difficult without also discussing forgiveness, and some would maintain that the primary purpose of an apology "is forgiveness and, ultimately, reconciliation between the offender and the offended" (Andrieu 2009: 5). As Govier puts it, "Like reconciliation itself, apology looks *backward* to what has been done and *forward* to commitment to reform, practical amends, and a better relationship" (2006: 69). Yet others argue that "there is no need to reconcile or have compassion in order to accept an apology" (Card 2004: 214). Further, while forgiveness may "lead to parties resolving their differences to the extent that a renewed form of relationship is possible, nothing in the concept of forgiveness requires parties to reconcile" (Clark 2008a: 202). Clark explains further that it is possible to forgive someone but still be reluctant to engage with that person. He argues that "forgiveness requires only that a victim should forgo feelings of resentment and a desire for direct revenge against the perpetrator" (2008a: 202). However, in the final chapter, I argue that strong notions of reconciliation are demanding ones that include forgiveness.

Apology generally precedes forgiveness, yet there are instances of people's remarkable forgiveness that comes immediately after a violent attack and without an apology. I think it is hard to analyze the real nature of this type of forgiveness. For many, it is a way of avoiding falling into the trap of bitterness and despair. The potential of apology can restore dignity; as Warner points out, "In several languages, the word apology does not exist independently of the word for forgiveness" (2002: 4). Many amazing examples are available of individual apologies being given in postwar settings, and their effect on others' lives is profound. Eugene de Kock was the commanding officer of the counterinsurgency unit of the South African police, a unit that kidnapped, tortured, and murdered many antiapartheid activists in the 1980s and 1990s. At the South African TRC, he said,

> I wish I could do much more than "I'm sorry." I wish there was a way of bringing their bodies back alive. I wish I could say, here are your husbands. . . . But unfortunately . . . I have to live with it. (in Gobodo-Madikizela 2002: 22)

However, saying "sorry" is significant in the acknowledgment of wrongdoing, by forming the basis for an apology.

Political Apologies

The examples of apology and acknowledgment of wrongdoing given so far have come from individuals. Some mention of the rise in political apologies and how these change the common historical narrative is also needed to understand the impact of apology. Political apologies are concerned with repairing broken trust between hostile groups or states that have caused harm, particularly through imperial colonialism. Typically, they are part of restorative justice practices. A host of political apologies have been offered by a wide range of political leaders toward an extensive variety of harmed peoples and for a variety of reasons—including Japanese American survivors of internment, the stolen generation of Australian Indigenous people, the relatives of Holocaust victims, relatives of Irish famine victims, and the suppression of indigenous peoples' rights to language, cultures, and spiritual practices. Specific reasons for public, political apologies vary also. Generally, they concern the violations of community norms and suppression of rights.

For example, in 2001 Xanana Gusmão, then the de facto East Timorese leader, told Australian Broadcasting Commission radio,

> The perpetrators . . . must recognize their mistake and ask for forgiveness. . . . The communities already told me bring them back. We will live together, we will punish them in our way, we will demand from them: "Oh, you burnt this house, help us and we will rebuild together." (CAVR 2005: Part 9, 2)

This did happen for many. In the community reconciliation procedures, to be examined more fully in Chapter 8, a deponent from the Aileu district of Timor-Leste attended district and village meetings to confess about the fighting and burning of houses. He said, "Through the process we could apologize and they forgave us. We fixed the roof—it wasn't a punishment but a sign of reconciliation. After reconciliation we felt better" (CAVR 2005: Part 9, 34).[1]

A victim from the Aileu district commented as follows on community reconciliation processes:

> I feel very happy with the process because now we can live in peace. Before I couldn't really talk to the [deponents]. I wanted them to declare what they did. I felt I said what I needed to say. Now I feel freer. (CAVR 2005: Part 9, 33)

These last two examples are personal, not political, but they set the background for the public, political apology made by then Indonesian president Abdurrahman Wahid, who apologized in 2011 for the violence in Timor-Leste during the twenty-four-year occupation by Indonesian forces. He made it clear that his apology was primarily to the "victims" and their families. These narrative accounts support the idea that forgiveness and reconciliation are mutually related. Forgiveness may ease "the rise of reconciliatory relations between parties that once destroyed each other. Likewise, reconciliatory political acts may hasten the occurrence of collective forgiveness" (Montiel 2000: 99).

When then Australian prime minister Kevin Rudd apologized to Indigenous Australians on February 13, 2008, it was, in his words, an attempt "to turn a new page in Australia's history by righting the wrongs of the past and so moving forward with confidence to the future"; his apology was "for the laws and policies of successive Parliaments and governments that have inflicted profound grief, suffering, and loss on these our fellow Australians" (Rudd 2008: 167). Jackie Huggins, a prominent Australian Indigenous leader, notes the event poignantly when she writes that "it was a moment when the nation held its collective breath and exhaled in sharing outpouring of emotion and joy" (2008: xiii). Similarly, in 2010, representatives of tribal organizations in New Zealand expressed the sentiment that apologies may bring a measure of solace and perhaps a sense of closure to the living who wish to see the memories of their ancestors honored and respected. Here we begin to hear common stories about receiving an apology as the first step in the healing process. For the Māori peoples, the apology goes "a long way with our elders to atone for the past. It does not mean we forget the past, but it gives the Crown an opportunity to make amends" and for movement toward healing (Murphy 2011: 54).

What can we make of acts of political apology that lead to forgiveness? Mark Amstutz reminds us how demanding political forgiveness is, given that it requires political actors to confront their culpability "through the acknowledgment of truth, the expression of remorse, and a willingness to offer reparations" (2005: 5). This indeed is demanding, and one wonders if he is asking too much from victims when he suggests that "victims must refrain from vengeance, express empathy, and respond to repentance by reducing or eliminating the offenders' debts or the deserved punishment or both" (2005: 5). Understanding his point is perhaps easier when he suggests that the reasons why victims should give up resentment and anger toward offenders is so that they no longer view them "as evil monsters but as human beings—morally responsible agents who are capable of change" (2005: 11). In this sense, "To forgive is to regard a wrongdoer as a moral agent who, in a particular context and often with mitigating excuses, has acted wrongly" (Govier 2002: 59). In allowing "the wrongdoer a fresh moral start" it becomes possible "to accept the wrongdoer as a human being with positive potential, capable of entering with oneself into a relationship of moral equality" (Govier 2006: 96). I do not want to overstate this. Sometimes the evil committed is so gross that it is inappropriate to give the wrongdoer such an opportunity to enter into any relational context with the person who has suffered because of the wrongdoer's actions. Also, pressures placed on victims to forgive can manipulate the vulnerable who are not ready to do so, which simply perpetuates injustices. Expecting a victim to cease resentment can be "dehumanizing in the sense of adding the burden of guilt to one already carrying a heavy yoke" (Montiel 2000: 97).

In terms of political apologies, the wrongdoer is a state, political leader, dominant political party, member of the security forces, or tribal grouping, and thus should be able to demonstrate changes through new laws, policies, or practices. Such changes prove the genuine nature of the apology and can contribute to healing and rectifying injustices.

Acknowledgment

In the literature on apology, due attention is not always given to the significance of acknowledgment. I argue that acknowledgment is the crucial first step that should precede apology and forgiveness. For apology it involves acknowledging wrongdoing and harm caused. For forgiveness it includes acknowledging the humility and courage needed to ask for forgiveness and the willingness to let go of resentment. I believe that underlying this acknowledgment is a crucial dimension to the recognition of mutual respect. Acknowledgment is part of restoring dignity to those who have been humiliated or depressed. "When we acknowledge something, we mark our knowledge or awareness of that thing, and we mark that knowledge to someone" (Govier 2009: 36)—sometimes to ourselves, usually toward an other. As Govier puts it, "Acknowledgment is articulated or embodied awareness" (2009: 41). In this context, acknowledgment arises because there are abhorrent things to admit. The refusal to acknowledge wrong and the suffering it causes is harmful, because denial damages people's abilities to feel and treats people as if their stories are not worth hearing or do not count. It might not be an outright refusal to acknowledge wrong and harm. With discord over interpretations of narratives, people interpret events differently. If people believe they are right, according to their narrative, there is no wrong to admit. With others, there is direct denial, the "refusal to give up one's narrative and the sense of identity and purpose that that narrative provides" (2009: 44).

Acknowledgment is powerful. It can be acknowledgment that a victim or communities of victims have been wronged or that a perpetrator, a group, or a state has done wrong. As Govier argues, to receive acknowledgment that certain things did happen, and that "they were wrong and should not have happened, is to receive confirmation, validation, of one's dignity and status as a human being, and a moral being of equal worth" (2003: 85). When there have been profound wrongs, acknowledgment is important to victims in providing recognition of the effect of these wrongs on self-dignity. Further, if the wrongdoer gives a narrative account of the wrongdoing, the injured party gets to hear about the context in which the injury occurred. Understanding this context may assist healing.

Trudy Govier and Colin Hirano (2008) discuss the shifts that victims need to undergo in feelings toward and in beliefs about the sort of person the offender is. They consider the relationships between "words, actions, and attitudes" to see whether it is saying, "I forgive you," or changes in attitudes of the victim that determine whether the offender needs to acknowledge wrongdoing. They present an interesting defense of "invitational forgiveness" as a good case, using the late Nelson Mandela's unilateral political gestures of forgiveness that were not offered in response to white South Africans' apology, because none was made. Mandela's words to his former enemies after his release from prison in 1990 are profound.

> I knew that people expected me to harbor anger towards whites. But I had none. In prison, my anger towards whites decreased, but my hatred for the system grew. I wanted South Africa to see that I loved even my enemies, while I hated the system that turned us against one another. (in Govier 2002: 68)

This type of forgiveness does not presume acknowledgment from the wrongdoer. Rather, Mandela's response can be interpreted as offering forgiveness to the white community as an "invitation . . . to morally acknowledge the wrongs of apartheid and change their ways" (Govier and Hirano 2008: 430). Curiously, many white people did not believe they had done any wrong, so they were surprised at offers of forgiveness. Similarly, Martin Luther King Jr.'s sermons and public talks in the 1960s indicated willingness to see no irredeemable enemies as barriers to relationships. What these examples show is that invitational forgiveness spurs engagement to consider a forthcoming positive relationship. "Invitational forgiveness can defuse the combative and confrontational emotions and attitudes that are often so prevalent after a serious wrong is inflicted" (Govier and Hirano 2008: 433). At this stage, the narrative is critical. The goal of invitational forgiveness is to elicit a response; hence communication is crucial. This goal may appear problematic to those who consider that forgiveness should not be sought because it is a gift, or those concerned with imbalanced power relations, which happens with many gender violence cases. Certainly, "Invitational forgiveness fails when it does not help to restore a positive relationship between victim and perpetrator" (2008: 437). Given the moral complexity of conflicts, "Mutuality undercuts the notion that a 'victim' is entirely pure whereas the 'offender' is entirely evil" (Govier 2002: 49).

Different motivations of self-interest, remorse, shame, or necessity of working with survivors sometimes drive ex-combatants, released prisoners, amnesty applicants, or defendants to ask for mercy or forgiveness. Acknowledgment of wrongdoing is fundamental to this drive. Until some of the narrative is understood, it is not possible to know whether these people act from the heart or merely from expediency.

Acknowledgment in the fullest sense is a crucial first step to many types of healing. Jean Baptise Kayigamba, a survivor of the Rwandan genocide in which most of his family were killed, sees it as crucial that survivors tell what they have witnessed firsthand and narrate their experiences. Being a witness in this sense is different from bearing witness to the suffering of others. Kayigamba states that "it would be wrong to forget" and writes, "When others learn and acknowledge what we survivors lived through, this helps restore some of the humanity that we lost during the genocide" (2008: 34). He writes of a poignant moment when his mother noticed that one of her neighbors was wearing one of her wedding shoes, which had been stolen in a killing spree in Gikongoro in 1959. She knew that to try to claim them back would trigger reprisal attacks against the family. Thirty-five years later, the genocide occurred. Kayigamba writes, "I resent bitterly that the world betrayed my people in their hour of most desperate need by refusing to intervene to halt the genocide" (2008: 40). In reflecting on the way that survivors of the genocide are urged to forgive and forget the crimes committed against their families, he expresses resentment at being asked to forgive. Acknowledgment comes in many forms and has to include strong emotions. Acknowledged anger can often precede a fight for justice rather than impunity in the name of reconciliation.

A different example of acknowledgment can be seen in the questioning of John Ackerman in the South African TRC. His wife was killed in a 1993 grenade attack at a mainly white church, the St. James Church massacre, in Cape Town. His questioning to the likely perpetrator of this violence was very specific:

> My wife was sitting next to me in the front pew. She was wearing a long blue coat. . . . I want you to tell me if you saw her. Do you remember firing at my wife? If you don't remember I'll accept it, but I want to know if you saw her, if you remember firing at her. (in Gobodo-Madikizela 2002: 24)

This might strike some readers as peculiar, a man simply wanting to know if his wife's probable killer remembers killing a woman who was wearing a blue coat. However, it brings to light the intense need for clarification on personal matters that seem trivial, but which are not to the person involved. Rather, they bring together the intensely evocative nature of conjoined narratives. The coat might have been a gift from the husband, worn at a special occasion that brings back poignant memories, or simply be the coat the woman always wore to church. To summarize this section, we can conclude that an apology is significant; it can achieve so much in acknowledging wrongdoing and harms caused.

Why Is Forgiveness Meaningful?

While it has been impossible to discuss apology without elaborating on its relationship to forgiveness, the task now is to clarify further what forgiveness really involves. It is easy to begin with what forgiveness is not. It is not a case of forgetting the crime or harm. It is not "forgive and forget," nor does it mean that the victim needs to cease being angry, come to like the offender, or excuse the offense. Forgiveness is not always appropriate. I have already explained that some acts of wrong-doing are so damaging to a person's dignity that either forgiveness seems impossible, or for some, it comes only after a long period of reflection and support from others. Marguerite La Caze (2006) gives the example that there is no good reason why Australian Aboriginal peoples should forgive non-Aboriginal people for past and present injustices. The reason is that forgiveness is an act of generosity, but apology is "a duty based on respect" (La Caze 2006: 457). She qualifies her point that an apology is not always accompanied by forgiveness, nor does forgive-ness always occur after an apology. Forgiveness is an enormous topic; here I concentrate on three aspects that highlight connections between peace, justice, and reconciliation: the features and types of forgiveness, reasons for forgiveness, and stories of forgiveness.

Features and Types of Forgiveness

Claudia Card suggests that forgiveness has five features: renunciation of hostility, compassionate concern for the offender, acceptance of the offender's apology and contrition, remission of punishment, and an offer to renew relationship or accept the other (2004: 213). Realistically, Card qualifies these features by saying that most perpetrators do not welcome forgiveness or become contrite; hence, these demanding fea-tures rarely are realized in full. Again, they stand as an ideal. Yet there are many notable cases of offenders asking for forgiveness and coming close to embodying the five features. In the South African TRC, Colonel Schobesberger, the former chief of staff of the Ciskei Defense Force, apologized for the Bisho massacres of 1992 and asked the victims for forgiveness, saying that "to get the soldiers back into the community, to accept them fully, to try to understand also the pressure they were under then. This is all I can do" (in Boraine 2000: 355). After a short time of stunned silence, the audience, which included relatives of the victims of the massacre, burst into applause at the apology and acknowledgment of suffering. The applause was a symbolic sign of willingness to accept the apology and thus to forgive. Forgiveness is not a substitute for justice; otherwise, in the absence of justice, resentments continue, kindling future conflict. However, the act of requesting forgiveness is an important step in reducing hostilities and working toward revised relationships wherein justice might be revisioned.

Nigel Biggar distinguishes between two types of forgiveness. First, he discusses a unilateral, unconditional, inner releasing of resentment, which he calls "forgiveness-as-compassion" (2011: 203). With unilateral forgiveness, there is no acknowledgment by a wrongdoer who may be unapologetic, indifferent, absent, or dead. Given the emphasis on self-preservation I wonder about its motivation as an act of compassion. Biggar's defense is that "people who have been relieved of grievance are generally freer to take creative risks of sympathy or compassion" (2011: 206). This point is reasonable. Second, there is "forgiveness-as-absolution" (2011: 203), which is reciprocal and conditional on some expression of repentance as an opening of the space needed to begin reconciliation. Biggar applies these understandings to Northern Ireland, where some have expressed regret at the suffering caused by killings, but expressing regret is not necessarily being remorseful. A narrative view of this regret recognizes that there are conflicting stories about causes, responsibilities, victims, and aggressors. Biggar's take on Northern Ireland is interesting, in maintaining that reconciliation can only occur between persistent enemies—that is, "between those who *continue* to disagree passionately about what has caused the Troubles and about who is basically to blame for them" (2011: 204). Accommodation and coexistence might be minimal, but weak forms of reconciliation are possible under these conditions, despite the remaining abundant disagreements.

Others argue that "it is through the experience of forgiving offenders that victims are empowered and can gain access to all that a restorative process offers" (Kohen 2009: 401). The rationale for this view lies in the degree to which a victim can let go of the power of the offense and move from victim status to survivor. Part of letting go is releasing oneself from the crippling effects of long-term resentment toward the offender. Making these choices can be empowering. Nothing can wipe out the memory of a horrible act, as the stories related throughout the book show, but the freedom of release from painful emotions is liberating. All this can occur without the offender knowing, which is very relevant in many instances, particularly with the case of rape in war. In political contexts, apologies may facilitate political compromise or be the preconditions to begin negotiations over serious issues like land or compensation. Particularly with indigenous peoples, such negotiations can speak to their "sacred values" (Atran 2010) and thus acknowledge their dignity.

Something we do not often think about is self-forgiveness, which addresses damaged self-respect. Robin Dillon (2001) provides useful examples of the need for self-forgiveness. Raped women mostly do not want to testify because of their feelings of shame, which is quite understandable. Self-respect is crucial to dignity, and its undermining is debilitating. Underlying self-respect is the Kantian idea that all persons are worthy of respect, despite what they have done or have had done to them. For former combatants or returnees, forgiving oneself means being "no longer crippled by negative conceptions of oneself" (Dillon 2001: 55). Another strange act of forgiveness comes when "a woman might need to forgive the child whom she gave birth to as a result of rape" (Schott 2004: 208) in order to accept the child and provide loving care. In this case, forgiveness not only assists the mother but also helps to break the cycle of communal hostility to difference if the child is from a mixed racial or ethnic group. There are many types of forgiveness, and all contribute in their differing ways to furthering more peaceful, just relationships that are open to the idea of being reconciled.

Reasons for Forgiveness

Reasons for asking for forgiveness differ. The story of Simon Wiesenthal, then a prisoner in a concentration camp, is an oft-told illustration of the massive effect of the Holocaust. Wiesenthal worked in a local hospital, where he once met a dying German soldier, Karl. Karl told Wiesenthal how his unit had killed up to three hundred Jews on the Eastern Front, and admitted,

> I know that what I have done to you is terrible. In the long nights while I have been waiting for death, time and time again I have longed to talk about it to a Jew and beg forgiveness from him. . . . I know that

what I am asking is almost too much for you but without your answer
I cannot die in peace. (in Wiesenthal 1998: 57)

Wiesenthal left the room without speaking to the dying soldier,
leaving the moral dilemma unanswered for the reader.

Similar acts of violence affect people differently. In 1985, South
African security forces intercepted a car, abducted the antiapartheid
activists inside, and murdered them in cold blood.[2] The men became
known as the Cradock Four. At the South African TRC, one of the widows of the victims, Nyameka Goniwe, said, "I can't forgive and forget
. . . or go on with my life until I know the actual killers" (in Gobodo-
Madikizela 2002: 16). Doreen Mgoduka, a widow of the Motherwell
bombing that killed three police and an informer, met Eugene de Kock.
De Kock explained to the widows what actually happened. In the process
of hearing the story and reconnecting with the facts surrounding their
husbands' deaths, they could finally release their husbands emotionally.
Mgoduka said that she was able to mourn appropriately, which enabled
her to free herself in accepting death. Pearl Faku also met de Kock and
was touched by his sorrow that he could not bring their husbands back.
Despite not looking at him, she felt that his apology was genuine. With
uncontrollable tears and overwhelmed by emotion, she nodded, "As a
way of saying yes, I forgive you. I hope that when he sees our tears, he
knows that they are not only tears for our husbands, but tears for him as
well" (in Gobodo-Madikizela 2002: 17). Again, this expression of empathy is a remarkable indication of the human potential to rise above self-
interest, despite deeply difficult personal circumstances.

In the messiness of life, there are unorthodox ways to grasp the
essence of forgiveness and the variations in approach. Jo Berry was the
daughter of Sir Anthony Berry, who died in 1984 when a bomb set by
the Irish Republican Army hit the Grand Hotel in Brighton where a
Conservative Party conference was occurring. The target had been then
prime minister Margaret Thatcher. Patrick Magee had set the bomb.
Berry befriended her father's killer. She said,

> Patrick opened up and became a real human being. We shared a lot of
> the struggles and how he felt and the cost to him of taking a violent
> stand. He wanted to know the kind of man my father was. My seven-
> year-old daughter got me to ask him why he killed her granddad, and
> he was shaken. (in Smith 2004: 10)

When Berry was asked whether she had forgiven Magee, her
response was interesting. Instead of forgiveness, which to her implied

some sort of ending, she said, "I want to be able to feel angry—so I prefer to say I can understand" (in Smith 2004: 10).[3] As noted already in the previous chapter, feeling anger is often a spur toward working for justice.

Zvi Bekerman and Michalinos Zembylas conducted research on the emotional complexities of teaching contested historical narratives in schools, where strong emotions like anger, resentment, and feelings of injustice align with "hegemonic narratives" (2012: 124). Their particular focus is on Palestinian, Jewish, and Greek-Cypriot schoolteachers who work with children who are living in conflict. Bekerman and Zembylas asked the teachers directly about their perspectives on forgiveness as a pedagogical practice and gained a variety of responses. In providing their narratives, "Several Palestinian and Jewish teachers emphasized that the first step to forgiveness was to recognize the other as a victim and understand his or her pain" (2012: 171). Further, in acknowledging each other's victimization, there is a chance of forgiveness. Esther argued that, when some things like bombs and the killing of children cannot be forgiven, "all that is left . . . is offering recognition to the other" (in Bekerman and Zembylas 2012: 172). She explained the operative aspect is that "when you are asking for forgiveness from someone, you are saying, 'I am sorry for doing this, I realize I was wrong. I also think that from now on I can act differently'" (in 2012: 172).

The Greek-Cypriot teachers placed more emphasis on remembrance. John, recalling the historical trauma suffered said that "it's impossible to forget this trauma, and I don't see any possibility of forgiveness," so he explained, "I think we should remember and stay adamant about not forgiving those who caused us so much suffering" (in Bekerman and Zembylas 2012: 175). The Greek-Cypriot teachers also emphasized justice. As Niki noted, "Bring justice for all and then perhaps we'll talk about forgiveness" (in 2012: 177). Schools can play an important role in fostering the mutual recognition of different identities, responsibilities for atrocities, and the need for justice for all. As we have seen, the story of forgiveness comes about because of a story of trauma. When people are traumatized, typically they occupy a space of silence dominated by living haunted memories. Speaking out about trauma to someone willing to listen makes the trauma recognizable. Such "testimonial narratives" should aid the victim in integrating the trauma into their lives and invite others to "bear witness to another's pain and suffering" (Gobodo-Madikizela 2008b: 175). The nature of trauma caused by war's damage is variable, so the reasons for forgiveness are diverse.

Stories of Forgiveness

Grappling with stories of forgiveness requires an understanding of narratives that are filled with strong emotions that emerge in multiple ways. A prime value of forgiveness is that it enables us "to reconnect and recognize the common humanity of the other," and the granting of forgiveness strengthens our commonality (Minow 1998: 14). La Caze suggests that "forgiveness is based on love" (2006: 456) in a similar way that Arendt says that "only love can forgive" (1974: 309). That is, forgiveness is a form of creative renewal, permitting one to renounce inner rage. While an emphasis on love seems strange—even inappropriate, given the types of acts to which forgiveness is directed in postwar contexts—La Caze qualifies her definition of a forgiveness based on love as one that is "understood as sympathy for the other" (2006: 456). Sympathy and love are different. I believe that you can sympathize without loving, but you cannot love without also demonstrating sympathy.

Practical narratives bring the potential power of forgiveness to the fore. Thomas Brudholm and Arne Grøn (2011) write of a Rwandan man named Innocent Rwililiza, whose wife and son were murdered in the Nyamata church massacre during the 1994 genocide. Rwililiza was skeptical about forgiveness, blaming humanitarian organizations for "importing forgiveness to Rwanda," and wrapping it in money to try to persuade people to change (in Brudholm and Grøn 2011: 160). Accusing these "whites in all-terrain turbo vehicles," he told the researchers that "when we talk among ourselves, the word *forgiveness* has no place; I mean it's oppressive" (in Brudholm and Grøn 2011: 160). Forgiveness should never be imposed. The relationship between forgiveness and reconciliation is intricate, but they need to be analytically distinguished. Consolate Mukanyiligira, coordinator of a Rwandan widows' group for survivors, told researcher Radha Webley in 2003 that Rwandan people feel "obliged to reconcile because we are neighbors," but there is little trust (in Govier 2006: 205). That is, there are pragmatic reasons why the forgiveness aspect to reconciliation is often stressed—when it is essential for people to coexist, to enable them to keep working together. When the motivation to work together is solely pragmatic, including sometimes simply to continue to receive aid funding, it usually means that the forgiveness has not been realized to the full, so any move toward reconciliation is half-hearted. On the other hand, sometimes during the process of working together, significant changes of attitudes can occur.

Laura Skovel, in following the Sierra Leone TRC of 2003, found a similar response. Even in the aftermath of shocking amputations, people were told they should forgive those who had harmed them. They had been taught they needed to forgive so that the country could reconcile. When she probed their response further and used different language, the responses changed. The issue of trust had not been central to the official reconciliation discourse. When she asked them if they forgave the wrongdoers and were they reconciled, people answered in the affirmative. When she asked, "Well, do you *trust* those people? Could you *trust* them again?" (in Govier 2006: 203), they answered, "Oh no, we do not trust them, of course not. It will be a long time before we can trust them again" (in Govier 2006: 203). Such a finding defends Govier's view that one of the fundamental attitudes underlying relationships that is most significant in a reconciliation process is trust. As I showed in the previous chapter, trusting relationships are built over time and with great effort and good intention, including having the space to air conflicts as well as to build reconciliation instead of resentment.

One well-documented case of apology and forgiveness is that of Winnie Madikizela-Mandela's exchanges in the TRC in South Africa, where she was giving testimony that linked her to the kidnapping and murder of Stompie Seipei, a fourteen-year-old activist, and also to the murder of Abubaker Asvat, the doctor who treated Stompie, as well as numerous other acts of violence. Initially, she was stubborn, denying all allegations of human rights abuses made against her, saying that the accusations were "ludicrous" and "ridiculous" and that she had "fought a just war" (in Krog 1999: 257). One frustrated lawyer burst out, "The truth in your hands is like putty which you simply mold to suit your own ends" (in Boraine 2000: 248). Desmond Tutu stressed that the commission was not a court of law; the purpose was to discover the truth, not to produce a guilty or not guilty verdict. He made a personal statement to her, affirming their prior close relationship. He then placed his plea to her firmly within the language of morality and the need to struggle "to establish a new, a different dispensation characterized by a new morality, where integrity, truthfulness, and accountability were the order of the day" (Tutu 1999: 134). Tutu accredited her role in the history of the African struggle. He pleaded with her to be more cooperative, particularly to admit that something went wrong. Tutu begged her to apologize, to ask for forgiveness, and he looked at her directly, saying, "You don't know how your greatness would be enhanced if you were to say sorry, things went wrong, forgive me, I beg you" (in Boraine 2000: 252). Madikizela-Mandela's response was,

> I will take this opportunity to say to the family of Dr. [Abubaker] Asvat, how deeply sorry I am; to Stompie's mother, how deeply sorry I am—I have said so to her before a few years back, when the heat

was very hot. I am saying it is true, things went horribly wrong. I fully agree with that and for that part of those painful years when things went horribly wrong and we were aware of the fact that there were factors that led to that, for that I am deeply sorry. (in Boraine 2000: 252; Digeser 2001: 144–145; Tutu 1999: 135)

The emotionally charged hearing adjourned. Boraine felt that Tutu's personalizing of this case was "unwise" (2000: 253). Had Madikizela-Mandela conceded accountability through applying for amnesty, this might have led to a pardon.

Digeser (2001: 145) points out three significant features of her statement: it shows an element of taking responsibility and some willingness to show humility, and it meets the minimal threshold of justice. Whether family and friends of the two murdered people perceived this as such is another matter. Tutu instinctively used her "culture of clan honor and shame" and, by begging her publicly he was honoring her as an equal because "in the culture of honor, you are answerable for your honor only to your social equals" (Krog 1999: 260). Insincere apologies do nothing positive to address wrongdoing and harm caused. Saying "sorry" is significant, "because a proper apology must use a term that accepts responsibility in the sense of acknowledging that one has an obligation to make amends" (La Caze 2006: 450). That is, "When we become responsible *for* something, we have a set of obligations to care for those who have suffered the wrong and to try to make reparations" (La Caze 2006: 452).

The relationship established between the one who forgives and one who is forgiven is personal, although not necessarily private, "in which *what* was done is forgiven for the sake of *who* did it" (Arendt 1974: 241). Arendt's point is that some acts are so evil that forgiveness is not morally appropriate, but, where it is, forgiveness can break repetitive cycles of vengeance. She argues, "Without being forgiven, released from the consequences of what we have done, our capacity to act would, as it were, be confined to one single deed from which we could never recover" (1974: 237). Gobodo-Madikizela's interpretation is that these acts "are unforgivable because no yardstick exists by which we can measure what it means to forgive them, and there is no mental disposition we can adopt towards them that would correct the sense of injustice that their actions have injected into our world" (2008a: 333). Ordinary wrongdoings are deserving of forgiveness, but willful evil acts may be unforgivable. Minow claims further that "to forgive is to let go of vengeance; to avenge is to resist forgiving" (1998: 21). Stories of forgiveness can surprise. They often defy expectations and are hard to explain. Again, they reveal the potential strength inherent in human nature.

What Is the Gift of Forgiveness?

The idea that forgiveness is a gift is becoming more accepted, but what does it mean in practice? Marie-Claire, a Rwandan genocide survivor, gave one response when she said, "I have already forgiven the killers" (in Clark 2010: 282), and she explains to Phil Clark that "it was not necessary for the perpetrators to ask for forgiveness, explaining instead, 'God forgives, therefore we must forgive'" (in Clark 2010: 285). What is involved in this incredible statement? Forgiveness is a prerogative held by the victimized. It is not a right to be claimed, because to expect survivors to forgive is to impose another burden. Forgiveness can never restore the losses, particularly of loved ones, but "the gift of forgiveness is important because it provides a means by which victims and offenders can restore an authentic moral self-worth" (Amstutz 2005: 43). Forgiveness is not owed, nor can it be demanded. It "is both free and costly" (Smyth 2008: 72).

The attitudes of those who are able to forgive mirror Jacques Derrida's idea of the paradox of forgiveness, whereby *"forgiveness forgives only the unforgivable"* (2002: 32). Derrida emphasizes that forgiveness *"should* remain exceptional and extraordinary, in the face of the impossible" (2002: 32). He is indicating that "monstrous crimes"—those crimes that we would have classified as "unforgivable" or where there is no remorse shown from the wrongdoer to the victim, where the victim has been so deeply dehumanized that they lose the power to speak the words of forgiveness—are becoming increasingly "visible, known, recounted, named, archived by a 'universal conscience' better informed than ever" (Derrida 2002: 33). This visibility of crimes against humanity is particularly evident given increasing access to the Internet and broadly interconnected social media accounts. Unforgivable wrongs denote the enormity of the harm caused, what a moral community rightly refuses to find acceptable. Richard Bernstein makes a powerful point in emphasizing that what is deemed unforgivable and forgivable is always contestable. He explores "what we actually do when we ask ourselves should we forgive what is (or what we take to be) unforgivable" (2006: 402). Bernstein suggests that we do not just bounce between incompatible positions, but we go through deliberative processes. In indecisive moments, when we juggle seemingly contradictory options, we struggle to come up with the best possible decision. The decision may well be enormous; we agonize over it, make up our mind, change it, and come up with a different reason for a responsible judgment, given "the difficulty of forgiving the unforgivable" (2006: 403).[4]

There are many remarkable instances of the gift of forgiveness. Mama K from Nyanza is a Tutsi survivor of the Rwandan genocide.[5] Only three of her eight children survived the genocide. She now works for an organization that helps genocide victims. She has openly forgiven some of the men responsible for her children's deaths. Mama K spoke of her refusal to forgive a man named Jean Muhire who killed her mother, at a stage where he had not confessed to his crimes. Later, Muhire confessed during the gacaca trials. She told the researchers that there are two categories of people:

> Those that ask for forgiveness and those that do not. Remember that. Those who confess, who actually feel sorry for what they did, they are the ones you can forgive. Those that do not feel bad, they do not want forgiveness and you cannot forgive them. (in Phillips 2007: 460)

Victims have the moral right to forgive, or to delay or deny forgiveness.

A host of examples highlight the deliberate, almost immediate choice to forgive. These apparently random examples are replicated in many other countries. Amy Biehl was a Stanford University student who was stabbed in a Cape Town township in 1993. Peter and Linda Biehl returned to Cape Town to work with their daughter's killers. Peter Biehl stated his intentions "to extend a hand of friendship in a society which has been systematically polarized for decades" (in Gobodo-Madikizela 2002: 26). Linda Biehl declared she had no hatred and was only concerned to help the young men rebuild their lives. Gordon Wilson, in the immediate aftermath of an Irish Republican Army bomb at the 1987 Remembrance Day service that killed his daughter, said, "I bear no ill will. I bear no grudge. That dirty sort of talk is not going to bring her back to life" (in Biggar 2011: 203). Gloria Terikien was abducted from her village of Rorovana in Bougainville and taken to the bush in 1992 by the Bougainville Revolutionary Army. Years later at a reconciliation ceremony she spoke to one of the army guerrillas who had bullied her for a year and half in the bush. She said,

> I forgive you before you even ask for it. I have put it all behind me. I am now settled down again and I do not want to think about this any-

more. I don't want to talk about it. All I want to say is "I forgive you" and put it behind me. (in Howley 2002: 12)

Reflecting on why she was forgiving, her motivation was that her children should understand that she did not carry hatred in her heart because, as she said,

If I carry hatred in my heart, then I am doing more damage to myself than to the person whom I hate. We must all learn to forgive and get on with our lives if we are going to be useful again. (in Howley 2002: 13)

This was a gift to the man who had bullied her, to her children, and ultimately to herself. In analyzing such examples, it is difficult to pinpoint why some can make such declarations while others shy from it, finding it impossible to do so.

Ulrike Poppe, an East German dissident who had twice been imprisoned by communist authorities, asks this question: "What's all this talk about forgiveness and reconciliation? I now live on the same street as the man who informed on me. I didn't know him then and I certainly don't want to know him now" (in Biggar 2011: 200). For some, apology comes easily and forgiveness follows. For others, an apology is impossible and forgiveness is undesirable. Some victims link forgiveness with reconciliation. Others, like Poppe, neither can imagine it nor want it. I take up variations of these options further in Chapter 8. In the next chapter I examine whether it is really possible to practice compassion in contexts where so much deep trauma has been inflicted on others.

* * *

In exploring the question of what apology and forgiveness can achieve, the answer is, a great deal. This chapter began with examining examples of obstacles to apology and forgiveness. I looked particularly at the temptation for revenge, arguing that, while revenge sometimes is motivated by justice, ultimately revenge harms others and undermines the development of sustainable peace. In exposing the significance of apology, I argue that acknowledgment of wrongdoing and harm suffered is a crucial first step—that when acknowledgment precedes apology and prompts forgiveness, these three virtues stand as a firm basis for the possibility of reconciliation. I showed that there are many reasons for forgiveness and many examples of incredible stories that show different degrees of forgiveness. Not all actions are forgivable, because forgiveness really is a gift, an act of grace that can be bestowed or withheld.

Notes

1. The point here is simply that apology and forgiveness should have practical outcomes. I explain their relationship with "feeling better," healing, and reconciliation more fully in Chapter 8. CAVR is the abbreviation for Comissão de Acolhimento, Verdade e Reconciliação.

2. Two were schoolteachers, one was a railway worker who led a youth movement, and the other was a visiting headmaster.

3. Since then, Patrick Magee has joined with Jo Berry in a project called Building Bridges for Peace. See www.buildingbridgesforpeace.org.

4. In a mark of wonderful humor, Bernstein suggests that the late Derrida might have begun an "on the other hand" type of argument, to which he responds, "So, Jacques, please forgive me" (2006: 405)!

5. The name has been changed by Phillips, as has Muhire's to follow.

7

Can Compassion Be Practiced in Postconflict Contexts?

In this chapter I make a case for why compassion should be accepted as a crucial practice in postconflict settings. This task is not easy, given the extent of disagreement and distorted relationships that remain in these settings. Again, as with the preceding chapters, I begin this chapter by looking briefly at some of the obstacles to demonstrating compassion—in particular a hardness of heart that resists reaching out to others and the hypocrisy that accompanies political rhetoric. Such resistance is often revealed in a single-mindedness to get one's own way, or to ignore or undermine anyone stepping in one's path. In outlining practices of compassion, the underlying principles I stress are, first, the common vulnerability we all have to suffering, simply by virtue of being human, and second, an acceptance of our moral obligations toward others who are suffering. I explain how a cosmopolitan ethics underlies the responsibilities we owe to others—that is, how our common humanity leads to ethical duties. I clarify and contrast differing examples of sympathy and empathy. Justice and care debates are infrequently included in peace studies and transitional justice literature. Drawing on these debates, my prime argument is that, contrary to common thinking, compassion need not be limited to the private sphere, because indeed it can play a crucial public, political role in responding to the human cry for help. Development of the ultimate test of this argument lies in the final section, where I suggest what is entailed in responding to someone who previously was an enemy.

What Are the Obstacles to Compassion?

Obstacles to demonstrating compassion are numerous, mainly because the motivations of those who commit horrific acts of violence are plentiful and quite contrary to the values implicit in compassion. They include malice, revenge, hatred, and, as already outlined in Chapter 3, what can only be described as evil. Trying to understand the mindset of perpetrators of violence is to seek to comprehend the incomprehensible, how one human can willfully harm another human. The sort of compassion and empathy discussed in this chapter is thus concerned with building or rebuilding relationships in circumstances where offenders have shown remorse and when it is essential for victims, orphans, and widows to live close to former combatants, genocide perpetrators, or paramilitary members. Fear remains. My central argument in this chapter is that, without some sort of empathetic connection to the other, there is only hope of coexistence, but little anticipation for a stronger notion of reconciliation, the focus of the final chapter. The obstacles to realizing these connections are formidable, and thus it is essential to avoid arguments that are naively idealistic.

A narrative example of the difficulty in contemplating softening one's response to the enemy is apt. Jaballa Matar was a former Libyan diplomat who became a dissident and opponent of the Gaddafi regime and disappeared in the prison system. His son, Hisham Matar, a Libyan novelist writes, "When you steal a man and lock him away like that, you take with him every word he was going to utter. The wait hardens the heart" (in Barrowclough 2012: 30). Yet the son was determined to try to keep an open heart, as he explains: "It is easy to underestimate the demands of an open heart. That, for example, I have to find a way to try to regard my father's torturer as my brother: to not allow the oppressor to lose me my right to be human" (in Barrowclough 2012: 30). In this chapter, this notion of being human is fundamental to my defense of the need for compassion, as I explain more fully shortly. Suffice it to say here that feeling a shared humanity underlies this novelist's narrative. Indeed, what the novelist reveals here is that, in retaining vengeful thoughts, a person is reduced to the motives of the avenger, and personal integrity is lost.

One chief obstacle to developing compassion in political life lies in the seeming hypocrisy of numerous politicians. Many of those who are influential in the public sphere espouse positive virtues of care in their media speeches, but then in policy issues that affect people's welfare, they formulate harsh regulations that crush the human spirit. One example that is the cause of great shame and grief to many Australians such as myself is recent Australian government responses to asylum seekers. The vast majority of these people come from war zones. In Australia, the five top source countries for asylum seekers who arrived by small boats in 2012 were Afghanistan, Sri Lanka, Iran, Pakistan, and Iraq. The 1958 Migration Act declares that it is not illegal to seek asylum in Australia. People seeking asylum in Australia arrive in much smaller numbers than in Canada, the United States, and the UK. Asylum seekers who arrive by boat to Australia make up less than 2 percent of Australia's annual immigration, but politicians use the issue as part of a post-9/11 scare campaign about potential terrorists arriving and employ the military to police ocean borders. The language of many Australian politicians from the major political parties is harsh when they refer to these people as "illegals" or "queue jumpers."[1] Asylum seekers are processed offshore and placed in detention camps where journalists and lawyers are banned. The Australian Human Rights Commission (2013) published a report on asylum seekers and refugees, maintaining that Australia has one of the most restrictive immigration detention systems in the world. There is worrying evidence that Australia is not upholding its international obligations toward asylum seekers or refugees. The nature and procedures of mandatory detention with inadequate conditions, social exclusion, and offshore processing cause grave mental harm in already traumatized people. The report shows that on September 30, 2013, there were 6,403 people seeking asylum in Australia who were in closed detention facilities, and approximately one in six of them were children. There are many viable alternatives to this disgraceful mandatory detention, with community care facilitating a smoother transition to life in Australia once refugee status is granted. If compassion is not shown to the most vulnerable in a nation, the nation deserves international criticism.

Why Does Common Humanity Lead to Duties?

Global suffering continues on a massive scale. As Catherine Lu puts it bluntly, people continue "to suffer the fate of flies in indifferent, thoughtless, or reckless human hands" (2006: 1). While natural disasters obviously result in humanitarian crises, there are too many instances of brutal, neglectful, tyrannical regimes, as well as terrorists and violent groups that contribute to cruelty, deprivation, intense poverty, and needless suffering. That is, human activity often creates humanitarian disasters. Humans are cruel to other humans, particularly in war. With such widespread misery, pleas go out to the international community from social media, aid organizations, the diaspora, and sometimes from those living amid the violence to step in to defend ailing humanity. The important question to consider is: What ought to be the duties of humanity in the international order? Writings on humanitarian action are couched in the strong language of moral duties, obligations, and responsibilities, particularly the duty to alleviate suffering and provide aid. The idea of duties is broad, encompassing "remedial duties" in the light of poverty; "duties to protect" for those who are victims; "duties not to inflict harm" through exploitation, environmental degradation, and military aggression; and "duties to avoid certain human targets," particularly civilians (Erskine 2008: 1).

I maintain in this chapter that cosmopolitan ethics, to be explained shortly, provides a viable normative foundation on which to base our answers to the question of what our duties toward humanity are in such a troubled world. These answers connect peace with justice. Underlying this foundation is the view that

> human beings are united by a common human condition marked by vulnerability to suffering. In this sense, humanity is one. Yet human individuals are also unique centers of consciousness, purpose, and agency. In this sense, humanity is many. Any defensible moral theory must do justice to humanity as one and many. (Lu 2006: 9)

In this sense, the dedication to preventing and alleviating human suffering that is intrinsic to humanitarianism acknowledges the equality of human vulnerability. That is, as humans, we all have an equal risk of vulnerability that comes with health, age, and eventual death. War increases vulnerability, and thus the massive injustice of unnecessary suffering. It is not unreasonable to attribute moral blame to "passive injustice"—that is, those instances where individuals or officials did little to prevent wrongdoing or failed to mitigate suffering (Lu 2006: 105). What I stress throughout this book is recognition that agency is shared by all humans, although we are distinctive in the different ways that we are deprived of opportunities to act on agency, or have access to adequate opportunities to enjoy agency. What makes abuse, torture, and violence inhuman is not only the obvious cruelty imposed by the acts and the harm caused, but that these acts crush the vitality of the human spirit, thereby depriving people of their capacity to engage in meaningful self-chosen acts that is intrinsic to living a full human life. Lu is correct to argue that nothing is controversial about asserting that "every human being who is born ought to live in security and with dignity," including enjoying adequate nourishment, clothing, shelter, health care, education, and the opportunity to lead "a meaningful and productive life in community with others" (2006: 164–165). Such security enhances a just peace. With this common humanity in mind, I explore here the basis to understanding our duties to others and what might constitute a cosmopolitan ethics. This basis extends the narrative understanding of the self, developed throughout the previous chapters.

Cosmopolitan Ethics

My discussion begins with a broad outlook on humanitarianism, an obvious site for compassion, then narrows to examine equal moral standing between individuals who once were enemies. My purpose is to elaborate further on the underlying reasons for the duties of care toward others, so that I can answer the chief question of this chapter: Can compassion be practiced in postconflict contexts? The notion that humanitarian emergencies demand a response from distant strangers is a modern notion. It emerges with cosmopolitan ethics. "That human beings intrinsically have ethical obligations to one another as such requires both a notion of transcending kinship, nationality, even acquaintance, and a notion of 'bare life' dissociable from specific cultures and webs of relationships" (Calhoun 2008: 78). Not to accept these obligations commits us only to consider those to whom we are close. Craig Calhoun suggests that humanitarianism came to be associated not only with "advancing human welfare but with softening roughness of the human condition" (2008: 80). Yet Calhoun cautions us on the view that connects humanitarianism too closely to cosmopolitan politics, because he suggests that, while such a politics is embedded in global interconnections, it often reflects a distanced view of the global system that misrecognizes the particularity of distant troubles. His point is, and I agree with it, that one cannot respond intelligently to actual crises without understanding the specifics of differing narratives of nationality, ethnicity, religion, and culture—all major factors that often underlie extreme tensions.

The type of humanitarianism under discussion is not the consequence of great need following natural disasters of flood, fire, famine, hurricanes, landslides, or tsunamis. These disasters affect millions of people each year and require great assistance from the international community. While environmental and ecological factors influence the propensity for some of these disasters, the humanitarian emergencies that occur during conflict generally arise from different factors. For example, the humanitarian emergencies of Rwanda, Bosnia, and Sudan did not simply arise because of ancient ethnic hatreds, poverty, or the potential for evil prowling around in human nature. "They are results also of geopolitics and shifting patterns in a long-distance trade: colonialism, the end of the Cold War, and oil" (Calhoun 2008: 85). Calhoun is not discrediting the way that cosmopolitanism plays an important part in responding to such emergencies, but he is qualifying that responses need to be grounded in more than emotive warm feelings about global interconnectedness. Local ties to community, culture, ethnic, and religious identification shape our values and who we are; that is, the local shapes our particular narratives. We have already seen in earlier chapters that localized views often produce narrow-minded worldviews that in their obstinacy refuse to see the point of view of another, thereby contributing significantly to violent conflict. However, these particular ties are not only contingently given—that is, to some degree we inherit our cultural roots—but rather, they are morally constitutive of our narratives, of who we are as unique individuals living in particular groups. I am deliberately bringing together the importance of the concrete and the particular to the universal and common humanity in an increasingly globalized world.

What type of cosmopolitan ethics, then, can underlie a humanitarian outlook, remain rooted in one's multiple social connections, and justify the duties we have to suffering strangers? To answer this, I draw heavily on the proposal by Toni Erskine of an alternative "embedded cosmopolitanism" that can both "sustain an account of moral agency, judgment, and value as radically situated in particularist associations," while simultaneously remaining "inclusive and self-critical enough to take seriously the equal moral standing of compatriots, comrades, foreigners, and foes alike" (2008: 3–4). Erskine seeks to explain "how we might foster recognition of the equal moral standing of 'strangers,' 'foreigners,' and 'enemies' across conventional, territorial communities without denying the moral force of these communities" (2008: 6). Erskine's arguments depend on a specific account of the moral agent, who, like my account, is a human actor with capacities for deliberating over possible actions and their consequences. Because such actors "possess such capacities, they can reasonably be considered bearers of duties and held accountable for their actions (and failures to act)" (2008: 24).

This is an account of the agent who is embedded in social relationships. We have seen in earlier chapters that such embeddedness in ethnic, religious, and cultural ties can restrict moral agents from adopting a

critical perspective of the cultural norms that tie us to immediate relationships and communities, but do not necessarily facilitate human
flourishing. We have seen how entrenched ties perpetuate nationalist,
ethnoreligious extremism that provokes violent conflict with those who
have different cultural roots. Erskine argues that it is possible "to construct an ethical framework that recognizes value as constituted by, but
not bounded within," particular strong ties as well as separate communities (2008: 40). Because the self is defined by more than one significant relationship, the situated self can challenge cultural traditions that
may limit a broader perspective from developing. Put simply, an embedded cosmopolitanism can begin "from a particularist account of the
moral agent and envisages as one's goal the global sphere of equal
moral standing" (Erskine 2008: 40). A feeling of solidarity should arise
with fellow moral agents with whom we share membership in a multi-
tude of morally constitutive communities.

It is undoubtedly more difficult to acknowledge the equal moral
standing of an enemy, violent opponent, or someone with whom there is
no consensus on shared understandings of religion, ethnicity, culture, or
politics. How then are these ideas on a cosmopolitan ethics applied? Are
they at all realistic in our reflections on transitional justice contexts?
The prohibition against torture and noncombatant immunity are norms
of restraint in war, and both outline standards of treatment to be
respected, even with perpetrators of abuse and supposed enemies. International conventions that embody these norms enable us to declare that
the notorious Abu Ghraib activities by US army personnel of sexual
abuse and torture of prisoners in a Baghdad prison during the 2003 US-
led war in Iraq, and the detention of terror suspects held in legal limbo
at Guantanamo Bay, are wrong, shameful, disgusting, and totally unacceptable. Only through recognizing the equal moral standing of remote
strangers, even those considered as enemies, can solidarity of common
humanity be realized and such a judgment of morally unacceptable
actions be made.[2] We are embedded, situated, and embodied in multiple
relationships and communities, and from this basis, obligations to the
other are realized.

Responsibility to Others

My goal in this chapter is to move closer to an understanding of what
motivates practices of compassion in order to determine the extent to
which compassion can play a healing role in postwar and transitional
justice contexts. To reiterate, in the global community there is a grow-

ing awareness of the urgent need to protect civil liberties and respond appropriately to suffering. There are international conventions that accept the consensus about the inherent moral worth of humans and the obligation of states to protect that status. The motivation to respond to suffering with compassion can translate practically where there is acceptance of the responsibilities we have to assist others. I am suggesting that this acceptance is more likely to occur when there is an understanding of the moral self as emerging through complex, changing relationships with others. Such a relational ontology alters the approach to harm and suffering by encouraging acceptance of being implicated somehow in the human tragedy of needless suffering, and wanting to see human flourishing instead. This is a "responsibility understood as ongoing practices and actions of responsiveness and care towards particular others" (Robinson 2006: 234). Within international relations theory, Ken Booth (1999: 62–63) presents a strong defense of links between universality, connections with others, and ethical responsibilities. He argues that a concentration on the wrongs suffered by victims shifts subjectivity to the victims, which has the crucial effect of humanizing people who have felt powerless. As a result, when confronted by gross human rights abuses, Booth maintains that we have no grounds for suggesting that they are not of concern to us. Indeed, he argues that if one chooses not to act when faced with human wrongs, a justification for noninvolvement is required. Such an approach is based on a strong commitment to our common humanity and assumes a relational ontology.

Another way to look at the link between humanization and responsibility to others is to begin with what humans are capable of. It is worth revisiting Martha Nussbaum's capabilities approach here. She defends an approach that addresses the social minimum of meeting basic human needs and rights through developing universal human capabilities. She asks, "What activities characteristically performed by human beings are so central that they seem definitive of a life that is truly human?" (1999: 39). Nussbaum is looking at the gaps between humanity in its full potential and the reality of people's lives. She develops ten central human functional capabilities: life; bodily health; bodily integrity; senses, imagination, and thought; emotions; practical reason; affiliation; other species; play; and control over one's environment (1999: 41–42; 2000: 78–80). While Nussbaum argues that these capabilities are universal, she agrees that there are particular cultural differences in the ways these capabilities are revealed. Nussbaum argues that individuals and governments have moral obligations to uphold justice for people outside their national boundaries. She suggests that in grasping the full "humanity of distant human beings" in all their dignity, we can "begin to ask the hard questions about the contingency that affects people's lives more than any other, the contingency of birth location" (Nussbaum 1999: 7). Being born into a war location affects people's narratives substantially. Whether listening to storytelling of those living in these locations extends opportunities for people to develop their capabilities freely depends not merely on hearing the stories but in taking responsibility for responding to the needs arising from these accounts. This listening to the storytelling can occur in truth commissions, community hearings, grassroots workshops, churches, and receptive local and international NGOs.

Iris Marion Young also argues "that obligations of justice arise between persons by virtue of the social processes that connect them" (2006: 102). The Internet and social media make sure we are only a click away. There is little excuse for ignorance about what is happening in the world around us. The more we are aware of the woundedness evident in many narratives, the more we should become aware of the responsibilities that accrue. Awareness of anguish "is a sign of ethical responsibility towards the other" and invites "victims and villains to share in the common idiom of humanity" (Gobodo-Madikizela 2008b: 177). Such woundedness can draw the villain into a relationship with the victim. Obviously, as I repeatedly have maintained, there are harms so heinous that this relationship is inconceivable, and properly so. In other cases of lesser harms, it may be "the victim's pain that awakens remorse in the perpetrator, and it is remorse that lays the ground for the emergence of empathetic sensibilities expressed on the part of the victim towards the perpetrator" (2008b: 177). This relationship can only form if the victim-survivor is ready for it; it should never be forced.

To summarize this section, because of our common humanity—where we are equal in self-dignity and have equal chance of vulnerability—I argue that we have a responsibility toward those who are suffering. Cosmopolitan ethics accepts this universal common humanity in the context of particularized situatedness. The responsibility to alleviate suffering is a moral duty. Given that suffering is so prevalent after violent conflict, the need for compassion is great. I need to qualify the nature of this responsibility to others. It differs according to our place and ability to respond. Clearly, international peacebuilders and NGOs working in conflict and postwar zones are highly suited to knowing how to respond, particularly when they listen carefully to what local groups inform them is needed. Academics, writers, journalists, and creative performers can respond by raising awareness of what is happening to fellow humans because of war. Concerned, well-informed citizens can donate to and actively prompt influential donors, international NGOs, regional organizations, and governments to support just peace rather than war. I proceed now to explain why this duty to others is more likely to be realized when it is accompanied by corresponding emotions, virtues, and practices related to compassion.

Is Empathy Appropriate in Postconflict Contexts?

Before establishing what compassion entails, it is useful to distinguish it from sympathy and empathy. Sympathy is demonstrated through the sharing of emotions. The idea of sympathy is embedded into most religious traditions, as a responsibility to the other. However, what about a response "toward those who seem to test our sense of belonging or to defy available norms of likeness" (Butler 2009: 36)? The question is pertinent wherever there are differences that remain a root cause of conflict, typically differences of ethnic, religious, racial, or cultural dissimilarity. As noted, what is more recent is the notion that suffering demands a response, including a response from distant strangers like us. Judith Butler is explicit: "Responsibility requires responsiveness" (2009: 50). What principles underlie these duties of responsiveness? I am reiterating a twofold answer of mutual vulnerability to suffering and equal dignity arising from common humanity. So, why are sympathy and empathy important in fulfilling responsibilities toward others? Also, is empathy an appropriate response to those suffering from war trauma? What about people who have been coerced into committing a crime during war? Are they deserving of empathy?

The moral responsibility to assist those in need demands a commitment to action that goes beyond feelings of pity. In pity, the voice of Benhabib's (1992) "concrete other" is absent; the listener or hearer experiences the suffering as resembling their own pain. Pity, while not without merit, can be self-indulgent. It is not going to contribute greatly to improving people's lives in repressive or violent regimes. Mercy differs. "As soon as we allow someone to gain something they did not deserve, or do not have a right to, we have an act of mercy" (Babic 2000: 89). Mercy occurs whenever someone is punished less severely then they deserve, or a debt is suspended. "Merciful actions must be motivated by *compassion*" (Meierhenrich 2008: 210), which motivates its subject to leniency. Merciful actions aim to relieve distress. Such actions are appropriate in personal relationships, but acute judgment is needed for mercy to be applied in criminal prosecutions. Mercy is inappropriate; indeed it is unjust for extreme crimes of torture, rape, and murder. Mercy is applicable when someone is sentenced disproportionately to his or her crime, or where an innocent person is falsely charged. At least with sympathy one does not try to imagine oneself as the other person. "Rather, one feels *for* the other and tries to understand and respond to his feelings and situation, but in doing so one recognizes that his perspective is different from one's own" (Mackenzie 2008a: 126). Sympathy thus differs from empathetic imagining, where one actually seeks to imagine what it would be like to be the other person.

If we take a narrative understanding of selfhood, with empathy "one must be able to imagine how the other would respond were they in the situation one imagines" (2008a: 126), and the result of this imagining can only be partial. With empathy, a person visualizes the particular perspective of another person. Jodi Halpern and Harvey Weinstein (2004) explain that the major function of empathy is to particularize the suffering and thus to challenge dehumanization, as the narrative emphasis throughout the book has attempted to do. These authors conducted extensive interviews in Bosnia and Herzegovina in 2002 and reached a startling conclusion: "We could not find a single example of what we would term empathy" (2004: 570).[3] Certainly there was evidence of people living as neighbors without destroying each other, but the problem with coexistence is that without empathy it is superficial, because under the surface is lingering hatred, mistrust, and resentment. They summarize barriers to empathy as including ethnic group pressure and discrimination, feelings of betrayal, mistrust, ongoing fear, stereotypes, and violence. Despite not finding much evidence of empathy, I am suggesting that empathy is necessary in order to reconceptualize a rehumanized view of the other. As I outline in the next chapter, this rehumanization of former enemies is a critical component of reconciliation. Some contend that for reconciliation to be realized, "an empathic connection must occur" (2004: 567). For these connections to develop, Christine Sylvester outlines an idea of "empathetic cooperation," mentioned in Chapter 5, which she explains is a "method for managing, working with, respecting, and surpassing rigid standpoints, positions, and issues without snuffing out difference" (2002: 244). We have seen how differences can appear stark, between Hutus and Tutsis, Indigenous and non-Indigenous people, colonized and colonizer, landowners and peasants, Irish Catholics and Northern Irish Protestants who identify as British, and the list goes on.

I draw attention to some instances of empathy. In his memoir of life as a Serb coming from an Eastern Orthodox religious tradition during the war in Bosnia and Herzegovina, Savo Heleta writes of the many people who showed empathy toward his family:

> In every war and on every side, there are those who hate, those who don't care, and there are good people. Helped by the good people, brave and caring individuals, both known and unknown to my family, we survived the horrors of the war and starvation. I came to realize that a single person can often make a difference between life and death, hope and despair. The people who helped my family would never admit they did anything special when they helped us. After the war, my mother gave thanks to some of them for all they had done for us; they didn't believe that their caring gestures were out of the ordinary. And yet a loaf of bread, a hiding place, or a word of support, again and again, made the difference for us. (Heleta 2008: 228)

Consider another example: the stories and experiences of Cypriots as they have been crossing the Green Line since 2003 to visit their old houses and neighborhoods, which were occupied by the other. Maria Hadjipavlou (2007: 67) writes that when she spoke in the Cypriot dialect to Mustafa, a Turkish-Cypriot taxi driver who had been to see his town and house in the south, he found everything changed and in ruins. His house had been demolished, and a restaurant now stood on the site. His reaction was pragmatic despite being painful:

> When I came here I was not married. Now I am a grandfather and my children and grandchildren were born on this side. I don't want to go back. Who can give me my thirty years back? No politician can. I want to cooperate with the Greeks and I like them but cannot go back to Limassol now. (in Hadjipavlou 2007: 67)

The author writes of another instance of witnessing a Turkish-Cypriot owner who visited his house in the south, and the present owner felt uncomfortable and embarrassed at occupying the other's house. The Greek Cypriot said, "Do you hate me for living in your house all these years? You can have your house back, and I don't want any money for the changes and repairs I have made," to which the Turkish Cypriot replied,

> No, I don't hate you. I also live in a Greek house in Katokopia village [in the north] but unlike you I had no money to make any repairs. I also do not feel the house and orchard belong to me although I was given a title by our administration. It is not your fault for what hap-

pened but neither was mine. Thank you for taking care of my home and property all these years. You can visit me too. I am ready to give back the keys of the house to the Greek owners. (in Hadjipavlou 2007: 64)

Selma, a Turkish-Cypriot woman, shared a dream she experienced in 2004 where she asked herself,

Why do we need Greek Cypriots to empathize with us? Why do we want to impose our need on them? They have not suffered as much as we, and our hardships still continue to this day for the last thirty years. Maybe we lived separate so long that the need for empathy and understanding mean different things to each other. I woke up feeling lonely. (in Hadjipavlou 2007: 66)

What are these narratives saying? They confirm the importance of the particular, difference, situatedness, and context, so that even the impact of empathy and trying to understand another's perspective is both understood and interpreted differently by different individuals.

The capacity to empathize requires participation in shared reflective engagement with an other's personal life. This does not come easily. Pumla Gobodo-Madikizela tells a revealing story of her involvement with seven mothers whose sons were killed by the South African apartheid government's police, and who became known as the Gugulethu Seven. One of the police applying for amnesty was a black policeman, Thapelo Mbelo, who approached members of the South African TRC asking for a meeting with the mothers in order to apologize and ask for forgiveness. Gobodo-Madikizela met with the mothers and their families to prepare them and met also with Mbelo, who, once with the women, said that his apology came "from the bottom of my heart" (in Gobodo-Madikizela 2008b: 180). The women confronted him with their anger and pain. It is important to remind ourselves that anger, as Nussbaum expresses it, "is a reasonable type of emotion to have in a world where it is reasonable to care deeply about things that can be damaged by others" (2004: 13–14). Michael Ure extends this defense of the moral worth of anger by maintaining that "compassion is only possible if we sustain the judgments that underpin anger and distress over our undeserved misfortunes and apply these judgments to others" (2008: 288). I agree with Juha Käpylä and Denis Kennedy that "becoming morally outraged requires, and emerges from, a moral attention to distant suffering" (2014: 284). With this attention, compassion "can be transformed and empowered by anger when distant suffering is apprehended in its context, as a case of historical and political injustice"

(2014: 284). As I explain in the next section, a politics of justice and care can develop when there is a commitment to this attention.

As I am arguing, such judgments underpinning anger at injustices as well as the compassionate response for those suffering such injustices require accepting the mutual vulnerabilities involved in being human. Listening to stories that express anger in postconflict societies is crucial to understanding what counts as major injury requiring punishment, forgiveness, or reparation. Compassion thus "helps limit or temper anger so that it does not turn into the lust for vengeance" (Ure 2008: 294). Emma Hutchison and Roland Bleiker suggest that there needs to be "some form of emotional 'turning point'" that enables the cultivation of "new ways of thinking about trauma" (2008: 394). This point is pertinent because trauma assaults selfhood, so there is good reason to believe that extreme trauma such as suffering through war diminishes the capacity to show empathic bonds to others, because one's own needs are so pressing. Hence the requirement exists to create ethical spaces where empathic sensibilities that have been so deeply damaged through violent conflict can become reawakened, or in most cases freshly awakened.

The turning point for these women with whom Gobodo-Madikizela met came when the policeman said, "I would like to ask you to forgive me, my parents. . . . I ask your forgiveness, my parents" (in Gobodo-Madikizela 2008b: 181). In posing his response in this fashion, he was appealing to the sociocultural ethos that is abundant in the humanity of ubuntu, presenting himself as a child who begs his parents to readmit him into the community. One of the mothers, Cynthia Ngewu, said, "You are the same age as my son. . . . I forgive you, my son. . . . Go well, my child" (in Gobodo-Madikizela 2008b: 181). Such an empathic encounter between victims and a perpetrator is rare, but it led to the other women embracing Mbelo. Gobodo-Madikizela's conclusion is illuminating in that the "cultural dance" implicit in this communication "is primarily concerned about giving a human face to a man who is begging, not for the slate to be wiped clean, but for a chance to take the first steps towards rehabilitation and to live among fellow human beings" (2008b: 183). Meaningful encounters are about listening, hearing, and connecting with one another at critical points of differing narratives where there is potential for our humanness to come to the fore. Empathy is a crucial dimension in understanding particularity within common humanity. I maintain it is not merely an appropriate response in postconflict and transitional justice contexts, but more than this, it is essential as an emotional response that can lead to practical ways to assist those who suffer because of war damage to their humanity. Further, in the meaningful encounters explained above, reconciliation has some chance of occurring.

While I do not imply any feminine essentialist proclivity toward empathy, significant anecdotal and empirical evidence is present of women's empathetic actions. Many women are what Anderlini calls "bridge builders and voices from the middle ground" (2007: 86). That is, "The trust building, empathy, and humanizing that come from finding common experiences as women are powerful fuel for enabling women to tackle the core causes of conflict" (Anderlini 2007: 85). As an example, she cites Terry Greenblatt, former director of the Israeli women's peace organization Bat Shalom, who in 2002 said to the UN Security Council, "Even when we are women whose very existence and narrative contradicts each other, we will talk—we will not shoot" (in Anderlini 2007: 89). In explaining how women were quick to show compassion in the South African TRC, Gobodo-Madikizela (2005) suggests that empathy was a crucial feature of forgiveness that helped to realize collective signs of hope. Elsewhere, many women form alliances across radical differences to work practically toward meeting everyday extended family needs. Empathy is a virtue of care, and in transitional societies it can assist a movement toward justice. Both men and women are capable of expressing empathy.

Can Peace Include Justice and Care?

I position my defense of cosmopolitan ethics and the need for compassion in postconflict and transitional justice contexts within a framework of feminist ethics, an enabling framework that supports advocacy for both justice and care in order to achieve a peace with justice and security. Certainly, the starting point of feminist ethics is women's lives, but more particularly for our concerns, it addresses gender inequalities and exclusions, including gendered insecurities for all people. Feminist ethics seeks to break down the logic of domination that is crucial in advocating for peace. Rather than concentrating on its implications for women, I show how it proposes alternative relationships that struggle to overcome dominant, destructive modes of relating that are the norm in conflict and divided societies. These alternatives presuppose that both women and men should be empowered as moral agents to make informed decisions about matters that are dear to them (Porter 2013). It also accepts that "emotions of care and sympathy lie at the heart of the ethical life" (Nussbaum 1999: 14). As Elizabeth Spelman puts it, our emotions "can be highly revelatory of whom and what we care or do not care about. These emotions provide powerful clues to the ways in which we take ourselves to be implicated in the lives of others and they in ours" (1997: 100).

Feminist ethics, as I am using it, draws on a liberal justice perspective that values the justice that accompanies equal universal human rights entitlements. Feminist ethics also draws on a feminist care perspective that accepts that, given gender differences, the way human dignity is realized varies in particular contexts; particular attention to these differences is thus necessary. Justice and care have a complementary relationship of "two cross-cutting perspectives" (Gilligan 1987: 25). That is, both the ethic of universal justice and the ethic of particularized care interact and draw on general principles of justice as applied to all, and contextual details of care that apply to specific persons (Porter 1999: 17). The mutual interdependence of justice and care means that each ethic provides "enabling conditions" for the other ethic (Narayan 1995: 139). Formal justice procedures such as those handed down in a court without considerations of care may be harsh, but the crimes of ethnic cleansing, genocide, terrorism, torture, murder, and war rape require appropriate accountability, judgment, and prosecution. The care component comes in treating prisoners or those on trial respectfully, looking after their full range of basic human rights. Without justice, perpetrators of abuse continue with impunity, and thus the value of the care of victims is questionable. Both justice and care come into play in deciding on suitable reintegration programs for former combatants as part of postwar reconstruction of a society. Particularized care requires that, to be just, such reintegration might need different strategies for women compared with men, girls with boys, former commanders to those who carried out commands. The interplay between justice and care goes beyond recognition of people's equal vulnerability to suffering to an "active concern with enhancing their well-being" (Gould 2004: 42). Given the atrocities committed in war, this is a demanding concern. Accordingly, I seek to show how justice and care have explicit implications for the politics of peace and in responding with compassion to traumatized narratives.

A political defense of an ethic of care prizes compassion as a central value of caring, along with the qualities of "attentiveness, responsibility, competence, and responsiveness" (Tronto 1993: 127), all qualities already discussed in previous chapters. The application of this ethic in Western cultures to welfare provisions of aged care, child care, disability rights, education, and health is entirely appropriate but does not do much to help us understand whether or how it might apply to the care that is needed in transitional justice contexts. In earlier writings I have sought to extend the political domain in which the practice of compassion is deemed appropriate (Porter 2012b; 2007a; 2006). I maintain that a politics of compassion occurs when the universal principles of justice and the particular needs of people for care are linked in a public manner. The politics of compassion responds to the "practical, particular responses to different expressions of vulnerability" (Porter 2006: 99) that are multiple in postconflict and transitional justice environments. The underlying premise of shared humanity is the simultaneous universal vulnerability to risk and thus to suffering, and our common need as moral agents to maintain human dignity and self-respect.

In earlier discussions on truth commissions, we saw how in the telling of stories of pain, anguish, and loss, and in being listened to, there is an attentiveness that is fundamental to feminist ethics. However, when the victim or survivor has to confront his or her perpetrator, or see this person receive an unjustified amnesty without any feelings of remorse, it is not difficult to see why many victims or survivors do not necessarily equate gaining truth with justice, or for that matter with reconciliation. Further, in these instances, survivors are not receiving appropriate care. I am suggesting that what is needed is a very careful emphasis on what Fiona Robinson calls "a critical politicized ethics of care" (1999: 47), one that combines justice and care. Of course, this is idealistic; it rarely happens in full, but it provides a normative framework to work toward. The main component to Robinson's argument is the analytical scrutiny of the contextual relations within global politics. Such an approach enables a probing scrutiny of structures of power differentials, insecurities, and injustices, and the findings from this scrutiny should enable responses to situations of suffering that embody empathetic imagination. Justice and caring responses vary according to differing needs. In societies undergoing transition from conflict, they include rebuilding of infrastructure, reintegration into community life of former combatants, provision of education and health facilities, job training, equality legislation, trauma counsel, care of orphans and widows, gender justice, and confirmation of security.

Even during this rebuilding period, violent relationships among rival groups or between states continue to contribute significantly to domination, exclusions, inequalities, and greatly felt insecurities. Understanding the nature of these relationships is a prerequisite to making a sound judgment on how to rectify root causes of violence. In conducting this scrutiny, we can get to the heart of the root causes of conflict, for example, in the struggles between rebel insurgents and corrupt governments, the continual tit-for-tat murders between paramilitary organizations, and the constant fighting between rival ethnoreligious groups. I am not suggesting that understanding these antagonistic, violent relationships is an easy task. It is not. It is an intensely difficult undertaking, and breaking down the antagonism often appears an insurmountable enterprise. In developing a normative framework within which to work, the aspiration toward building a sustainable just peace with caring and reconciled relationships is kept alive. This critical approach places international peace within a framework that privileges social interdependence and the emotional connectedness that entails. I acknowledge that this sounds incredibly hopeful; mostly, translating reciprocity, respect, empathy, and understanding in practice in communities that have known long-term violence seems quite unfeasible. However, normative frameworks contain goals worth striving toward, even when the practicalities involved appear so unrealistic or excruciatingly difficult to achieve. Such frameworks can have an impact on the development of policies, laws, and new institutions within transitional justice processes. As many of the examples throughout the book highlight, there are incredible examples of justice and care merging in situations where no one would have imagined them springing to life.

Compassion

I have been talking generally about compassion without clarifying precisely what it entails. It is now important to do so.[4] "Compassion recognizes and responds to the humanity of the suffering victim" (Humphrey 2002: 94). Compassion involves an emotional identification with the anguish, despair, distress, grief, hardship, misery, and suffering that someone else is enduring. Often this identification can induce responses of repulsion, or someone may be so overcome by the horrors of listening to traumatized narratives that it can leave the person overwhelmed and thus impotent to act. As stated, there is a universal truth that all humans are vulnerable; we do not know when disaster, sickness, or great loss will strike. As I have already argued, this common, shared humanity is the grounds of vulnerability underlying the need for compassion and an obligation to respond to particular forms of suffering in appropriate ways. Given that suffering is an intrinsic part of the human condition, a crucial mark of acknowledging the full humanity of others comes in taking the suffering of others seriously, including considering what that particular instance of suffering means. In doing so, the need for compassion comes to the fore.

There are four dimensions of compassion that I wish to stress. First, compassion involves an emotional identification with what someone else is going through, whether extreme emotions or an unbearable sense of loss. Often these feelings of compassion can come through trying to imagine what our reactions would be if our own daughter, parent, son, or spouse was enduring similar pain. In this way, empathy is closely linked to compassion. "In compassion, I am moved by what *you* are going through, not what *I* am going through, concerned about *your* condition, not about *mine*" (Spelman 1997: 120). Those not living in a postwar context cannot have direct identification with those suffering, but limited forms of this identification are still possible.

Second, if compassion involves the capacity to feel for others and to some extent share these emotions, the degree to which this feeling can be shared is contestable. Without putting ourselves in the position of others, we are not being truly open to others. Certainly being open to difference exposes new beliefs, cultural practices, and political commitments, but many of these might leave us outraged or repulsed. Then there are forms of suffering that are so particular to the sufferer that identification as an outsider toward the sufferer can only be limited. Able-bodied people cannot really know what it is like to have lost a leg to a landmine or had one's hand chopped off by a child soldier. However, this is where empathy is a crucial part of compassion.

> Empathy taps the ability and willingness to enter into the feeling or spirit of something and appreciate it fully in a subjectivity-moving way. It is to take on board the struggles of others by listening to what they have to say in a conversational style that does not push, direct, or break through. (Sylvester 2002: 256)

It is worth questioning the extent to which we can share these feelings fully. Empathy is needed particularly to see the situation from the perspective of one who has previously been considered as the enemy, adversary, antagonist, or opponent. In such contexts, trust as discussed in Chapter 5 is needed. Empathy is excruciatingly difficult; it can be one-sided, and hence a mutual compassionate response is rare in transitional justice practices. Yet empathy may permit negotiators, mediators, or peacebuilders to enter partially into the mind of the enemy, even if it is only in a minimalist fashion of trying to understand motivations for recurring violent actions. This scrutiny of motivations is needed in order to break down structural causes of violence like poverty, marginalization, and illiteracy, thereby minimizing the continuation of such motivations. It is best undertaken by those with deep familiarity with the local conditions.

Third, there are differences between co-feeling and co-suffering. Co-feeling implies attachment "as identifying with and feeling the suffering of others" (Arendt 1973: 81). Compassionate co-suffering supposes a sense of shared humanity; somebody else's suffering is based on the sort of pain or loss that could happen to anyone. There are often steps in the process of compassion. The compassionate person feels some of the pain of another. They try to identify imaginatively and thus empathetically with the sufferer in order to understand what might relieve their pain. This attentiveness to the sufferer's needs allows the compassionate person to discern how best to respond. Clearly, this knowledge of suitable responses will be meaningful between those who are interacting in post-conflict settings. It is harder to respond well from a distance.

The compassionate response is indeed the fourth crucial dimension. Responses are needed to address the harms of the axing of limbs; the effects of landmines or bomb blasts; the decades needed to come to grips with the enormity of genocide; the shame of rape, HIV/AIDS, and children born from an act of violence; the fear and uncertainty of terrorist attacks; the debilitating maiming of tribal spearings; the confusion of being displaced; and the massive loss of property, jobs, livelihoods, loved ones, and self-dignity that occurs in the long-term consequences of war. Any responses that do not utilize the "intelligence of compassion in coming to grips with the significance of human suffering is blind and incomplete" (Nussbaum 1996: 49). Further, as Nussbaum qualifies, compassion involves empathetic identification, where "one is always aware of one's own *separateness* from the sufferer" (1996: 35). Such separateness is an important safety valve for humanitarian, medical, and aid workers; international peacebuilders; and local leaders who are responding compassionately to such a mass of harms. Without this separateness, workers could be overwhelmed by their emotions. Compassionate judgment requires responses to harms that affirm human dignity. These responses can integrate justice and care in furthering peace.

Expressions of these judgments vary considerably, which is not surprising. As one example, Deborah Mindry writes on the diversity of women's transnational networks and how women often articulate their relationships to one another in terms of being part of "the global family" (2001: 1193). In working with black, white, Indian, and colored women in South Africa who were working in NGOs, Mindry found that these women "frequently expressed the belief that they brought compassion and understanding regarding the shared humanity to their relationships" (2001: 1198). By this they meant that they felt close to the every-day lives of people as well as feeling the struggles of other women and their families and communities. She stresses that grassroots involve-ment is an ethical zone, a site of need where local struggles are con-nected to the global. Many of these coalitions do not begin as political, but as already mentioned, simply grow out of the necessity to respond to the urgency of meeting basic needs or overcoming crises of insecu-rity. In the process of doing so, and in connecting with other groups in solidarity in seeking to overcome power struggles to obtain resources, these women become politicized co-sufferers. This is the story of many women's groups in multiple conflict and postconflict zones. It is not that men do not demonstrate compassion or work in similar networks, because they do. Rather, expressions of compassion appear to be more conspicuous in women's groups, despite ideological, ethnic, or religious differences within these groups.

Countless other inspiring stories make one hope that talk of a com-passion that combines justice and care need not be dismissed as apolit-ical or naively idealistic, or limited to women's traditional activities. Roméo Dallaire, commander for the UN Assistance Mission for Rwanda, tells of the moment when he personally dedicated himself to bringing a UN peacekeeping mission to Rwanda. He came across a smelly, dirty camp of displaced persons. He watched a young Belgian Red Cross worker and was impressed by her calm compassion, and he thought that "it was obvious that she could see through the dirt and despair to their humanity" (2004: 64). Dallaire found the scene deeply disturbing as it was the first time he had witnessed such intense suffer-ing firsthand. He went from watching an old woman dying alone in the camp to joining a group of resilient children who were playing soccer with a ball made of twigs, and they were eager to have him join their game. He played with them and resolved at that moment to do his best for the sake of the children.

Annalise Acorn (2004) suggests some interesting normative condi-tions that are needed for restorative compassion. She is trying to counter the illusory and seductive convergence of love, harmony, and justice that obviously do not exist in postconflict contexts. She stresses that restorative justice seeks creative ways to put things right, which is always highly context-sensitive. She suggests that what is needed is "a vivid awareness of the complexity and concreteness of the inner lives of others" (2004: 138), along with the realization of mutuality and humil-ity. As Acorn writes, we are implicated "in the dual conditions of human existence: pain and the possibility of flourishing" (2004: 140). I maintain that normative frameworks of justice and compassion allow these dual conditions to remain in the foreground of our moral imagination. Furthermore, peace not only can include justice and care, but I argue that it must do so if it is to respond meaningfully to people's needs of inner healing and practical support.

Responding to the Enemy

How on earth does one defend, let alone apply an appropriate response to, the enemy, the perpetrator of violence, the one who has killed your spouse, or raped your daughter, or chopped off the ears of your baby son? It is indeed a seriously vexing question, not one to be taken lightly. In fact, it is an outrageous question, not one for which I have any easy answers. All I can say is that there are remarkable instances of individuals who are able to show caring responses in extraordinary ways. We are accustomed to considering that compassion is something we show only to our nearest and dearest, those, we might argue, who truly are deserving of our care. It is also easy to understand the need to demonstrate compassion toward those who have been wronged or have suffered through the trials and violence of war, particularly when compassion is linked to practical concerns of compensation, redress, or reparations. Of course, victims who suffer are worthy of compassion. But an enemy, an evil person: Should we support the idea of showing care to them, and if so, what might it mean?

The only defense of the possibility of showing some care to be made, I believe, is one based on our equal worth as humans. As stated, this principle of equal moral dignity justifies noncombatant immunity and the prevention of torture. Within violent societies, the violation of dignity is profound. Responding to victims is undemanding in the sense that it is obvious that victims need compassionate responses. In taking narratives seriously, this principle of equal moral dignity has to include the voice of abusers as well as the abused. If everyone deserves to be treated with dignity, this includes the appropriate treatment of perpetrators of violence and former combatants as well as the compassionate care of victims and survivors. As I mentioned in earlier chapters, sometimes former combatants, offenders, paramilitary members, perpetrators, prisoners, and terrorists do feel regret and change their values and practices. Sometimes they change while in the prison system or in displaced persons camps, often through programs of reintegration or education involving the international community. A commitment to norms of human dignity accepts "the possibility of moral change in any human being. To regard ex-combatants as irredeemably evil is to disregard their humanity" (Govier and Verwoerd 2004: 376).

Having said this, many perpetrators of violence do not change their attitudes or practices, particularly in contexts of recurring violence. They do not demonstrate remorse for their evil actions. They do not accept any blame for the harm they have caused victims to suffer. Therefore, punishment is their due, which remains consistent with the principles of justice and equal moral worth. As moral agents, we are responsible for the decisions we make, including bad ones. Appropriate care toward the perpetrator of abuse who has not shown remorse requires careful acts of justice, which include fair trials, proper punishment, and reasonable, humane treatment of those in prisons or on probation, with meaningful strategies of reintegration into the community to follow, where justified.

Gobodo-Madikizela asks a pertinent and important question: "What are the circumstances that might invite the emergence of empathy with another who is responsible for one's pain and suffering?" (2008a: 344). Where there has been deep pain and harm and where victims continue to suffer long after the political conflict has formally ended, what is needed to change the dynamics of the intersubjective engagement between victims and perpetrators? Gobodo-Madikizela's answer to this is fascinating. She suggests that when perpetrators express feelings of remorse, it can present them as the "wounded other" (2008a: 344). This woundedness demonstrates decent concern toward the other. As stated above, this idea is interesting because most literature talks solely of victims as those who have been wounded and have emerged as survivors. There is less writing on former combatants, fighters, genocide perpetrators, and abusers who have changed, who have genuinely felt troubled by their evil actions, particularly the harm they have caused to others. Indeed it is sometimes seeing firsthand the victim's pain that prompts shame in the perpetrator and begins a slow empathic change toward the other. As highlighted in earlier chapters, many examples of extraordinary acts of compassion have emerged through truth commissions, reconciliation workshops, and everyday interactions. As demonstrated, we find these examples through stories—stories often of the almost impossible idea of a perpetrator showing remorse and asking a victim for forgiveness and, further, the victim granting this release. Taking a narrative foundation for speaking and being heard, compassion is a crucial response to the narrative of the person who is suffering. Through compassionate responses dignity is restored. The display of compassion brings together justice and care and can facilitate a preparation to contemplate reconciliation, the focus of the final chapter.

To return to the question this section began with regarding a fitting response to those who commit gross violations, I argue that compassion is inappropriate because perpetrators of abuse demonstrate inhumanity. Only through responding to the humanity of the suffering victim can compassion be reasonably displayed. In those rare situations when perpetrators admit their wrongdoing, realize the harm caused, and change their ways, it may then be possible to show compassion to their newly found humanity.

* * *

In this chapter I have shown that compassion can be practiced in limited ways in postconflict contexts. After discussing obstacles to compassion like a hardness of heart and political hypocrisy, I explored the rationale for why we have duties to alleviate suffering. I showed that our human vulnerability and our common shared dignity underlie a responsibility to others. I argue that empathy is appropriate in postconflict and transitional justice contexts because of the enormous need to respond to the trauma of those who suffer. Related to this argument is my further claim that peace must include parallel considerations of justice and care. Certainly demonstrating compassion toward victims comes easier than caring responses toward those who carried out violence, but I make a distinction between those perpetrators of violence who have demonstrated remorse and have changed their practices and those who have not. For the latter group, justice and care include fair treatment, including reasonable prosecution and punishment.

Notes

1. The Australian Greens are a notable exception and demonstrate compassion in their policies.

2. The "love the sinner, hate the sin" message fits this idea.

3. Specifically, they held ninety key informant interviews, twenty-four focus groups, and surveys of eight hundred people in Mustar, Bosnia and Herzegovina; four hundred people in Vukovar, Croatia; and four hundred in Prijedor, Bosnia and Herzegovina.

4. See also Porter (2007a; 2006) for earlier iterations of arguments on the politics of compassion.

8

What Happens in Reconciliation?

My entire argument in this book has been leading to the conclusion that reconciliation, in all of its different guises, is an ideal worth striving for. Not all readers will accept this conclusion, so I need to explain my argument more fully. I begin by contrasting differing understandings of reconciliation, and indeed there is a vast range. I classify this range in four ways of looking at reconciliation: in terms of relationships, processes, cultures, and a spectrum of possibilities. My argument supports John Paul Lederach's (2004) idea that truth, justice, mercy, and peace interact in multifarious spaces, and the goal is to work collaboratively to find culturally meaningful practices, places, and processes in which reconciliation and a sustainable just peace can flourish. Culturally differing examples of what constitutes the place where reconciliation happens are fascinating. Through outlining select examples, I highlight the way that healing of broken souls is requisite to strong notions of reconciliation. I am building further on Sara Cobb's (2013) idea that a narrative lens enables analysts and peacebuilders who are promoting reconciliation to attend to the stories told in postwar and transitional justice settings. All persons involved in reconciliation processes have their own stories to tell; thus, they bring to these processes their own narrative that connects with other narratives. Attention to the detail of intersecting narratives permits a deeper understanding of differences and similarities in the life stories of those avoiding or seeking reconciliation.

What Is Reconciliation?

It is no wonder that reconciliation is hard to define and that there is no real agreement on what is required in coming to terms with the past. Many different emotions, concepts, and practices come together in the reconciliatory moment. Sometimes, there is not one particular moment that pinpoints the changes required by reconciliation; rather there are a series of encounters as part of an ongoing process. Before launching into an outline of some views of reconciliation that recognize its difficulty but acknowledge its worth as a goal, it is wise to consider a different view. For example, Susan Dwyer suggests "that we think of human reconciliation quite generally in terms of tensions" (1999: 85) between different beliefs, values, interpretations of events, and responses to them. Many theorists and practitioners believe that it is precisely because these tensions amount to obstacles in building workable relationships that we require reconciliation. However, Dwyer's emphasis is on the fact that we live our lives as narratives, and making sense of these narratives is important. Thus, on her terms, reconciliation is basically "the process whose aim is to lessen the sting of tension: to make sense of injuries, new beliefs, and attitudes in the overall narrative context of a personal or national life" (1999: 96). She acknowledges that this is a modest picture, directed toward multifaceted narratives.

A narrative perspective on reconciliation can show contrasting themes. As Adrian Little argues, "Reconciliation narratives can be just as defensive and misleading as they are transformative, unifying, and illuminating" (2011: 86). He maintains that part of the function of reconciliation narratives is not simply to foster unity but to open up a space for disagreement and contestation in contexts where traumatic events must be narrated. This approach is realistic. Certainly, space for dissent is needed in transitional societies moving from conflict to more open politics, and I maintain that discussions within this space are more likely to be reasonable when relationships have been reconciled or are in the process of becoming reconciled. Little's research in Northern Ireland in 2006 demonstrates considerable divisiveness among differing narratives that spread not merely along ethnonational lines but also within these categories. That is, in Northern Ireland there is an "absence of shared narratives" (2011: 94). I argue more fully later that this absence is not an insurmountable hurdle in all postwar contexts; rather it is indicative of the need to develop further mutual respect of differences that permits the disagreement that Little suggests is necessary, and thus moves relationships closer toward reconciliation.

Having outlined two positions that stress tensions and contestations, it is important to clarify what reconciliation is not. I show later why it is neither forgiveness nor healing, although elements of these may or may not occur in individual narrative understandings of reconciliation processes. It is not simply dialogue, listening to testimonies, or memorializing the past; yet, again, these might be included as part of the process. As we will see, there are necessary ambiguities in the concept and practices, particularly given cultural adaptations. However, one thing I believe is certain: reconciliation is an ongoing, dynamic process, involving complex individual, social, and political relationships that strive to develop reconciled narratives. Reconciliation is indeed extremely difficult to achieve; however, I seek to show that all steps toward it are worthwhile.

Talk of reconciliation often is vague. Hence to clarify our understanding, I highlight four predominant ways to theorize the practice of reconciliation. Reconciliation can be understood primarily as reconciling relationships, as a process, as a culture, or as a spectrum of possibilities. I examine each of these ways of understanding reconciliation, noting that it is hard to distinguish them neatly because of the many overlaps across these four aspects.

Reconciling Relationships

The first typical conceptualization of reconciliation is in terms of reconciling relationships. It is important to determine who exactly must be reconciled. What I am discussing in this chapter is the reconciliation between former enemies, antagonists, or violent opponents. These people have not only felt deep anger, bitterness, hatred, and resentment toward others for a whole range of diverse reasons, but they have acted on these emotions in ways that have been cruel, debilitating, wounding, or murderous. Some have issued orders to others to commit barbarous acts; others have committed them. While usually the violent acts are physical, they also can be verbal or written acts that are vindictive and ruin reputations or self-confidence. Even contemplating getting these people together is fraught with massive anxieties. Take into account that people's individual and communal narratives are complex, burdened with tensions and inexplicable incoherencies, and the task of reconciling relationships seems daunting. The nature of the task is particularly challenging because conflict disrupts individual, group, and communal narratives. Talk of reconciliation must go beyond mere rhetoric or loose analysis.

I defend the idea that there must be strong moral reasons why people are willing to begin the difficult journey toward reconciliation, for it is indeed a journey with a rocky path; many sidetracks lead people away from the main route and cause distractions as obstacles arise on winding pathways. The terrain is unpredictable, with a few high points in the road, and occasional glimpses of spectacular background scenery, but mostly there are uncomfortable, bumpy, realistic lows on the long journey. Sometimes relationships get stuck, unable to move on through the force of radical disagreement. Reconciliation must signal a new stage of relationships, or at times a novel start. For many, it may be the first time an amicable relationship between former opponents is contemplated. There usually is some decisive encounter, moment of history, event, occasion, or decision to put aside previous hostilities and estrangement, or it can be a range of these options. Often, this change comes about with an emotional event such as the first time stories are shared and the mutual acknowledgment of different types of suffering is exchanged. This change does not come about easily. Frequently, the change happens in informal settings where people can relax and not feel as though they are being watched. The settings might be in a pub, retreat, forest, or tent; around a kitchen table; under a tree; on the grass; or on a mat in a hut. Where there has been some sort of prior relationship, as neighbors or as fellow citizens, the moral repair of relationships involves building trust as noted in Chapter 5, because in "decent relationships, trust is always necessary" (Govier 2006: 21). Often, this trust can develop between individuals, but such trust requires support from structures of society, including civil, legal, and political structures that are open to changed relationships in a new reconciled polity.

It is illuminating to read the words of Juan Méndez, a survivor of torture and detention during an Argentinean military dictatorship, on the significance of relationships in the reconciliation process. He understands reconciliation, the goal of reckoning with past human rights violations, "to mean the long-term setting aside of disputes between factions that have divided a nation" (Méndez 2001: 28). Without the removal of such antagonisms there is no way to prevent the recurrence of these abuses. I keep stressing that it is not the removal of differences or disputes that is necessary for reconciliation to occur, but the removal of the undercurrent of violence that erupts when differences are taken too seriously or are not taken seriously enough. The removal of the antagonism that previously surrounded the differences is crucial. In the broadest sense, "Reconciliation involves the rebuilding of fractured individual and communal relationships after conflict, with a view to encouraging meaningful interaction and cooperation between former antagonists" (Clark 2008a: 194). Reconciling relationships in all their various forms is fundamental to revisioning postconflict societies where a just peace prevails.

Process of Reconciliation

Different authors define reconciliation differently. Those who stress the importance of process generally see dialogue as a crucial means to move beyond the tyranny of violence. Hence, in restoring, building, or rebuilding fractured relationships, the process of reconciliation seeks to enable dialogue with people for whom communication previously has faltered or been nonexistent. Some of these obstacles revolve around the fact that "reconciliation and (cultural or political) difference are occasionally seen as incompatible alternatives" (N. Porter 2003: 6). This hurdle is evident particularly in places such as Northern Ireland, where "cultural differences are fiercely protected to the point where appeals to commonality frequently are seen as requiring unacceptable compromises" (2003: 11). In Northern Ireland, where some might argue that peace without reconciliation resonates to many, because it is convenient and not particularly demanding, the reasons for this view can include political apathy, fear of the other, fear of losing influence, or because of suffering acts of injustice or humiliation (N. Porter 2003: 39–45). Norman Porter thus argues that "peace without reconciliation, whether deriving from indifference, fear, or bitterness, is a radically inadequate position" (2003: 45). It is inadequate because it leaves unresolved the deeper problems that created an absence of peace in the first place.

Instead, Norman Porter, in defending an ideal of "strong reconciliation," suggests that this requires three main things: "(1) it requires *fair interactions* between members of opposing groups; (2) it requires that we overcome our antagonistic divisions by occupying *common ground*; and (3) it requires the presence of society in which all citizens have a sense of *belonging*" (N. Porter 2003: 94–95). The goal of fair interactions is a multilayered requirement between members of opposing groups, traditions, or political parties. It includes a willingness to conduct interactions at all levels in a spirit of openness to express views and tell stories, and to be listened to with respect. In the process of reconciliation, differences must be taken seriously if relationships are to be meaningful. "Reconciliation's requirement of fair interaction calls for the *cultivation of civic virtues* among citizens and their political representatives" (N. Porter 2003: 102). Disagreements remain through the risk of open dialogue, which includes listening as well as talking, but in accepting the importance of the process of reconciliation, the antagonism of differences should be minimized in trying to maintain peace. "The moral value of respect implies an obligation to offer reasons to others who are of a different tradition who may simply disagree" (Philpott 2012: 113). The complexity of the process of reconciliation involves the importance of respectful dialogue, including listening to and taking seriously disagreements that come about because of fundamental differences between political parties and other major players seeking to reconcile their views, including putting aside the antagonism that the differences had caused.

Brandon Hamber and Gráinne Kelly, also writing from Northern Ireland, define reconciliation "as the *process* of addressing conflictual and fractured relationships" (2009: 291). They suggest five interconnected strands. The first strand accepts that there will always be different beliefs, but as with Norman Porter's view above, Hamber and Kelly consider that it is possible to develop "a shared vision of an interdependent and fair society" (2009: 291). Second, there is an acknowledgment of the losses and the truths of the past and the various roles that individuals and institutions have both played. Such honesty does not come easily. Indeed, sometimes it only comes partially, or not at all. Third, relationships must redress mistrust, prejudice, and intolerance. Fourth, significant changes of attitudes are required in order to develop a new respectful culture where human rights prevail and there is a sense of belonging. Fifth, there needs to be "substantial social, economic, and political change" (Hamber and Kelly 2009: 292). In their research on the conceptualizations and implementation of community reconciliation in Northern Ireland in 2003 at the political and grassroots levels, interviewees were vague as to their perceptions of reconciliation, which included some whose work was funded under the reconciliation banner. Interestingly, "Few could articulate a vision of what a reconciled society would look like," but they did talk about community relations, good relations, or community cohesion (Hamber and Kelly 2009: 296).

Others who work on the process of reconciliation in the Middle East include Daniel Bar-Tal and Gemma Bennink, who suggest that reconciliation is a product of secure peace and "requires forming a new, common outlook on the past" (2004: 18). They suggest that this process only starts when the psychological changes of developing mutual trust, sensitivity, consideration of others' interests, and mutual recognition begins to improve. We have seen in earlier chapters how challenging it is to initiate this process in transitional justice contexts. Effective processes progress when there are simultaneous top-down and bottom-up changes occurring with political elites and grassroots groups supporting these processes. Phil Clark, writing on Rwanda, also emphasizes reconciliation as "both a process and an endpoint"; thus it is "both backward and forward-looking" (2008a: 194). Some processes lead to a definite endpoint, an identifiable moment when participants in the process can recall the exact occasion or place where the process seemed to bring them together with some common purpose. Other processes occur over a long period of movement toward reconciliation, with many setbacks preventing progress.

What sort of process is reconciliation? Paul James develops two underlying arguments for thinking about reconciliation as an open-ended process. First, a sustainable process of reconciliation requires practices "across different levels of social integration or 'ways of relating,'" including face-to-face and extended relationships; second, there needs to be "an active sensitivity to different 'ways of being,' including the tensions and contradictions between them" (James 2008: 118). Establishing face-to-face contact that is genuinely open to the differences of others, including those differences that have been instrumental in causing conflict, as outlined in earlier chapters, is immensely difficult. Former enemies may have had no contact with each other during the height of the violence. Coming together after violence, slowly taking tentative steps, is part of the open nature of the reconciliatory process. Indeed, Ernesto Verdeja recognizes "that reconciliation is a complex, multileveled process that is best understood as *disjunctured* and *uneven*, with multiple moral claims often in competition with one another" (2009: 3). His normative conception of reconciliation relies on shared beliefs of moral respect and acceptance among past opponents.

The contrasting theories on the process of reconciliation are important; their efficacy is tested in practice. Xanana Gusmão, former president of the Democratic Republic of Timor-Leste, writes of reconciliation as "a long process," and while he suggests that it involves more than forgiving, he suggests that the process entails "the courage to admit our mistakes and to forgive" (2005: 26). Gusmão defends the idea "that no one should hold bitterness towards the enemies" given that they also were instruments of an oppressive system (2005: 26).[1] For many, this seems to offer a demanding view of reconciliation. How does one release long-held bitterness? Is this release helpful to victims of injustice? Ethiopian Hizkias Assefa suggests that there are five key elements to the process of reconciliation: acknowledgment of harm done, expression of remorse, asking for or granting pardon, alleviating the effects of the harm, and "defining a new mutually beneficial relationship that addresses the root causes of the past conflict and guarantees the past mistakes will not be repeated" (2005: 637). Whether there can ever be such guarantees is debatable. Assefa does stress the affective process of reconciliation in that it involves feelings of denial, guilt, and shame, which are not easy to turn into acknowledgment, humility, and remorse in revised narratives. The process of reconciliation certainly is demanding and rarely is realized in a full sense.

Culture of Reconciliation

In addition to stressing relationships and reconciliation as a process, other theorists emphasize the importance of developing a culture of reconciliation. Andrew Rigby explains that a culture of reconciliation cannot be confined to the symbolic realm, but "must be embodied and lived out in new relationships between people at all levels of society" (2001: 189). Sometimes a power-sharing arrangement such as occurred in Northern Ireland after the 1998 Good Friday Agreement is the context in which a new system of equality and respect for difference can begin to emerge, and with it a changing social and political culture that, at least in theory, should permit reconciliation to flourish. However, without working through the remaining deep cleavages between divided communities that caused the violent conflict, the tensions that Dwyer refers to above hover close to the surface. It does not take much for them to erupt. Coexistence is necessary, as former adversaries have to live near each other, work together, and share social spaces; hence an accepted culture of reconciliation is crucial. Beside the idealistic, normative reasons for reconciliation, there are pragmatic reasons to build a culture where decent relationships exist.

Sadako Ogata, former United Nations High Commissioner for Refugees, writing of her experience of those returning to Bosnia, says that "neither my colleagues nor I had ever been exposed to so much hatred" (in Chayes and Minow 2003: xiv). The commission was preparing roofs, doors, and windows of shelter for returnees, but great courage is needed to return to a community from which one has been expelled. She recalls the story of a Serbian woman who had gone back to a Bosnian-dominated community. The woman told Ogata "that when she returned, the house was intact, but what was frightening was that none of her former neighbors would talk to her" (in Chayes and Minow 2003: xiv). Ogata reminds us that this is the reality for starting places for reconciliation. The reality lies in people's lived narratives and their willingness or otherwise to begin to build a culture of reconciliation, even when great resistance or remaining hostility prevails.

Spectrum of Possibilities

If we have established so far that reconciliation is an open process that needs to change cultural attitudes and practices in order to build decent, reconciled relationships, what is the end game? What should we be satisfied with? Are there half measures or degrees of reconciliation? Trudy Govier (2006: 13) writes of "a spectrum of possibilities" in interpreting what reconciliation involves—from rich "thickness" of unity, harmony, healing, forgiveness, decent relationships, truth, and acknowledgment, to "thinness" where there is little emphasis on changed attitudes, but there is a cessation of violence and democratic, institutional changes. This contrast overlaps with Norman Porter's (2003) ideas of "strong" and "weak" reconciliation. Govier defines reconciliation as "a coming together after a rift that has undermined the capacity for decent cooperation between the people involved" (2006: 18). She is realistic in explaining the context of alienation and suspicion that makes it hard for people to trust each other. She stresses the role of trust in other people in believing "that they will act in ways that are generally constructive and not harmful to us" (2006: 19). She gives practical examples, such as the fact that people understandably will only come to a meeting if security is not at risk. This is particularly significant in rural or mountainous regions, as well as in urban estates where paramilitary groups have a strong presence. In other examples, in seeking facts, witnesses need to be reliable. In legal proceedings, judges and officials need to be trustworthy—that is, not corrupt but competent. Treaties only make sense if all signatories keep their word and honor the promises to which they have agreed. Monitors have to be trusted. Fundamental to reconciliation is the acknowledgment of wrongdoing, and also that those who were harmed possess human dignity and merit equal human rights. In contextualizing this spectrum of possibilities, the central focus of reconciliation processes is to shift "relationships away from anger, hatred, and grievance in the direction of acceptance and trust so as to build the capacity for collaboration and sustainable peace" (Govier 2006: 144). I suggest that on the journey toward reconciliation, there are midpoints and stepping-stones to cross in the full gamut of possible degrees of reconciliation. Often there is slippage from thick, strong progress back to thin, weak, fragile ties. Trust has to be rebuilt, truth told instead of lies, and new movements toward reconciliation initiated.

For example, David Crocker also talks of a range of meanings of reconciliation that lie on a spectrum, ranging from "thinner" to "thicker" conceptions (2003: 54). He contrasts "simple coexistence" with former enemies who begin to obey the law instead of killing each other, with a "liberal social solidarity" where former enemies at least respect each other as fellow citizens, to a "democratic reciprocity" that "implies a willingness to hear each other out, to enter into a give and take about matters of public policy, to build on areas of common concern, and to forge principled compromises with which all can live" (Crocker 2003: 54). This range of measures is similar to Rajeev Bhargava's distinction between a weaker sense of "reconciliation as resignation"—where people can live together despite past hostility but there is not a lot of change in people's relationships—and a stronger sense of reconciliation, where there is acknowledgment of wrongdoing, moral parity is restored, and relationships are congenial (2012: 371). Bhargava considers the strong sense to be utopian because of the enormous difficulties involved in transforming antagonistic identities. It is certainly idealistic, but I consider it imperative to strive toward the stronger understandings of reconciliation, including developing deep and meaningful relationships. However, not everyone shares this view.

Toshihiro Abe also is critical of what he calls the naïve view of reconciliation that, in striving for mutual understanding, "relies on key concepts such as moral repair, mutual empathy, transformation of identity, and re-categorization of the we/them category" (2012: 789–790). He questions how changing mutual understanding and new identifications of the self can occur when parties are so deeply estranged. Instead, he advocates "durable adversarial relationships" (2012: 795) where "disagreement, discontent, distrust, and resilience" all find a place in the context of a democratic ethos (2012: 796). I have argued in earlier chapters of the need to create safe spaces to express disagreements openly, and many hostilities remain in transitional justice societies. But I believe that it is possible to hold a normative view of reconciliation that permits disagreements to be aired without the need for discontent or distrust to emerge. I have shown in previous chapters why trust, which is hard to build and easily broken, is needed for open dialogue to be meaningful. I agree that the strong conceptualization of reconciliation is immensely difficult to achieve in practice at the robust, thick end of the spectrum, but nevertheless I contend that the goal is worth striving toward. The reason is that it permits the possibility of a society of vulnerable humans, willing to work together to create a just and peaceful society, despite holding massively different political views. Many disagree with my view.

Ernesto Verdeja (2009) also is critical of both "minimalist" and "maximalist" approaches. He suggests that a minimalist approach views reconciliation "as simple coexistence between former enemies" (2009: 12). This approach is based on thin proceduralism of how to survive in the present, so crucial issues of dealing with the past are blocked out. Attention to the needs of victims thus is ignored, as too are issues of vengeance that must be dealt with if former enemies can relate interpersonally. In contrast, maximalists assume there will be remorse, repentance, and forgiveness, with Desmond Tutu's role in the South African TRC an obvious example. Instead, Verdeja advocates a process of reconciliation working at "the political, institutional, civil society, and interpersonal levels" (2009: 20). He stresses that reconciliation is practiced in narrative contexts, with specific actions and actors. At the center of his argument is the crucial concept of mutual respect—that is, the recognition of others' worth, including previous enemies. Concepts and practices already discussed in previous chapters—like truth, accountability, recognition of victims' needs, and the rule of law—promote respect. Thus, a society that seeks to be reconciled must create the conditions and institutions wherein citizens will be recognized as bearers of moral worth and dignity. Respect for others should be a reciprocal norm. When former enemies recognize and start to accept each other as members of the same polity, and work together on common goals, then we begin to see reconciliation in action.

In adopting this view, I am endorsing Paul James's idea of "slow reconciliation" (2008: 115), moments that suggest the possibility of reconciliation. James also makes a distinction between "negative reconciliation," which can be seen "as a process of forgiving and forgetting," and "positive reconciliation," which is "a never-concluding, often uncomfortable process of remaking or bringing together of persons, practices, and meanings in ongoing 'places of meeting'" (2008: 117). I talk more of reconciliatory spaces later, but it is useful to explain James's clarification of these places because the ideas overlap. James suggests that places of meeting "require the active possibility of return over time and the possibility of layering of truths and the contestation of meaning" (2008: 117). In these places, there are manifold tensions, wherein previous enemies are still recovering from varying degrees of trauma, and enmity remains. But, in keeping the idea of the "moral imagination" (Lederach 2005) alive, and in celebrating every new reconciliatory moment as the possibility of a new future with a transformed narrative, disagreements and tensions are not shelved; instead they can be absorbed as part of the moment, but without their usual accompanying antagonism.

How then does the idea of a spectrum of possible degrees of reconciliation play out in practice? Carlos Sluzki describes stages of reconciliation, with each stage symbolized "by a set of narratives, stories that people tell about the situation" (2003: 28). In the conflict stage, emotions of hostility and contempt are expressed in conversations, and the narrative that dominates is that "hostility is the only option" (2003: 24). Resentment, anger, and mistrust remain with coexistence, as people talk about the past and new grudges often emerge. Coexistence is positive in that parties can live together without open acts of violence, but the dominant narrative comprises variations of the idea that "we are ready for hostile acts when needed" (2003: 24). The rules of engagement still fall into a zero-sum-game deadlock. Such a notion is not terribly demanding because it simply involves restraint from adversaries. The next stage Sluzki suggests is collaboration over common projects such as sharing the development of a crop on neighboring boundaries or rebuilding a bridge. Women from opposing parties can wash their clothes in the same river despite feeling ambivalent toward the other. Underlying the dominant narratives is the idea that "hostilities are a fall-back option" (2003: 25). When activities begin to emerge in common, such as designing a dam to facilitate irrigation in all parts of the territory, cooperation starts to emerge and a narrative develops that peace is desirable and thus "hostilities would be a major disadvantage" (2003: 25) in disrupting prospects for sustainable peace. In the next stage of interdependence, the parties are involved in planning activities toward the collective good. There is an acceptance of the past and some cautious trust, which enables narratives that display a consensus that "hostilities would be foolish" (2003: 25–26). With the next stage of integration, solidarity has grown and there is good intent toward others. Narratives of hostilities have been disbanded. Sluzki stresses that, while the process can stagnate at any stage, and as I have already suggested there is often much slippage and tumbling backward to an earlier stage, it follows a sequence where stages rarely are missed, and where each stage constitutes the beginnings of the next one. What is important about Sluzki's outline for my purposes is that it conceptualizes the entire process toward reconciliation in shifts of prevailing narratives, from stories of persecution to stories of progress and confidence building. As noted, dominant stories become entrenched in community narratives that emerge in multiple levels, not merely as national, political narratives, but also in civil society stories in cultural pursuits, education, and sports, as well as in extended family and social networks.

In this section I have outlined four differing understandings of reconciliation. These have included emphases on reconciling relationships, processes, cultures, and a spectrum of degrees of reconciliation. I have noted the value in these four different ways to conceptualize reconciliation, and I keep contending that, while it is incredibly challenging to achieve fully, reconciliation at each of the four levels is worth striving for, because it signals hope for new relationships in a just and peaceful future.

Is Healing Intrinsic to Reconciliation?

In discussing reconciliation, it is fundamental to keep clarifying why it is important and who is reconciling with whom. Whose stories need to be told to whom and for what purpose? The underlying need for reconciliation lies in the fact that "it is impossible to overstate the extent to which severe physical, emotional, and psychological trauma characterizes many postconflict communities" (Clark 2008a: 199). As Clark explains, this trauma involves feelings of helplessness, an inability to engage with others, and expressions of anger, mistrust, paranoia, and vengefulness. He thus defines healing as requiring "rehumanizing survivors and perpetrators to overcome the negative identities they assumed during conflict" (2008a: 201). What then is the relationship between this need for healing of wounded souls and reconciliation in all its varied forms?

The type of healing needed depends on the nature of the harm suffered. Norman Habel (1999) addresses issues of healing by maintaining that it is only through listening to stories that the extent of suffering can be understood. For example, as a white Australian, it is important for me to acknowledge Australia's shame in the terrible suffering that was inflicted by the majority on the Indigenous minority. Acknowledgment and apology are necessary. The forgiveness factor in the healing process is significant in giving public assurances that grudges will not persist against the wrongdoer. However, as I have demonstrated in previous chapters, a lot is asked from the injured party. As emphasized in Chapter 6, acknowledgment and apologies are crucial first steps. Forgiveness "enables parties to embrace each other again as fellow human beings with a just future together" (Habel 1999: 41). Habel uses a poignant example of the words of an Australian Indigenous mother who is one of the stolen generations who were taken from their communities. The words on a memorial sculpture read, "And every morning as the sun came up the whole family would wail. They did that for 32 years until they saw me again. Who can imagine what a mother went through? But you have to learn to forgive" (in Habel 1999: 41).[2] Authors disagree on the significance of forgiveness as part of the healing dimension to reconciliation, with some arguing that it "is a constituent element of reconciliation" (Meierhenrich 2008: 206), a necessary but not sufficient condition. While forgiveness sometimes is a part of the process of reconciliation, it is often a one-way act—unlike reconciliation, which always involves relationships. Reconciliation, then, is conceptually separate from forgiveness, so that even when an apology is not forthcoming or forgiveness seems to be not possible, tentative moves toward reconciliation may be.

As maintained in the previous chapter, the need for healing does not arise solely from victims. Sara Cobb shows insight on this point when she writes,

> From a narrative perspective on reconciliation, the aesthetics of a "better" story would be one in which the humanity of the perpetrator was explored, not to assist him in redemption, but to ensure that the stories about the development of violence and the perpetrator's own moral descent circulate in the public sphere. (Cobb 2013: 270)

This humanizing of violent offenders does not excuse gross acts of evil. To the contrary, a story presenting perpetrators of abuse "as human beings would require the social construction of them as human beings who were human enough to know they were crossing a line, a moral line" (Cobb 2013: 270). For example, take child soldiers. Cobb suggests that asking questions is important, about whether the children knew what they were doing; what they later told their parents if they were still alive; whether they really knew the difference between right and wrong; or, after reflection on the violence, when they first understood that they violated moral standards. And further, how did they justify these acts? What aspects of violence haunt them? What do they regret? As Cobb puts it, "These questions construct the perpetrator as having a morality," as knowing they have done wrong, as someone who has learned the difference between right and wrong and therefore has regrets (2013: 270–271). I keep qualifying that we cannot presume that remorse, the desire for healing, or even awareness of the immorality of violence toward others actually occurs with perpetrators of abuse. Most often, it does not. Hence I am outlining the possibilities where it may occur and in the hope that it might.

Cynthia Ngewu, whose son was one of the Guguletu Seven killed by the South African police, is an example of someone who gained healing through release of bitterness toward the man who killed her son. I recounted the story in Chapter 3, but it is pertinent to retell here. In revealing her story to the South African TRC she said,

> This thing called reconciliation . . . if I am understanding it correctly . . . If it means this perpetrator, this man who has killed Christopher Piet, if it means he becomes human again, this man, so that I, so that all of us, gets our humanity back . . . Then I agree, then I support it all. (in Minow 2002: 25–26)

What Ngewu is indicating is that reconciliation involves the healing of perpetrators as well as victim-survivors. She said,

> What we are hoping for when we embrace the notion of reconciliation is that we restore the humanity to those who were perpetrators. We do not want to return the evil by another evil. We simply want to ensure that the perpetrators are returned to humanity. (in Boraine 2000: 353)

Healing for victims and perpetrators who have expressed remorse is important. Given that many former perpetrators take on key roles in new political structures, much to the dismay of victims and their families, this healing is a crucial, understated aspect to reconciliation. Many of these new politicians have not fully grasped what is needed to leave aside the undercurrent of violence of the past.

Consider a different example. Solomon Nsabiyera Gasana defines himself as "a survivor of conflict in the Great Lakes region" and writes that "as a witness to and victim of violence, I personally struggled for years with my inner woundedness" (2008: 145). As a Congolese Tutsi, his family "lived in total poverty" after losing all of their cattle through fighting, and he reveals that "the bitterness of my parents taught me to hate those who drove us to such destitution" (2008: 150). Accordingly, he bore grudges and had an inner desire for revenge toward those who had crushed his community. He says that "the narrative of hatred and fear dominated the daily conversations" in his community, reinforcing people's trauma (2008: 151–152). Like others, he is skeptical of simplistic interpretations of reconciliation that assume that, simply because Rwandans are cooperating together on development objectives, they have rebuilt relationships. Rather, there often are other motivations coming to the fore, like personal gain. Interestingly, his "journey of healing" (2008: 152) began with involvement in peacebuilding. For

Gasana, he needed to explore past narratives, which included the shared history between Tutsi and Hutu. In openly sharing with others and tending to others' emotional wounds and feelings of sorrow, he began to be released from the grip of the past, particularly his "own bondage of self-pity, sorrow, anger, and hatred" (2008: 153). As he struggled with the idea of forgiveness for the offenders' hatred, and through compassion found it possible to do so, he writes, "I moved toward a place of reconciliation, where I believed it was possible to live and interact with the people whom I previously hated" (2008: 154). The point in outlining one person's narrative in detail is to high-light that forgiveness or healing does not equal reconciliation, but in many cases, they make it easier by preparing the path. I am certainly envisaging reconciliation as a long journey on a rocky, meandering road. Gasana gives an account of how, through connecting with Hutus in his work and in visiting some in prison and listening to their stories, these "were acts of reconciliation" (2008: 155). In recalling a World Vision group therapy workshop, he heard stories from Hutus who were overwhelmed by their shame and expressed disbelief at their heinous acts. He writes that "these confessions made me humanize Hutu, people whom I previously viewed as beasts" (2008: 155). His point is that, in a traumatized society, without healing there will be little change.[3] Healing is an integral part of reconciliation for victims and for those perpetrators who demonstrate remorse and are willing to join others on the journey toward reconciliation.

Are Truth, Justice, Mercy, and Peace Part of Reconciliation?

Having established the central role that reconciliation plays in societies transitioning from conflict, I connect reconciliation with some of the central themes that I have developed throughout this book. To do so, I build on John Paul Lederach's articulation of three working assumptions that ground reconciliation. First, there is the "notion that *relationship* is the basis of both the conflict and its long-term solution" (Lederach 2004: 26). Second, in order to address the past without getting stuck in a vicious cycle, "Engagement of the conflicting groups assumes an *encounter*" that acknowledges the trauma of loss, grief, and anger that accompanies pain, memory of injustices, experiences, and validation of each others' stories (2004: 26). As already discussed above, the encounter is a significant moment or series of moments, when changing relationships is discernible. Lederach's idea of an encounter grasps the notion of a space where "both the past and the future can meet" (2004: 27). Third, "Reconciliation requires that we look outside the mainstream of international political traditions, discourse," and practices if we are to find creative ways to locate these spaces (2004: 27). This action requires inspired use of the moral imagination, a concept used often in earlier chapters. These three assumptions underlie a rich notion of reconciliation.

Lederach provides a useful example that brings these three assumptions together. During the 1980s he was working with a conciliation team that mediated negotiations between the Sandinista government and the Yatama, the indigenous resistance movement of the Nicaraguan east coast. The conciliation team accompanied the Yatama leaders as they returned to their home area to explain the agreement they had reached with the Sandinistas. At the start of each village meeting the Nicaraguan conciliators read Psalm 85:10 from a Spanish version of the Old Testament, which reads, "Truth and mercy have met together; peace and justice have kissed" (Lederach 2004: 28). At a training workshop later, Lederach asked the conciliators more about this text. They said that, while truth requires "honesty, revelation, clarity, open accountability, and vulnerability," alone it is insufficient (2004: 28). With mercy, images surfaced of "compassion, forgiveness, acceptance, and a new start," yet alone, mercy covers up; it moves on too quickly without attending to the importance of justice, "of making things right, creating equal opportunity, rectifying the wrong, and restitution" (2004: 28). With peace came images of unity and well-being, as well as feelings of respect and security that are a farce if they only benefit some. On asking the participants what to call the place where truth, mercy, justice, and peace all meet, one answered, "That *place* is reconciliation" (2004: 29). These ideas resonate with the arguments developed throughout this book. They are worth elaboration.

Lederach stresses the significance of this social space, where people come together. He summarizes the interrelationships between the active concepts:

> Truth is the longing for acknowledgment of wrong and validation of painful loss and experiences, but it is coupled with Mercy, which articulates the need for acceptance, letting go, and a new beginning. Justice represents the search for individual and group rights, for social restructuring, and for restitution, but it is linked with Peace, which underscores the need for interdependence, well-being, and security. (Lederach 2004: 29)

Drawing on these ideas, Lederach summarizes the three paradoxes that reconciliation addresses. First, "Reconciliation promotes an encounter between the open expression of the painful past . . . and the search for the articulation of a long-term, interdependent future" (2004: 31). As such, it overlaps with dual goals of transitional justice to deal with the past in order to move to a transformed future. Second, "Reconciliation provides a place for truth and mercy to meet" where the quality of the relationship is a priority (2004: 31). As I stressed earlier, in my view this needs thick, strong, maximalist connections. Third, "Reconciliation recognizes the need to give time and place to both justice and peace, where redressing the wrong is held together with the envisioning of a common, connected future" (Lederach 2004: 31). Reconciliation is not an abstract concept; rather it is closely linked to interconnected practices, encounters, and places that are needed for decent relationships to flourish.

Tamar Hermann extends some of these ideas further, positing a comprehensive "idea of reconciliation as a 'locus,' the place where truth (acknowledgment, transparency, revelation, and clarity) meets mercy (acceptance, forgiveness, support, compassion, and healing), justice (equality, right relationships, rectification, and restitution), and peace (harmony, unity, well-being, security, and respect)" (2004: 45–46). In this social and political space, there is room for a joining together, rather than a dualistic fragmentation of a win-or-lose mentality, or a justice rather than peace approach. Concessions may be needed to overcome the intransigence of polarized views that block the space from opening. Patricia Lundy suggests that in a politicized context, like Northern Ireland, evidence suggests the importance of "sequencing" truth recovery efforts, with "intercommunal truth recovery being the first necessary 'building block'" in developing the self-confidence that is necessary to tackle contentious issues surrounding different accounts of truth (in Aiken 2010: 180–181). Dealing with blockages is time-consuming, personally demanding, and often risky, but essential to opening the spaces.

Daniel Philpott (2012) develops a substantive argument on the links between justice and an ethic of political reconciliation. At the basis of this ethic "is the restoration of right relationship within or between political communities" (2012: 16). Conceived this way, Philpott suggests that reconciliation involves "a multiplicity of practices that each redress wounds of injustice in a particular way" (2012: 49). Philpott addresses the outlooks that are hostile to reconciliation or believe that it is paternalistic or sacrifices justice. His is a strong view: "Reconciliation equals justice that entails a comprehensive restoration of relationship" (2012: 15). In this view, with all activities that restore right relationship, whether they are acts of truth, forgiveness, or mercy, Philpott argues that "reconciliation *is* justice" (2012: 53). This position draws on the two sides to justice as both right conduct and right response to wrong conduct. Philpott's substantial definition of the ethic of political reconciliation is as follows:

> It is a concept of justice that aims to restore victims, perpetrators, citizens, and the governments of states that have been involved in political injustices to a condition of right relationship within political order or between political orders—a condition characterized by human rights, democracy, the rule of law, and respect for international law; by widespread recognition of the legitimacy of these values; and by the virtues that accompany these values. (2012: 58)

Right relationship is thus what political reconciliation is all about. Political reconciliation "involves victims, perpetrators, and members of the community who variously accuse, defend, demand, narrate, recognize, learn, listen, affirm, show remorse, acknowledge, forgive, and empathize" (2012: 60). The practices Philpott identifies that are most likely to affect reconciliation include building socially just institutions to address the violation of human rights; acknowledging victims' suffering; reparations that attend to actual harm to victims; punishment that confers recognition of victim dignity; apology that conveys respect to the victim; and forgiveness, signaling a willingness to construct a new relationship (2012: 171–174).

With regard to the relationship between truth and justice, Emir Suljagić, one of the few male survivors of the Srebrenica genocide, resists reconciliation. He says, "I never wronged anyone. I did nothing wrong. Reconciliation means we have to meet halfway, but that's offensive. I was wronged and almost my entire family was killed. I care about justice and truth" (in Subotic 2009: 149). His story is an important reminder of the crucial weight that victims give to justice as being an integral requirement of meaningful reconciliation. Horacio Verbitsky, a Chilean journalist, makes a similar point when he asks, "Reconciliation by whom? After someone takes away your daughter, tortures her, disappears her, and then denies having ever done it—would you want to 'reconcile' with those responsible?" (in Sooka 2006: 322). This is indeed a massive question, and any abstract response to it could be accused of insensitivity. Verbitsky talks of the political discourse on reconciliation as "immoral" in denying the reality of people's horrific experiences. In highlighting narratives I have sought to avoid the depersonalization of disembodied theory in order to link a narrative understanding of trauma- tized identities with theories and practices of peace, justice, and recon- ciliation. In taking personal narratives seriously I continue to struggle with Verbitsky's question; the answer does not come easily.

I return to the idea that the reconciliation process contains identity, truth, and justice principles alongside the suffering dimension and the forgiveness factor. When former enemies begin to engage with each other, there is a process of redefining antagonistic identities in order to re-create, and sometimes simply to create for the first time, a construc- tive way of relating. For this engagement to happen, the cultural identi- ties of both parties in conflict must be valued equally. A partial transfor- mation of attitudes also is necessary. Habel suggests that the truth principle affirms that there cannot be any "serious reconciliation" where stories of the truth remain suppressed. The "justice principle requires that past injustices, losses, and evils inflicted on the weaker party are addressed by a mutually agreed procedure" (Habel 1999: 37). Restoring the dignity of the wronged party is a crucial part of this process. Some maintain that reconciliation promotes justice in "vindicating the victims, and restoring them to their former, pre-violations selves" (Sarkin and Daly 2004: 692). However, in many cases, there is no return to a former self; the violation disrupts and alters self-understanding. Identity, truth, and justice come together in reconciliation.

Reconciliation is demanding. Jean Baptiste Kayigamba, a Tutsi sur- vivor of the Rwandan genocide who lost his parents, two sisters, five brothers, as well as close friends in the genocide, writes a deeply per- sonal narrative of how he has "tried, day by day, to come to terms with the devastating personal legacies of these experiences" (2008: 33). He is wary of reconciliation. He writes that, because survivors live alongside neighbors whom they know participated in the genocide, a "new culture of impunity comes under the guise of calls for reconciliation" (2008: 40). Kayigamba's claim is that without justice, attempts to reconcile will prove futile. The message of the need for justice as part of reconcil- iation is made pointedly. Here I differ from Philpott's position stated earlier, that "reconciliation *is* justice" (2012: 53). Justice in my view is not equivalent to reconciliation, but without justice, those who are seek- ing to reconcile necessarily struggle. I would agree more with Assefa, who maintains that "justice is at the core of reconciliation" (2005: 639). His reason for this is that it is necessary to address the issues that led to unjust relationships in order to address the needs of victims. Sometimes, the struggle for justice brings people together. For example, a Serb woman named Dobrinka and a Croat woman named Marija both lost sons in the war. On their initial meeting in 1997 they hated each other. They met as part of a project related to finding those who went missing during the war in Croatia. What they hold in common is a shared commitment to justice. "To hold values reciprocally is the basis of genuine respect for each other as moral agents" (in Halpern and Weinstein 2004: 579). In this section I have deliberately drawn on a wide range of writers to show the common view that truth, justice, mercy, and peace are interconnected features in building the process and culture of reconciled relationships. In each different reconciliatory moment, different weight is given to each of these features.

Where Are Reconciliatory Spaces?

What then is so special about reconciliatory spaces? How would we know their essential ingredients? Where are these reconciliatory spaces to be found? The concept of "places of meeting" that James (2008: 117) describes and I have outlined above has manifold examples. They include actual face-to-face spaces to negotiate over differences, institutionalized spaces where communities confer over radical differences, tribunals, and commissions.[4] Often these formal spaces are dominated by legal proceduralism, whereas the personal sharing of narratives is more likely to break down the binaries between victim and perpetrator and between former political antagonists. This sharing of narratives usually is fraught with tensions; often there is deep uncertainty, including about how each story will be perceived. For some, the tensions are so deep that they shy away from reconciliation. For example, Juliane Okot Bitek, a Ugandan woman, has reservations about any notion of reconciliation that diminishes the experiences of survivors or assumes that prior relationships are necessarily worth reconciling. Instead, she sees the challenge "to create a whole new understanding of the current circumstances that hinges on an imaginary place and peace without the burden of the past bearing on the everyday" (2012: 395). Women often play a significant role in reconciliation initiatives that can imagine a different peaceful space for communities. For example, in the Pacific Islands, in Bougainville in the mid-1990s, women from local churches worked to address the practical impact of the crisis on women and helped to kick-start the peace negotiations. In the Solomon Islands in 1999, women initiated a Reconciliation Peace Committee with work that continues. In Fiji numerous women's groups play significant roles in holding peace vigils, opposing the coups, and securing venues for dialogue to keep working toward reconciliation.

Elsewhere, international programs in Rwanda that seek to foster reconciliation are strengthening the beginning of new narratives. Through the use of theater, drama, play, art, income-generation schemes, conflict resolution training, or healing workshops, these programs seek to open participants to express their own narratives and to learn about others' narratives. Not all programs have been culturally sensitive, but many are. Duhozanye (To Console Each Other) is a group of Hutu and Tutsi women who came together in mourning, as I discussed in Chapter 5. They had all lost family members, many had been raped and borne children, and then they worked together to solve the problem of their immediate survival needs and how to care for the numerous orphans. A critical moment occurred when a Tutsi woman who had a sister-in-law who was a Hutu widow asked for this woman to be allowed to come and mourn with them. This moment is indicative of the need for an encounter to create the reconciliatory spaces to which I refer. This is a "serendipitous" moment that Lederach (2005) suggests is part of the moral imagination, where something triggers a release in someone's thoughts that permits the unimagined to happen. The relational attachments that developed in this Rwandan group became foundational to the community—in building houses and in starting an agricultural cooperative, a school for orphaned children, and a craft center. Through collective mourning, these women have developed a collaborative narrative that provides a place for reconciliation between Hutu and Tutsi women. Cobb refers to this as an indigenous, bottom-up "narrative transformation" (2013: 103). Identities can be reinvented as different but not opposed to working with different groups, so that there is reciprocal sincerity that confirms belonging to a distinct group while also making social connections to different groups; and with this reciprocity, reconciliation grows. Cobb interviewed some of these women in 2000 as part of the Imagine Coexistence Project. In telling their stories of loss, rapes, giving birth to a child of their rapist, pain, and mourning together, all the speakers felt legitimized. This reciprocal legitimization of unique narratives is crucial to reconciliation. Multiple possibilities arise for reconciliatory spaces to emerge.

Culturally Different Spaces

Countries around the globe are engaged in transitional justice processes that have little in common except that their governments tout the rhetoric of reconciliation as a remedy for their country's shortcomings. Reconciliation initiatives understandably appear attractive because they respond to the diverse needs of different nations, including incorporating legal and political, public and private needs, and moral and pragmatic considerations. Inadequate consideration is often paid to the best cultural way to promote reconciliation. Roxana Waterson (2009) explains how significant traditional rituals can be in reconciliation processes. She maintains that symbolic and ceremonial elements within these processes can "create a space in which order, calm, and a sense of emotional support might prevail," and that rituals help "to channel and focus emotions" (2009: 35). Particularly in traditional customary reconciliation practices, there can often be a sense of theater whereby many disenfranchised people dramatize and perform their own suffering in these spaces.

In view of the fact that reconciliation is always culturally context-specific, Hayner asks how we might gauge its progress. This question is important for societies undergoing a transitional justice process. She suggests that three central issues should be taken into consideration (2011: 189). The first is how to deal with the past in the public sphere. Levels of bitterness and the ability of people to discuss past abuses civilly with former opponents are critical considerations. Different cultures handle these concerns differently. Second, progress is gauged by the strength of relationships between former opponents. Always referring back to the past and reiterating bitter memories is not helpful. In many cultures, the past has dominated not only conflicts but attempts to move closer to reconciliation, when the move falters because antagonists constantly harp back to the past. Third, there needs to be some way to deal with many versions of the past, involving "reconciling contradictory facts or stories" (Hayner 2011: 189). Cultural differences exist in how stories feed into the meanings and practices of reconciliation. In many cultures, traditional conflict resolution mechanisms, such as cleansing rituals, customary trauma healing, religious services, and dramatization, are used as part of reconciliation processes. In Pacific cultures, such public expression of peace and reconciliation is valued highly. Hence, in Bougainville, armed militants of the Bougainville Revolutionary Army and the pro-Papua New Guinea Resistance forces joined together for an exchange of pigs and shells and the symbolic breaking of bows and arrows (Maclellan 2004: 535). This form of customary reconciliation is crucial in stopping the cycles of payback and feuding.

Meierhenrich (2008) outlines four central background concepts to understanding cultural differences in reconciliation. First there is the notion of equilibrium, or restoration of balance, that can be found in many differing cultures. He uses examples of the Lozi in Barotseland, western Zambia, who were striving to achieve a solution acceptable to all the parties in dispute through balancing the differing expectations. Second, conciliation seeks to resolve disputes in ways that are acceptable to the parties. Third, alternative dispute resolution is used cross-cultur-ally, with significant cases in 1975 between the Hopi and Navajo Indian tribes. The fourth central concept is restorative justice, bringing together victims and offenders; this practice particularly can pave the path, laying the groundwork for the development of reconciliation. Cultural practices of restorative justice are fascinating. In some of the major peace agree-ments in Somaliland, reconciling parties agreed to exchange fifty wives. The practice is symbolic. "You give a daughter to someone you trust, honor and wish to maintain an interaction with" (Farah and Lewis 1995: 55). Particularly when there has been loss of life, the offer of a marriage-able partner is a customary atonement. In the African context, the notion of ubuntu, or the intertwining of humanity, plays a significant role in providing a rationale for restoring victim and perpetrator. In Guatemala, many church institutions supported victimized indigenous women so that the atrocities of sexual violence were recognized in the interests of fur-thering reconciliation. In Timor-Leste, traditional leaders were crucial in giving credibility to the community reconciliation procedures that formed a vital part of the Commission for Reception, Truth, and Recon-ciliation (CAVR, Comissão de Acolhimento, Verdade e Reconciliação). Whatever the cultural form, the goal is to build a just peace in a society where people work successfully in common pursuits.

In Northern Uganda, the Juba Peace Talks (2006–2008) called for traditional justice to heal the wounds and appease the spirits. In a reli-gious ceremony of reconciliation, the tradition of stepping on an egg was used to welcome the former fighters back into their communities. In the Acholi culture, the *matooput* ritual involves an investigation into the conflict, with the wrongdoers giving an account of their action and admitting responsibility in making some sort of restitution. "The offender and the victim then share a drink made of bitter hops for wit-nesses to indicate and confirm that reconciliation has occurred" (Sarkin and Daly 2004: 672). In talking with people in Uganda, Joanna Quinn found that people meant a variety of things when they used the term "reconciliation," including, "the actual resolution of conflict, bringing the war to an end; building a lasting peace; reintegrating rebel soldiers and child abductees; amnesty; reconstruction of the physical property damaged in the conflict; compensation; and repaired relationships"

(2009: 183). She summarizes this as a search to capture connections of social capital and social cohesion where trust, reciprocity, and associations bridging social divisions can thrive.

In interviews with forty-five experts working on community-based reconciliation in Northern Ireland during 2008, Nevin Aiken found that the majority of his participants cited the reduction of structural and material inequalities as "crucial to the promotion of intergroup reconciliation, most often noting that this distributive work has served as a kind of 'minimum baseline' from which all other reconciliatory activities have been able to build" (2010: 174). This finding demonstrates again how significant notions of justice are to reconciliation; as one person said, "You cannot build a positive environment if one side feels they are getting the short end of the straw. There has to be equity" (Ray Mullan in Aiken 2010: 174).[5] This point is extremely important, because in Northern Ireland, as in many other places, much of the continual violence occurs in areas of economic disadvantage where sectarian behavior is particularly conspicuous. Aiken repeatedly heard interviewees stress the powerful reconciliatory potential when contact is combined with "opportunities for engagement in safe and sustained dialogue processes" (2010: 185). Of course, storytelling of narratives is a prime way to humanize the other. Through listening to the narrative, crude stereotypes can be dismantled and new understandings can emerge. Dialogue in the service of reconciliation involves "opening up reflexive spaces within which silenced, anxious, or angry voices can be heard" (Bishop 2009: 180). Peter Bishop explains that reconciliation involves "a responsibility to 'the story of the other'" (2009: 180).

The exchange of gifts is a crucial part of reconciliation in many cultures. Volker Boege, in writing on postconflict Bougainville, suggests that these gifts "are an outward sign of reconciliation," where the exchange "takes place in the context of peace ceremonies that mark the culminating point of the whole process. The adversaries feast together, eating, drinking, dancing, chewing betel nut together, symbolically breaking spears and arrows, and so on" (Boege 2009: 33). Peter Mekea, representing the chiefs of Bougainville, reiterates the long-term embedding of reconciliation practices in their culture and says, "In its simplest form, it is just a question of two people saying, 'I did you wrong and you did me wrong. I forgive you and you forgive me'" (in Howley 2002: 102). In criticizing the West's preference for criminal punishment—jail, in particular—he reiterates the importance of the exchange of goods, especially, in his culture, the value of pigs and shell money. However, I keep stating that forgiveness, while crucial in the reconciliatory process, is not the same as reconciliation.

Phil Clark's fieldwork in Rwanda is pathbreaking in providing a detailed account of how the community hearings of the genocide, namely gacaca, operated.[6] Traditionally, the gacaca process was not so much a space for truth telling as a space to permit the speech needed to preserve primarily family relationships. Clark argues that gacaca represented "a holistic response to the legacies of the genocide," bringing together "interlocking personal, community, and national aims" (2010: 27). He explains that six key objectives emerged through both the design and operation of gacaca: truth, peace, justice, healing, forgiveness, and reconciliation (2010: 83). Through listening to the voices of the genocide survivors, much of the significance of gacaca becomes apparent. For example, there are links between truth and coexistence. Boniface, a genocide survivor, told Clark in 2003 that "at gacaca the truth frees us from the weight we have carried around since the genocide. Gacaca is important because it allows us to be together to hear the truth and to learn to live together again" (in Clark 2010: 90). Clark clarifies three different dimensions of truth, namely, "truth-telling, truth-hearing, and truth-shaping" (2010: 189). He explains that these three different dimensions of truth serve legal, therapeutic, and restorative purposes.

In Clark's telling of the narrative of the "gacaca journey," based on his firsthand observations, the complexity and efficacy of the journey both emerge. In May 2003, when twenty thousand confessed genocide perpetrators who had spent nearly a decade in prison were released into their communities, Clark persuaded camp officials to let him ride on the bus carrying seventy detainees to an undisclosed destination. One of those on the bus was Diomède, who was only ten years old during the genocide and "had confessed to being in a group of three boys who killed another boy with a machete" (Clark 2010: 109). The emotions on the bus ranged from jubilation to silent uncertainty. Clark had the opportunity to hold interviews with detainees over a period of six years. Laurent, who had confessed to killing three men and a woman, told him that "reconciliation doesn't come from the sky. It comes bit by bit. . . . It is much more than words—it is actions" (in Clark 2010: 112). Chantal, whose parents and cousins had been murdered, said, "There is no reconciliation here. There is no more violence, but there isn't reconciliation" (in Clark 2010: 124). Clark notes that many of the detainees used the concepts of forgiveness and reconciliation interchangeably. As one young detainee who confessed to a group killing of a woman when he was eleven said, "But I want to help the community forgive me at gacaca. . . . One day I hope the community will let me go back to my farm and start my life again" (in Clark 2008b: 306). For others, trauma was reignited. Géraldine, a fifty-six-year-old farmer, spoke of her increased levels of trauma when she said, "I have suffered nightmares because of what I hear at gacaca and the things it puts back in my mind" (in Clark 2010: 3). Yet there were cases of survivors who, as a gesture of reconciliation, adopted the person who killed their family members. The generosity of the human spirit knows no bounds.

Verdeja (2009) provides a marvelous example of this spirit from Mozambique after the 1992 peace agreement that ended sixteen years of vicious fighting. The *curanderos*, or traditional healers, were rural authority figures who played a key role in "reintegrating former soldiers who had murdered by 'rehumanizing' them, casting off the 'bad luck' that came from the victims' spirit" (Verdeja 2009: 10). What is important for the process of reconciliation is that this practice required an acknowledgment of guilt by the soldier and some sense of communal responsibility for the rehumanization. The rituals served as a community focus on reconciliation.

Patrick Burgess was director of the UN Transitional Administration in the East Timor Human Rights Unit from 2000 to 2002. He took a lead role in what was a historic event, "the first time that a UN peace-keeping mission had been directly involved in the establishment of a truth and reconciliation commission" (Burgess 2008: 141). He describes how the community reconciliation procedures worked in practice. Staff members from the CAVR visited villages to offer information and helped perpetrators write statements. Panels presided over cases in the villages where the violations had occurred. The panels were chaired by CAVR regional commissioners along with local leaders from women's groups, churches, or youth committees. On the day of the hearing, perpetrators were required to make a public acknowledgment of wrongdoing and apologize, and victims could ask questions and also suggest what might help them. Reparations requested by victims generally involved very small symbolic payments of rice or a pig to be sacrificed for the communal meal. The panel negotiated an agreed "act of reconciliation," which might have been a payment, apology, or community service. The local staff encouraged the idea of having a meal at the end of the hearing to finish on a positive note. The traditional practice of *adat*, where a large mat is unfurled by the spiritual elders who are often dressed in colorful traditional weavings and headdresses of feathers, gave it cultural meaning. Why? "The mat could not be rolled up until the dispute had been settled" (Burgess 2008: 146). Quite astonishingly, but in the spirit of reconciliation toward perpetrators, Burgess notes that "in several cases victims volunteered to join them in completing their community service as a demonstration of forgiveness and solidarity" (2008: 146). This is a positive example of a combination of traditional indigenous and formal procedures. Many participants "said that the incorporation of traditional ritual procedures had reinforced the agreement to reconcile and that forgiveness and repentance were taken more seriously within this ceremonial context" (Waterson 2009: 45). Again, the role of forgiveness in reconciliation is central.

Reconciliation cannot be forced. All forms of reconciliation may be engaged in grudgingly, but genuine gestures toward reconciliation are likely to be spontaneous. Time to develop trust is an important factor. Too often, resources are directed at specific programs encouraging reconciliation for people who are not ready and willing to join in this space. Susan Thomson undertook life history interviews in 2006 with Rwandan peasants. Her interviewees provided clear evidence that the policy of national unity and reconciliation, the backbone of the Rwandan government's reconstruction strategy, included a silencing of dissent, and thus the "perceived compliance with its dictates is tactical rather than sincere" (2011: 440). Thomson refers to "locally grounded and contextualized narratives in which Rwandans express themselves in their own words and as 'knowers' of their own life stories" (2011: 449). Aurelia, a thirty-nine-year-old widow, explained how she actively tries to avoid her local official who makes demands for reconciliation. All she wants is "recognition as a survivor of the genocide so I can get some [financial] support" (in Thomson 2011: 450). She gives examples also of "irreverent compliance," where, for example, Esther, a Tutsi survivor, forced to attend the returns ceremony of a Hutu individual whom she does not believe should have been released from prison, says that she "laughs out loud, or if that is not possible, I glare at him" (in Thomson 2011: 452). By attending the ceremony, she remains a law-abiding citizen, but she resists by expressing contempt, thereby undermining the process but retaining her agency and dignity. Tréso, a sixteen-year-old Tutsi boy, described to Thomson how he uses "withdrawn muteness" as his tactic for sabotage, the tactic of choice for many imprisoned Hutu (2011: 454).

* * *

In this chapter I have contrasted notions of reconciliation, explaining four different orientations that emphasize relationships, processes, cultures, and spectrums of possibilities in reconciliation. I argue that healing and forgiveness are intrinsic to reconciliation, but they need to be understood as distinctive practices. I have defended my position that truth, justice, mercy, and peace frequently coincide to provide some of the best opportunities for reconciliation to emerge. However, there can be nothing contrived about reconciliation, and some of the most interesting stories come about in surprising ways when people are open to new possibilities for reconciliatory spaces to come alive in culturally specific ways. These are creative spaces, emancipatory spaces that signal new beginnings. Stories of reconciliation arise because of the gross evil that people are capable of, yet they only come about because of the generosity of spirit that is intrinsic to human nature. Certainly, reconciliation is a tough ideal, but so too are all the other ethical principles it entails, including equality, human rights, freedom, and justice. Reconciliation needs strong advocates who are willing to engage in long-term processes of building relationships in all stages of peacebuilding. Narratives of peace, justice, and reconciliation express the wonders of human diversity.

Notes

1. Elsewhere, I have suggested that many Timorese have felt that the official line on reconciliation has worked against their active pursuit of justice. See Porter (2012b).

2. This quotation is particularly significant to me because it is on a "Fountain of Tears" sculpture in my hometown of Adelaide, South Australia, on the old site of Colebrook Home, where Indigenous children were kept.

3. John Steward worked with Gasana as a World Vision colleague. He also stresses the "value of healing rituals and telling personal stories" (2008: 171) but claims that speaking of deep pain is not easy, because "the wounds heal slowly" (2008: 187). He argues strongly that time alone is insufficient to heal the deepest wounds because *"only proactive, conscious healing heals"* (2008: 188).

4. I am not eliminating the potential of social media, particularly in peace and justice activism, but I am suggesting that most types of interaction that work toward reconciliation require direct, face-to-face contact.

5. Ray Mullan was program director of the Community Relations Council in Northern Ireland.

6. Clark's research in this publication draws on 459 interviews in the period from 2001 until 2010, when gacaca was completing its final cases.

9

Conclusion

Peace, justice, and reconciliation are connected, although each can exist in a partial sense without the others. Throughout the eight chapters of this volume I have shown that after violent conflict has ceased, there can be moments of peace, but sorting out ceasefires, disarmament, and the regrouping of disparate, once-hostile parties often leaves little time to deal with the pressing needs of deciding appropriate justice measures. Such high-pressure, volatile times offer only limited prospects for reconciliation. In different parts of the world, where peace has held for longer, the situation might differ. During a movement toward transitional justice, new laws are created, new constitutions are formed, and security is restored on the streets. People start to feel safe to return to the markets, mosques, temples, and schools, but one incident may trigger violence again, and the prospect of lasting peace disappears. Elsewhere, reconciliation may be pushed onto people from a transitional justice government that is keen on projecting a reformed image to the international community. While a negative peace might prevail, victims can feel underlying resentment that the pressure to reconcile is coming before justice is realized. Simmering bitterness and remaining feelings of injustice make meaningful reconciliation difficult to achieve. With these realistic qualifiers in mind, what does it really mean to connect peace, justice, and reconciliation? Throughout the book, I have argued that these three principal ideas and practices are connected for two central and interrelated reasons. First, each idea and practice strengthens and reinforces the others. Second, peace, justice, and reconciliation are necessary for sustainable peace to prevail. To conclude, I briefly summarize the arguments made throughout the book and recap the underlying bases to these two interrelated reasons.

Where peace, justice, and reconciliation exist, they build on each other. The route to positive peace, which is a sustainable peace, is to deal with the root causes of conflict. As noted, these causes are historically, geographically, and culturally different. They include fights over territory, resource wars, ethnoreligious antagonisms, corrupt or failing governments, or clashes between rival warlords, clans, rebels, paramilitary groups, or insurgency groups. Many of these basic sources of conflict have long, entrenched histories, so deeply held bitterness, hatred, and animosity take generations to break down. Momentary peace is fragile. Without dealing with these root causes, the slightest reminder of past revenge attacks; ongoing discrimination toward minority ethnic, religious, or political groups; or new triggers of enmity that explode for all sorts of reasons can spark another round of violence. Here we see the need for peace to be connected to justice.

Many of these causes of conflict are rooted in a felt sense of injustice. Injustice experienced in everyday lives is manifest through inequalities, deprivation of human rights, repression, and marginalization, all of which are heightened consequences and regularly are causes of violent conflict. For peace to be sustained, justice is essential. At the root of justice is a notion of fairness—receiving what one is due. As the preamble to the UN Declaration of Human Rights adopted in 1948 says, "Recognition of the inherent dignity and of the equal and inalienable rights of all members of the human family is the foundation of freedom, justice, and peace in the world" (UN General Assembly 1948). The preamble acknowledges that disregard for human rights has resulted in "barbarous acts." It reaffirms the faith of the peoples of the United Nations "in fundamental human rights, in the dignity and worth of the human person, and in equal rights of men and women." The thirty articles that make up this declaration confirm the importance of the fundamental link between peace and justice.

Justice comes in many forms. To reiterate, retributive justice includes legal punishment and accountability and is necessary to make wrongdoers answerable for their wrongdoing and to prevent impunity, where perpetrators of abuse gain license to commit crimes with no responsibility to be accountable for the terrible harms they have caused. Distributive justice aims to distribute social goods and resources in a fair way that does not lead to inequalities, and can include special measures of affirmative action toward those who have been disadvantaged through structural violence. After conflict, reparations are a form of justice to compensate victims for the harms that result from crimes committed against them. The narrative examples used throughout the book mainly focus on restorative justice, the justice that attempts to restore right relations among the remorseful wrongdoer, the wronged person, and the community. Obviously some abuses are so abhorrent that it is inappropriate for the victim to contemplate having any contact with the abuser, because retributive justice is required for serious harms caused. However, in transitional justice contexts, restorative justice, with its traditional, culturally distinctive indigenous practices, increasingly is seeing positive responses that move people toward realizing a sense of justice as well as providing the groundwork for reconciliation to flourish.

Reconciliation is elusive; it is not easy to define, and it is enormously difficult to practice. I noted in Chapter 8 four main ways of understanding reconciliation. First, reconciliation is fundamentally about building or rebuilding workable relationships with diminished degrees of antagonism. Given that differences of ethnic background, religious beliefs, or political ideologies separate opposing parties, breaking down the hostility of differences while respecting the integrity of difference to identity is important. Second, reconciliation is a process that doesn't happen overnight. It is part of the long-term nature of peacebuilding, an ongoing activity. Third, developing a culture of reconciliation, where reconciled relationships become more normal and accepted than fighting ones, increases the chance of peace being sustained. It means that when diverse views are expressed, grounds of trust already exist, so that problematic differences can be worked through dialogically, without resorting to violence. Fourth, reconciliation can occur across a spectrum of possibilities. These range from simple coexistence where people cease to kill each other, but there is minimal change of attitude; to a middle position where relationships are becoming healthier, but distrust still prevails and lies are told surreptitiously to cover the past; to a rare but valuable strong reconciliation, where dialogue is open, mutual respect of differences is granted, and fair relations are the norm.

In the most visible signs of such strong reconciliation, great hope is present for a changed future. People feel secure. However, all transitional justice contexts are fraught with the dual tensions of dealing adequately with the past while seeking to develop a new, just, peaceful future. Terrible issues relating to processing the past do not disappear easily. As the narratives provided in the previous chapters have shown, the past has a strong influence on who we are in the present. When the past has been dominated by war, violent conflict, and terrible abuses, any processing of the past is traumatic and takes time. However, in this idealistic transformed period where strong reconciliation exists, stories about trauma, loss, pain, and grief are listened to respectfully, even when the narrative that emerges seems starkly different from the one the listener experiences. Differences between the speaker and listener can be acknowledged as being important to different ethnoreligious, cultural, and political forms of identity, and as needing to be mutually respected. Support services for those who are still suffering are provided, and as we have seen, the range of support needed is vast, given that attention to particular needs is required.

I continue to paint an optimistic picture of what can happen when peace and justice merge with a durable form of reconciliation. Again, I reiterate, we should not be naïve about how difficult arriving at this position really is. I have repeatedly acknowledged the enormous obstacles that need to be overcome to even get close to this position. The reason I paint this picture is to keep the moral imagination alive in envisaging what transformed transitional justice communities might look like. In these communities, shame and guilt for the acts committed or sustained may remain, but the provision of truth commissions, trials, amnesties, community reconciliation procedures, and community support groups assist the telling and the witnessing of the stories behind the reasons for these powerful, crippling emotions. In such contexts, the telling of truthful stories is powerful.

Yet as explained, the deliberate withholding of stories is sometimes crucial to personal dignity, to ensure the safety of one's own life or the lives of loved ones, or even to keep a peace process alive. Self-chosen silence is particularly important for rape victims. Many women choose to be silent on the abuse suffered, which differs from the oppression of being silenced. It is a way to retain self-respect. Memories remain. Many memories are nightmares. Deliberate forgetting helps some people. Others can live with terrible memories if there is a promise of a liberating future. Actual signs of sociopolitical change are needed to sustain the promises made by politicians, many of whom were formerly engaged in the violence of the previous era. Both top-down and bottom-up social and political change is needed. For others, speaking and being listened to, as well as listening and recognizing differences, are ways to build trust and to overcome fear of the other. Trust often develops in formal contexts, through meeting together around a negotiating table or in seeing formally opposed parties who are willing to make some political compromise for the sake of the common good. Other times, trust develops informally, through sharing stories of the past conflict and trauma, and hope for the new revisioned future.

As part of these new practices in a commendable transitional justice context, the acknowledgment of wrongdoing plays a massive symbolic role in breaking down inevitable intransigence that occurs in peace processes. Similarly, offering an apology for harms caused is a powerful indication of a willingness to make amends and begin to engage with the demanding consequences of reconciliation. Those who have suffered choose whether to forgive. Some can't. Others find enormous release in forgiving and, to some degree, letting go of the stranglehold of the past. We are all vulnerable humans. Accepting the responsibility of caring for others, given our common humanity, leads to the unexpected—that compassion can be practiced in postconflict and transitional justice contexts through responding appropriately to the practical, spiritual, and psychological requirements that emerge from listening and paying attention to sufferers' stories. Sufferers' needs are varied and vast and may include at least the following: emotional counsel, trauma healing, HIV/AIDS medication, health services (including maternity assistance), and the acquisition of literacy skills and education. In some cases, destroyed huts or houses may need rebuilding, and care needs to be extended to orphans, widows, widowers, and those maimed through war. In other cases, there may be a need for reparations, or for prisoners, combatants, or displaced persons to be reintegrated into local communities. Compassion is more than an emotion; it requires a response.

Throughout the book, in connecting peace, justice, and reconciliation, I have used a narrative understanding of the self to highlight the importance of heeding particular stories that are told in conflict and postconflict contexts, particularly those environments that are making progress in their transitional justice processes. In prioritizing what happens to people in violent encounters, we have seen the real human costs of conflict. Thus, repeatedly, I have maintained that responding to human security needs is of paramount importance in transitional justice strategies. Responses require giving attention to gender, age, culture, geographic location, and all the distinctive ways that maximizing human security has specific cultural requirements. As we have seen in the previous eight chapters, there are many hurdles to overcome in realizing what can emerge when peace, justice, and reconciliation interconnect. I have sought to avoid painting an overly rosy picture of these connections. War is a terrible evil. Violent conflict destroys so much of what is good in humanity. However, I wanted to highlight positive stories that demonstrate how people's lives are transformed through telling their versions of the truth, developing trust with previous enemies, apologizing to those they have wronged, forgiving those who have wronged them, and receiving or giving compassion after listening to stories or being heard. Our individual, group, and national narratives are complex and fascinating. The challenge to continue working toward connecting peace, justice, and reconciliation remains. It is a demanding challenge, but one that is truly worthy of pursuit if a sustainable and meaningful peace is to become a reality.

References

Abbott, H. Porter. 2008. *The Cambridge Introduction to Narrative*, 2nd ed. Cambridge: Cambridge University Press.

Abe, Toshihiro. 2012. "Reconciliation as Process or Catalyst: Understanding the Concept in a Post-Conflict Society." *Comparative Sociology* 11: 785–814.

Acorn, Annalise. 2004. *Compulsory Compassion: A Critique of Restorative Justice*. Vancouver: University of British Columbia Press.

Aiken, Nevin T. 2010. "Learning to Live Together: Transitional Justice and Intergroup Reconciliation in Northern Ireland." *International Journal of Transitional Justice* 4(2): 166–188.

Allan, Pierre, and Alexis Keller. 2006. "The Concept of Just Peace, or Achieving Peace through Recognition, Renouncement, and Rule." In *What Is a Just Peace?* Ed. Pierre Allan and Alexis Keller. Oxford: Oxford University Press, 195–215.

Ambos, Kai. 2010. "The Legal Framework of Transitional Justice: A Systematic Study with a Special Focus on the Role of the ICC." In *Building a Future on Peace and Justice: Studies on Transitional Justice, Peace and Development*. Ed. Kai Ambos, Judith Large, and Marieke Wierda. Heidelberg: Springer-Verlag, 19–103.

Amstutz, Mark R. 2005. *The Healing of Nations: The Promise and Limits of Political Forgiveness*. Lanham, MD: Rowman and Littlefield.

Anderlini, Sanam Naraghi. 2007. *Women Building Peace: What They Do, Why It Matters*. Boulder, CO: Lynne Rienner Publishers.

Andrieu, Kora. 2009. "'Sorry for the Genocide': How Public Apologies Can Help Promote National Reconciliation." *Millennium—Journal of International Studies* 38(3): 3–23.

Apiyo, Nancy. 2012. "Ododo Wa: Our Stories." *Voices Magazine* 2 (October 24, 2012). http://justiceandreconciliation.com/2012/10/ododo-wa-our-stories/, accessed December 18, 2012.

Arendt, Hannah. 1973. *Men in Dark Times*. Harmondsworth: Penguin.

———. 1974. *The Human Condition*, 9th ed. Chicago: University of Chicago Press.

Aristotle. 1977. *The Nichomachean Ethics*. Trans. J. A. K. Thomson. London: Penguin Books.

Assefa, Hizkias. 2005. "Reconciliation: Challenges, Responses, and the Role of Civil Society." In *People Building Peace II: Successful Stories of Civil Society*. Ed. Paul van Tongeren, Malin Brenk, Marte Hellema, and Juliette Verhoeven. Boulder, CO: Lynne Rienner Publishers, 637–644.

Atran, Scott. 2010. *Talking to the Enemy: Violent Extremism, Sacred Values, and What It Means to Be Human*. London: Allen Lane.

Australian Human Rights Commission. 2013. *Asylum Seekers, Refugees, and Human Rights: Snapshot Report 2013*. Canberra: Commonwealth of Australia.

Babic, Jovan. 2000. "Justifying Forgiveness." *Peace Review* 12: 87–93.

Bachelard, Michael. 2012. "Confessions of a Bali Bomber." *The Age*, September 20, 2012.

Barrowclough, Nikki. 2012. "Interview: Hisham Matar." *Sydney Morning Herald*, May 12–13, 2012.

Bar-Tal, Daniel, and Gemma H. Bennink. 2004. "The Nature of Reconciliation as an Outcome and as a Process." In *From Conflict Resolution to Reconciliation*. Ed. Yaacov Bar-Siman-Tov. Oxford: Oxford University Press, 11–38.

Bastick, Megan, Karin Grimm, and Rahel Kunz. 2007. *Sexual Violence in Armed Conflict: Global Overview and Implications for the Security Sector*. Geneva: Geneva Centre for the Democratic Control of Armed Forces.

Baxi, Upendra. 1999. "Voices of Suffering, Fragmented Universality, and the Future of Human Rights." In *The Future of International Human Rights*. Ed. Burns Weston and Stephen Marks. New York: Transnational Publishers, 101–156.

Behuria, Radhika, and Nicola Williams. 2012. *Women's Perspectives of Peace and Security*. Bangkok: UNDP Asia Pacific Regional Centre.

Bekerman, Zvi, and Michalinos Zembylas. 2012. *Teaching Contested Narratives: Identity, Memory and Reconciliation in Peace Education and Beyond*. Cambridge: Cambridge University Press.

Benhabib, Seyla. 1992. *Situating the Self: Gender, Community and Postmodernism in Contemporary Ethics*. Cambridge: Polity Press.

———. 2005. *The Rights of Others: Aliens, Residents, and Citizens*. Cambridge: Cambridge University Press.

Bennett, Olivia, Jo Bexley, and Kitty Warnock. 1995. *Arms to Fight, Arms to Protect: Women Speak Out about Conflict*. London: Panos.

Berdal, Mats. 2009. *Building Peace after War*. London: International Institute for Strategic Studies.

Bernstein, Richard J. 2006. "Derrida: The Aporia of Forgiveness?" *Constellations* 13(3): 394–406.

Bhargava, Rajeev. 2012. "The Difficulty of Reconciliation." *Philosophy and Social Criticism* 38(4–5): 369–377.

Biggar, Nigel. 2003. *Burying the Past: Making Peace and Doing Justice after Civil Conflict*. Washington, DC: Georgetown University Press.

———. 2011. "Melting the Icepacks of Enmity: Forgiveness and Reconciliation in Northern Ireland." *Studies in Christian Ethics* 24(2): 199–209.

Bishop, Peter. 2009. "To Witness and Remember: Mapping Reconciliation Travel." In *Travel Writing, Form, and Empire: The Poetics and Politics of Mobility.* Ed. Julia Kuehn and Paul Smethurst. New York: Routledge, 180–198.

Bitek, Juliane Okot. 2012. "A Chronology of Compassion, or Towards an Imperfect Future." *International Journal of Transitional Justice* 6: 394–403.

Bloch, Corinne. 2005. "Listen to Understand: The Listening Project in Croatia." In *People Building Peace II: Successful Stories of Civil Society.* Ed. Paul van Tongeren, Malin Brenk, Marte Hellema, and Juliette Verhoeven. Boulder, CO: Lynne Rienner Publishers, 654–660.

Boege, Volker. 2009. "Peacebuilding and State Formation in Post-Conflict Bougainville." *Peace Review* 21(1): 29–37.

Bolten, Catherine E. 2012. *I Did It to Save My Life: Love and Survival in Sierra Leone.* Berkeley: University of California Press.

Booth, Ken. 1999. "Three Tyrannies." In *Human Rights in Global Politics.* Ed. Tim Dunne and Nicholas Wheeler. Cambridge: Cambridge University Press, 31–70.

Boraine, Alex. 2000. *A Country Unmasked: Inside South Africa's Truth and Reconciliation Commission.* Oxford: Oxford University Press.

———. 2005. "Transitional Justice." In *Making States Work: State Failure and the Crisis of Governance.* Ed. Simon Chesterman, Michael Ignatieff, and Ramesh Thakur. Tokyo: UN University Press, 318–338.

Borneman, John. 2002. "Reconciliation after Ethnic Cleansing: Listening, Retribution, Affiliation." *Public Culture* 14(2): 281–304.

Boulding, Elise. 2000. *Cultures of Peace: The Hidden Side of History.* Syracuse, NY: Syracuse University Press.

———. 2002. "Peace Culture." In *Toward a Compassionate Society.* Ed. Hahnaz Afkhami. Bethesda, MD: Women's Learning Partnership, 8–15.

Boulding, Kenneth. 1978. *Stable Peace.* Austin: University of Texas Press.

Boutros-Ghali, Boutros. 1992. *An Agenda for Peace: Preventive Democracy, Peacemaking and Peacekeeping.* New York: United Nations.

———. 1995. *Supplement to An Agenda for Peace: Position Paper of the Secretary-General on the Fiftieth Anniversary of the United Nations.* A/50/60/-S/1995/1. January 3. New York: United Nations.

Brahimi, Lakhdar. 2000. *Report on Peace Operations*, A/55/305-A/2000/809. New York: United Nations.

Brookings Institution. 2013. *Iraq Index: Tracking Variables of Reconstruction and Security in Iraq.* July 2013, http://www.brookings.edu/~/media/Centers/saban/iraq%20index/index20130726.pdf, accessed September 15, 2013.

Brounéus, Karen. 2010. "The Trauma of Truth Telling: Effects of Witnessing in the Rwandan Gacaca Courts on Psychological Health." *Journal of Conflict Resolution* 54(3): 408–437.

Brown, A. Widney, and Farhat Bokhari. 2001. "Afghanistan: Humanity Denied—Systematic Violations of Women's Rights in Afghanistan." *Human Rights Watch* 13(5): 1–25.

Brown, Kris. 2012. "'What It Was Like to Live Through a Day': Transitional Justice and the Memory of the Everyday in a Divided Society." *International Journal of Transitional Justice* 6: 444–466.

Brudholm, Thomas. 2006. "Revisiting Resentments: Jean Améry and the Dark Side of Forgiveness and Reconciliation." *Journal of Human Rights* 5(1): 7–26.

Brudholm, Thomas, and Arne Grøn. 2011. "Picturing Forgiveness after Atrocity." *Studies in Christian Ethics* 24(2): 159–170.

Buckley-Zistal, Susanne. 2006. "Remembering to Forget." *Journal of the International African Institute* 76(2): 131–150.

———. 2008. "We Are Pretending Peace: Local Memory and the Absence of Social Transformation and Reconciliation in Rwanda." In *After Genocide: Transitional Justice, Post-Conflict Reconstruction and Reconciliation in Rwanda and Beyond.* Ed. Phil Clark and Zachary D. Kaufman. London: Hurst, 125–143.

Burgess, Patrick. 2008. "Community Reconciliation in East Timor: A Personal Perspective." In *Pathways to Reconciliation: Between Theory and Practice.* Ed. Philipa Rothfield, Cleo Fleming, and Paul A. Komesaroff. Aldershot: Ashgate, 139–148.

Butler, Judith. 2009. *Frames of War: When Is Life Grievable?* London: Verso.

Cahn, Naomi, Dina Haynes, and Fionnuala Ní Aoláin. 2010. "Returning Home: Women in Post-Conflict Societies." *University of Baltimore Law Review* 39(3): 339–369.

Calhoun, Craig. 2008. "The Imperative to Reduce Suffering: Charity, Progress, and Emergencies in the Field of Humanitarian Action." In *Humanitarianism in Question: Politics, Power, Ethics.* Ed. Michael Barnett and Thomas G. Weiss. Ithaca, NY: Cornell University Press, 73–97.

Call, Charles. 2008. "Ending Wars, Building States." In *Building States to Build Peace.* Ed. Charles Call with Vanessa Wyeth. Boulder, CO: Lynne Rienner Publishers, 1–22.

Card, Claudia. 2004. "The Atrocity Paradigm Revisited." *Hypatia* 19(4): 212–222.

CAVR. 2005. *Chega! Final Report of the Commission for Reception, Truth and Reconciliation in East Timor (CAVR).* www.etan.org/news/2006/cavr.htm, accessed August 7, 2012.

Chan, Stephen. 2005. *Out of Evil: New International Politics and Our Doctrines of War.* London: I. B. Tauris.

Chayes, Antonio, and Martha Minow, eds. 2003. *Imagine Coexistence: Restoring Humanity after Violent Ethnic Conflict.* San Francisco: Jossey-Bass.

Clark, Janine N. 2011. "Transitional Justice, Truth, and Reconciliation: An Under-Explored Relationship." *International Criminal Law Review* 11(2): 241–261.

Clark, Phil. 2008a. "Establishing a Conceptual Framework: Six Key Transitional Justice Themes." In *After Genocide: Transitional Justice, Post-Conflict Reconstruction, and Reconciliation in Rwanda and Beyond.* Ed. Phil Clark and Zachary D. Kaufman. London: Hurst, 191–205.

———. 2008b. "The Rules (and Politics) of Engagement: The Gacaca Courts and Post-Genocide Justice, Healing, and Reconciliation in Rwanda." In *After Genocide: Transitional Justice, Post-Conflict Reconstruction, and Reconciliation in Rwanda and Beyond.* Ed. Phil Clark and Zachary D. Kaufman. London: Hurst, 297–319.

———. 2010. *The Gacaca Courts, Post-Genocide Justice, and Reconciliation in Rwanda: Justice without Lawyers*. Cambridge: Cambridge University Press.

Cobb, Sara. 2003. "Fostering Coexistence in Identity-Based Conflicts: Toward a Narrative Approach." In *Imagine Coexistence: Restoring Humanity after Violent Ethnic Conflict*. Ed. Antonia Chayes and Martha Minow. San Francisco: Jossey-Bass, 294–310.

———. 2013. *Speaking of Violence: The Politics and Poetics of Narrative Dynamics in Conflict Resolution*. Oxford: Oxford University Press.

Cockburn, Cynthia. 2004. *The Line: Women, Partition and the Gender Order in Cyprus*. London: Zed Books.

Copelon, Rhonda. 2000. "Gender Crimes as War Crimes: Integrating Crimes against Women into International Criminal Law." *McGill Law Journal* 46: 217–240.

Crocker, David A. 2003. "Reckoning with Past Wrongs: A Normative Framework." In *Dilemmas of Reconciliation: Cases and Concepts*. Ed. Carol A. L. Prager and Trudy Govier. Waterloo, Ontario: Wilfred Laurier University Press, 39–64.

Dallaire, Roméo. 2004. *Shake Hands with the Devil: The Failure of Humanity in Rwanda*. London: Arrow Books.

DasGupta, Sumona, and Meenakshi Gopinath. 2005. "Women Breaking the Silence: The Athwaas Initiative in Kashmir." In *People Building Peace II: Successful Stories of Civil Society*. Ed. Paul van Tongeren, Malin Brenk, Marte Hellema, and Juliette Verhoeven. Boulder, CO: Lynne Rienner Publishers, 111–116.

D'Costa, Bina. 2006. "Marginalized Identity: New Frontiers of Research for International Relations?" In *Feminist Methodologies for International Relations*. Ed. Brooke A. Ackerly, Maria Stern, and Jacqui True. Cambridge: Cambridge University Press, 129–152.

Derrida, Jacques. 2002. *On Cosmopolitanism and Forgiveness*. Routledge: London.

Digeser, P. E. 2001. *Political Forgiveness*. Ithaca, NY: Cornell University Press.

Dillon, Robin S. 2001. "Self-Forgiveness and Self-Respect." *Ethics* 112: 53–83.

Dwyer, Susan. 1999. "Reconciliation for Realists." *Ethics and International Affairs* 13: 81–98.

Eastmond, Marita, and Johanna Mannergren Selimovic. 2012. "Silence as Possibility in Postwar Everyday Life." *International Journal of Transitional Justice* 6: 502–524.

Eisenstein, Zillah. 1996. *Hatreds: Racialized and Sexualized Conflicts in the 21st Century*. London: Routledge.

El-Bushra, Judy. 2000. "Transforming Conflict: Some Thoughts on a Gendered Understanding of Conflict Processes." In *States of Conflict: Gender, Violence and Resistance*. Ed. Susie Jacobs, Ruth Jacobsen, and Jennifer Marchbank. London: Zed Books, 66–86.

El Jack, Amani. 2003. *Gender and Armed Conflict*. Brighton: University of Sussex, BRIDGE Institute of Development Studies.

Elshtain, Jean Bethke. 1998. *New Wine and Old Bottles: International Politics and Ethical Discourse*. Notre Dame, IN: University of Notre Dame Press.

Erskine, Toni. 2008. *Embedded Cosmopolitanism: Duties to Strangers and Enemies in a World of "Dislocated Communities."* Oxford: Oxford University Press.

Evans, Gareth. 2008. *The Responsibility to Protect: Ending Mass Atrocity Crimes Once and for All.* Washington, DC: Brookings Institution.

Farah, Ahmed Yusuf, and Ioan Myrddin Lewis. 1995. *Somalia: The Roots of Reconciliation.* London: Action Aid.

Ferguson, Neil, Mark Burgess, and Ian Hollywood. 2010. "Who Are the Victims? Victimhood Experiences in Post-Agreement Northern Ireland." *Political Psychology* 31(6): 857–886.

Freeman, Mark, and Priscilla B. Hayner. 2003. "Truth-Telling." In *Reconciliation after Violent Conflict: A Handbook.* Ed. David Bloomfield, Teresa Barnes, and Luc Huyse. Stockholm: International Institute for Democracy and Electoral Assistance, 122–139.

Gadamer, Hans-Georg. 1976. *Philosophical Hermeneutics.* Berkeley: University of California Press.

Galtung, Johan. 1964. "An Editorial." *Journal of Peace Research* 1(1): 1–4.

———. 2004. "The Security Approach and the Peace Approach: Some Cultural Factors Conditioning the Choice." World Culture Open, UN Meeting, Building Peace through Harmonious Diversity, October 9.

Garcia, Ed. 2004. "Empowering People to Build a Just Peace in the Asian Arena." In *Searching for Peace in Asia Pacific: An Overview of Conflict Prevention and Peacebuilding Activities.* Ed. Annelies Heijmans, Nicola Simmonds, and Hans van de Veen. Boulder, CO: Lynne Rienner Publishers, 23–36.

Gasana, Solomon Nsabiyera. 2008. "Confronting Conflict and Poverty through Trauma Healing: Integrating Peacebuilding and Development Processes in Rwanda." In *After Genocide: Transitional Justice, Post-Conflict Reconstruction, and Reconciliation in Rwanda and Beyond.* Ed. Phil Clark and Zachary D. Kaufman. London: Hurst, 145–169.

Gbowee, Leymah. 2011. "Nobel Lecture." Oslo, December 10. www.nobelprize.org/nobel_prizes/peace/laureates/2011/gbowee-lecture_en.html, accessed December 6, 2012.

Gibson, James L. 2004. "Does Truth Lead to Reconciliation? Testing the Causal Assumptions of the South African Truth and Reconciliation Process." *American Journal of Political Science* 48(2): 201–217.

Gilligan, Carol. 1987. "Moral Orientation and Moral Development." In *Women and Moral Theory.* Ed. Eva Feder Kittay and Diana T. Meyers. Totowa, NJ: Rowman and Littlefield, 19–33.

Gilmore, Leigh. 2005. "Autobiography's Wounds." In *Just Advocacy? Women's Human Rights, Transnational Feminisms, and the Politics of Representation.* Ed. Wendy S. Hesford and Wendy Kozol. New Brunswick, NJ: Rutgers University Press, 99–119.

Glasius, Marlies, and Mary Kaldor. 2006. "A Human Security Vision for Europe and Beyond." In *A Human Security Doctrine for Europe: Project, Principle, Practicalities.* Ed. M. Glasius and M. Kaldor. London: Routledge, 3–19.

Gobodo-Madikizela, Pumla. 2002. "Remorse, Forgiveness, and Rehumanization: Stories from South Africa." *Journal of Humanistic Psychology* 42(1): 7–32.

————. 2003. *The Human Being Died That Night: A South African Story of Forgiveness*. New York: Houghton Mifflin.

————. 2005. *Women's Contribution to South Africa's Truth and Reconciliation Commission*. New York: Hunt Alternatives Fund.

————. 2008a. "Trauma, Forgiveness, and the Witnessing Dance: Making Public Spaces Intimate." *Journal of Analytical Psychology* 53: 169–188.

————. 2008b. "Empathetic Repair after Mass Trauma: When Vengeance Is Arrested." *European Journal of Social Theory* 11(3): 331–350.

Goldblatt, Beth, and Sheila Meintjes. 1998. "South African Women Demand the Truth." In *What Women Do in Wartime: Gender and Conflict in Africa*. Ed. Meredith Turshen and Clotilde Twagiramariya. London: Zed Books, 27–61.

Goldstone, Richard J. 1996. "Justice as a Tool for Peace-Making: Truth Commissions and International Criminal Tribunals." *New York University Journal of International Law and Politics* 28(3): 485–503.

Gould, Carol. 2004. *Globalizing Democracy and Human Rights*. Cambridge: Cambridge University Press.

Govier, Trudy. 2002. *Forgiveness and Revenge*. London: Routledge.

————. 2003. "What Is Acknowledgment and Why Is It Important?" In *Dilemmas of Reconciliation: Cases and Concepts*. Ed. Carol A. L. Prager and Trudy Govier. Waterloo, Ontario: Wilfred Laurier University Press, 65–90.

————. 2006. *Taking Wrongs Seriously: Acknowledgment, Reconciliation, and the Politics of Sustainable Peace*. New York: Humanity Books.

————. 2009. "A Dialectic of Acknowledgment." In *Reconciliation(s): Transitional Justice in Postconflict Societies*. Ed. Joanna R. Quinn. Montreal: McGill-Queen's University Press, 36–50.

Govier, Trudy, and Colin Hirano. 2008. "A Conception of Invitational Forgiveness." *Journal of Social Philosophy* 39(3): 429–444.

Govier, Trudy, and Wilhelm Verwoerd. 2004. "How Not to Polarize 'Victims' and 'Perpetrators.'" *Peace Review* 16(3): 371–377.

Gusmão, Kay Rala Xanana. 2005. "Personal Story: 'A Vital Force.'" In *People Building Peace II: Successful Stories of Civil Society*. Ed. Paul van Tongeren, Malin Brenk, Marte Hellema, and Juliette Verhoeven. Boulder, CO: Lynne Rienner Publishers, 25–27.

Gutmann, A. 1992. "Introduction." In *Multiculturalism and "The Politics of Recognition."* Ed. Charles Taylor. Princeton, NJ: Princeton University Press, 3–24.

Habel, Norman C. 1999. *Reconciliation: Searching for Australia's Soul*. Sydney: HarperCollins.

Hadjipavlou, Maria. 2007. "Multiple Stories: The 'Crossings' as Part of Citizens' Reconciliation Efforts in Cyprus." *Innovation: The European Journal of Social Sciences* 20(1): 53–73.

Halpern, Jodie, and Harvey M. Weinstein. 2004. "Rehumanizing the Other: Empathy and Reconciliation." *Human Rights Quarterly* 26: 561–583.

Hamber, Brandon, and Gráinne Kelly. 2009. "Beyond Coexistence: Towards a Work in Definition of Reconciliation." In *Reconciliation(s): Transitional Justice in Postconflict Societies*. Ed. Joanna R. Quinn. Montreal: McGill-Queen's University Press, 286–310.

Harris Rimmer, Susan. 2010. *Gender and Transitional Justice: The Women of East Timor.* London: Routledge.

Hauss, Charles. 2010. *International Conflict Resolution*, 2nd ed. New York: Continuum.

Hayner, Priscilla B. 2011. *Unspeakable Truths: Transitional Justice and the Challenge of Truth Commissions*, 2nd ed. New York: Routledge.

Heleta, Savo. 2008. *Not My Turn to Die: Memoirs of a Broken Childhood in Bosnia*, 2nd ed. Saranac Lake, NY: AMACOM Books.

Hermann, Tamar. 2004. "Reconciliation: Reflections on the Theoretical and Practical Utility of the Term." In *From Conflict Resolution to Reconciliation.* Ed. Yaacov Bar-Siman-Tov. Oxford: Oxford University Press, 39–60.

Hewitt, J. Joseph, Jonathan Wilkenfeld, and Ted Robert Gurr. 2012. *Peace and Conflict 2012: Executive Summary.* College Park: University of Maryland Press.

Hoogensen, Gunhild, and Kirsti Stuvøy. 2006. "Gender, Resistance, and Human Security." *Security Dialogue* 37: 207–228.

Howley, Pat. 2002. *Breaking Spears and Mending Hearts: Peacemakers and Restorative Justice in Bougainville.* London: Zed Books.

Hudson, Heidi. 2005. "'Doing' Security as Though Humans Matter: A Feminist Perspective on Gender and the Politics of Human Security." *Security Dialogue* 36(2): 155–174.

Huggins, Jackie. 2008. "The Human Face of Indigenous Australia." In *Pathways to Reconciliation: Between Theory and Practice.* Ed. Philipa Rothfield, Cleo Fleming, and Paul A. Komesaroff. Aldershot: Ashgate, xiii–xvi.

Humphrey, Michael. 2002. *The Politics of Atrocity and Reconciliation: From Terror to Trauma.* London: Routledge.

Hutchinson, Emma, and Roland Bleiker. 2008. "Emotional Reconciliation: Reconstituting Identity and Community after Trauma." *European Journal of Social Theory* 11(3): 385–402.

Huyse, Luc. 2003. "Justice," In *Reconciliation after Violent Conflict: A Handbook.* Ed. David Bloomfield, Teresa Barnes, and Luc Huyse, Stockholm: International Institute for Democracy and Electoral Assistance, 97–115.

Ignatieff, Michael. 1993. *Blood and Belonging: Journeys into the New Nationalism.* London: Chatto and Windus.

Jabri, Vivienne. 1996. *Discourses on Violence: Conflict Analysis Reconsidered.* Manchester: Manchester University Press.

James, Paul. 2008. "Reconciliation: From the Usually Unspoken to the Almost Unimaginable." In *Pathways to Reconciliation: Between Theory and Practice.* Ed. Philipa Rothfield, Cleo Fleming, and Paul A. Komesaroff. Aldershot: Ashgate, 115–125.

Jenkins, Rob. 2013. *Peacebuilding: From Concept to Commission.* London: Routledge.

Joya, Malalai. 2009. *Raising My Voice.* Sydney: Pan Macmillan Australia.

Justice and Reconciliation Project. 2012. "Who Forgives Whom? Northern Uganda's Grassroots Views on the Amnesty Act." Policy Brief (June): 1–8. http://justiceandreconciliation.com/wp-content/uploads/2012/06/JRP-Amnesty-Policy-Brief-FINAL1.pdf, accessed January 2, 2013.

Kalayjian, Ani. 2010. "Forgiveness in Spite of Denial, Revisionism, and Injustice." In *Forgiveness and Reconciliation: Psychological Pathways to Conflict Transformation and Peacebuilding*. Ed. Ani Kalayjian and Raymond Paloutzian. Heidelberg: Springer, 237–249.

Kaldor, Mary. 1991."Rethinking Cold War History." In *New Thinking about Strategy and International Security*. Ed. Ken Booth. London: Harper Collins Academic, 313–331.

———. 2007. *Human Security: Reflections on Globalization and Intervention*. Cambridge: Polity Press.

Käpylä, Juha, and Denis Kennedy. 2014. "Cruel to Care? Investigating the Governance of Compassion in the Humanitarian Imaginary." *International Theory* 6(2): 255–292.

Kashyap, Rina. 2009. "Narrative and Truth: A Feminist Critique of the South African Truth and Reconciliation Commission." *Contemporary Justice Review* 12(4): 449–467.

Kaufman, Edward. 2005. "Dialogue-Based Processes: A Vehicle for Peacebuilding." In *People Building Peace II: Successful Stories of Civil Society*. Ed. Paul van Tongeren, Malin Brenk, Marte Hellema, and Juliette Verhoeven. Boulder, CO: Lynne Rienner Publishers, 473–487.

Kaufman, Zachary. 2010. "The Nuremberg Tribunal v. the Tokyo Tribunal: Designs, Staffs, and Operations." *John Marshall Law Review* 43(2): 753–768.

Kayigamba, Jean Baptise. 2008. "Without Justice, No Reconciliation: A Survivor's Experience of Genocide." In *After Genocide: Transitional Justice, Post-Conflict Reconstruction, and Reconciliation*. Ed. Phil Clark and Zachary Kaufman. London: Hurst, 33–42.

Kegley, Charles W., with Shannon L. Blanton. 2010. *World Politics: Trend and Transformation*, 12th ed. Boston: Wadsworth.

Kelman, Herbert C. 2005. "Building Trust among Enemies: The Central Challenge for International Conflict Resolution." *International Journal of Intercultural Relations* 29(6): 639–650.

———. 2010. "Looking Back at My Work on Conflict Resolution in the Middle East." *Peace and Conflict* 16(4): 361–387.

Kelsall, Tim. 2005. "Truth, Lies, Ritual: Preliminary Reflections on the Truth and Reconciliation Commission in Sierra Leone." *Human Rights Quarterly* 27(2): 361–391.

Kerr, Rachel, and Eirin Mobekk. 2007. *Peace and Justice: Seeking Accountability after War*. Cambridge: Polity.

Kleck, Monika. 2006. "Working with Traumatized Women." In *Peacebuilding a Civil Society in Bosnia-Herzegovina: Ten Years after Dayton*. Ed. Martina Fischer. Berlin: LIT Verlag, 343–355.

Kohen, Ari. 2009. "The Personal and the Political: Forgiveness and Reconciliation in Restorative Justice." *Critical Review of International Social and Political Philosophy* 12(3): 399–423.

Komesaroff, Paul. 2008. "Pathways to Reconciliation: Bringing Diverse Voices into Conversation." In *Pathways to Reconciliation: Between Theory and Practice*. Ed. Philipa Rothfield, Cleo Fleming, and Paul Komesaroff. Aldershot: Ashgate, 1–14.

Kreiswirth, Martin. 2005. "Narrative Turn in Humanities." In *Routledge Encyclopaedia of Narrative Theory*. Ed. David Herman, Manfred Jahn, and Marie-Laura Ryan. London: Routledge, 377–382.

Krog, Antjie. 1999. *Country of My Skull*. London: Jonathan Cape.

———. 2001. "Locked into Loss and Silence: Testimonies of Gender and Violence at the South Africa Truth Commission." In *Victims, Perpetrators, or Actors? Gender, Armed Conflict, and Political Violence*. Ed. Caroline Moser and Fiona Clark. London: Zed Books, 203–216.

Kurhasani, Valon. 2005. "Young Kosovars Help Themselves: The Kosovar Youth Council." In *People Building Peace II: Successful Stories of Civil Society*. Ed. Paul van Tongeren, Malin Brenk, Marte Hellema, and Juliette Verhoeven. Boulder, CO: Lynne Rienner Publishers, 167–173.

La Caze, Marguerite. 2006. "The Asymmetry between Apology and Forgiveness." *Contemporary Political Theory* 5(4): 447–468.

Langer, Lawrence. 1991. *Holocaust Testimonies: The Ruins of Memory*. New Haven, CT: Yale University Press.

Lapsley, Michael. 1998. "Confronting the Past and Creating the Future: The Redemptive Value of Truth Telling." *Social Research* 65: 741–758.

———. 2012. *Redeeming the Past: My Journey from Freedom Fighter to Healer*. Maryknoll, NY: Orbis Books.

Lederach, John Paul. 2004. *Building Peace: Sustainable Reconciliation in Divided Societies*. Washington, DC: United States Institute of Peace Press.

———. 2005. *The Moral Imagination: The Art and Soul of Building Peace*. Oxford: Oxford University Press.

———. 2008. "Cultivating Peace: A Practitioner's View of Deadly Conflict and Negotiation." In *Contemporary Peacemaking: Conflict, Peace Processes, and Post-War Reconstruction*, 2nd ed. Ed. John Darby and Roger MacGinty. New York: Palgrave MacMillan, 36–44.

Lederach, John Paul, and Scott R. Appleby. 2010. "Strategic Peacebuilding: An Overview." In *Strategies of Peace: Transforming Conflict in a Violent World*. Ed. Daniel Philpott and Gerard F. Powers. Oxford: Oxford University Press, 19–44.

Lederach, John Paul, and Angela Jill Lederach. 2010. *When Blood and Bones Cry Out: Journeys through the Soundscape of Healing and Reconciliation*. St. Lucia: University of Queensland Press.

Lemarchand, René. 2008. "The Politics of Memory in Post-Genocide Rwanda." In *After Genocide: Transitional Justice, Post-Conflict Reconstruction, and Reconciliation in Rwanda and Beyond*. Ed. Phil Clark and Zachary D. Kaufman. London: Hurst, 65–76.

Little, Adrian. 2011. "Disjunctured Narratives: Rethinking Reconciliation and Conflict Transformation." *International Political Science Review* 33(1): 82–98.

Lopez, George. 2009. "Dynamics Affecting Conflict, Justice, and Peace." In *Peace, Justice, and Security Studies: A Curriculum Guide*. Ed. Timothy McElwee, B. Welling Hall, Joseph Liechty, and Julie Garber. Boulder, CO: Lynne Rienner Publishers, 91–102.

Lu, Catherine. 2006. *Just and Unjust Interventions in World Politics*. New York: Palgrave Macmillan.

Luke, Hanabeth. 2012. *Shock Waves: Finding Peace after the Bali Bomb.* United States: Hanabeth.

Mack, Andrew, ed. 2005. *Human Security Report 2005: War and Peace in the 21st Century.* New York: Oxford University Press.

Mackenzie, Catriona. 2008a. "Imagination, Identity, and Self-Transformation." In *Practical Identity and Narrative Agency.* Ed. Catriona Mackenzie and Kim Atkins. Routledge: New York, 121–145.

———. 2008b. "Introduction: Practical Identity and Narrative Agency." In *Practical Identity and Narrative Agency.* Ed. Catriona Mackenzie and Kim Atkins. Routledge: New York, 1–28.

Maclellan, Nic. 2004."Regional Introduction: Creating Peace in the Pacific— Conflict Resolution, Reconciliation, and Restorative Justice." In *Searching for Peace in Asia Pacific: An Overview of Conflict Prevention and Peace-building Activities.* Ed. Annelies Heijmans, Nicola Simmonds, and Hans van de Veen. Boulder, CO: Lynne Rienner Publishers, 526–542.

Maguire, Peter. 2005. *Facing Death in Cambodia.* New York: Columbia University Press.

Maiese, Michelle. 2003. "What It Means to Build a Lasting Peace." *Beyond Intractability.* www2.beyondintractability.org/m/peacebuilding.jsp, accessed December 5, 2005.

Mamdani, M. 2001. *When Victims Become Killers: Colonialism, Nativism, and the Genocide in Rwanda.* Princeton, NJ: Princeton University Press.

Mani, Rama. 2005. "Balancing Peace with Justice in the Aftermath of Violent Conflict." *Development* 48(3): 25–34.

Maoz, Ifat. 2000. "An Experiment in Peace: Reconciliation-Aimed Workshops of Jewish-Israeli and Palestinian Youth." *Journal of Peace Research* 37(6): 721–736.

Marshall, Monty G., and Ted Robert Gurr. 2005. *Peace and Conflict: A Global Survey of Armed Conflicts, Self-Determination Movements, and Democracy.* College Park: Center for International Development and Conflict Management, University of Maryland.

McLean Hilker, Lyndsay. 2009. "Everyday Ethnicities: Identity and Reconciliation among Rwandan Youth." *Journal of Genocide Research* 1(1): 81–100.

Meierhenrich, Jens. 2008. "Varieties of Reconciliation." *Law and Social Enquiry* 33(1): 195–231.

Méndez, Juan E. 2001."National Reconciliation, Transnational Justice, and the International Criminal Court." *Ethics and International Affairs* 13: 25–44.

Mertus, Julie. 2000. "Truth in a Box: The Limits of Justice through Judicial Mechanisms." In *The Politics of Memory: Truth, Healing and Social Justice.* Ed. Ifi Amadiume and Abdullahi An-Na'im. London: Zed Books, 142–161.

Mindry, Deborah. 2001. "Non-Governmental Organizations, 'Grassroots,' and the Politics of Virtue." *Signs: Journal of Women in Culture and Society* 26(4): 1187–1211.

Minow, Martha. 1998. *Between Vengeance and Forgiveness: Facing History after Genocide and Mass Violence.* Boston: Beacon.

———. 2002. "Breaking the Cycles of Hatred." In *Breaking the Cycles of Hatred: Memory, Law and Repair.* Ed. Martha Minow. Princeton, NJ: Princeton University Press, 14–76.

Montiel, Cristina Jayme. 2000. "Constructive and Destructive Post-Conflict Forgiveness." *Peace Review* 12(1): 95–101.

Mouffe, Chantal. 2005. *On the Political*. London: Routledge.

Murphy, Michael. 2011. "Apology, Recognition, and Reconciliation." *Human Rights Review* 12(1): 47–69.

Narayan, Uma. 1995. "Colonialism and Its Others: Considerations on Rights and Care Discourses." *Hypatia* 10(2): 133–140.

Nelson, Hilde Lindemann. 2001. *Damaged Identities, Narrative Repair*. Ithaca, NY: Cornell University Press.

Ní Aoláin, Fionnuala. 2012. "Advancing Feminist Positioning in the Field of Transitional Justice." *International Journal of Transitional Justice* 6: 205–228.

Ní Aoláin, Fionnuala, and Catherine Turner. 2007. "Gender, Truth and Transition." *UCLA Women's Law Journal* 16: 229–279.

Nordstrom, Carolyn. 1997. *The Different Kind of War Story*. Philadelphia: University of Pennsylvania Press.

Nowrojee, Binaifer. 2008. "'Your Justice Is Too Slow': Will the ICTR Fail Rwanda's Rape Victims?" In *Gendered Peace: Women's Struggles for Post-War Justice and Reconciliation*. Ed. Donna Pankhurst. New York: Routledge, 107–136.

Nussbaum, Martha C. 1996. "Compassion: The Basic Social Emotion." In *The Communitarian Challenge to Liberalism*. Ed. Ellen Frankel Paul, Fred Miller, and Jeffery Paul. Cambridge: Cambridge University Press, 27–58.

———. 1999. *Sex and Social Justice*. Oxford: Oxford University Press.

———. 2000. *Women and Human Development: The Capabilities Approach*. Cambridge: Cambridge University Press.

———. 2004. *Hiding from Humanity: Disgust, Shame and the Law*. Princeton, NJ: Princeton University Press.

———. 2011. *Creating Capabilities: The Human Development Approach*. Cambridge, MA: Belknap Press of Harvard University Press.

Nzenza, Sekai. 2006. "African Grief." In *Postcolonializing the International: Working to Change the Way We Are*. Ed. Phillip Darby. Honolulu: University of Hawai'i Press, 145–152.

O'Hagan, Des. 2012. *Letters from Long Kesh*. Dublin: Citizen Press.

Oliver, Kelly. 2001. *Witnessing: Beyond Recognition*. Minneapolis: University of Minnesota Press.

Olonisakin, 'Funmi, Karen Barnes, and Eka Ikpe. 2011. *Women, Peace and Security: Translating Policy into Practice*. London: Routledge.

O'Neill, Onora. 1993. "Justice, Gender, and International Boundaries." In *The Quality of Life*. Ed. Martha Nussbaum and Amartya Sen. Oxford: Clarendon Press, 303–323.

Pappe, Illan. 2006. "The Bridging Narrative Concept." In *Israeli and Palestinian Narratives of Conflict: History's Double Helix*. Ed. Robert I. Rotberg. Bloomington: Indiana University Press, 194–204.

Paris, Roland. 2004. *At War's End: Building Peace after Civil Conflict*. Cambridge: Cambridge University Press.

Phelps, Teresa Godwin. 2004. *Shattered Voices: Language, Violence, and the Work of Truth Commissions*. Philadelphia: University of Pennsylvania Press.

Phillips, Rebekah. 2007. "Commentary: Ambiguity in Narratives of Reconciliation: A Commentary on Positioning in Accounting for Redemption and Reconciliation." *Culture and Psychology* 13(4): 453–460.

Philpott, Daniel. 2012. *Just and Unjust Peace: An Ethic of Political Reconciliation.* Oxford: Oxford University Press.

Pía Lara, María. 2007. *Narrating Evil: A Postmetaphysical Theory of Reflective Judgment.* New York: Columbia University Press.

Plato. 1971. *The Republic.* Trans. H. D. P. Lee. London: Penguin Books.

Pollard, Ruth. 2012. "The Duty to Expose Syria's Slaughter." *Saturday Age,* February 25: 15.

Porter, Elisabeth. 1999. *Feminist Perspectives on Ethics.* London: Longman.

———. 2000. "Risks and Responsibilities: Creating Dialogical Spaces in Northern Ireland." *International Feminist Journal of Politics* 2(2): 163–184.

———. 2006. "Can Politics Practice Compassion?" *Hypatia: A Journal of Feminist Philosophy* 21(4): 97–123.

———. 2007a. *Peacebuilding: Women in International Perspective.* London: Routledge.

———. 2007b. "Women's Truth Narratives: The Power of Compassionate Listening." *Critical Half* 5(2): 20–25.

———. 2012a. "Gender-Inclusivity in Transitional Justice Strategies: Women in Timor-Leste." In *Gender in Transitional Justice.* Ed. Susanne Buckley-Zistal and Ruth Stanley. Basingstoke: Palgrave Macmillan, 221–240.

———. 2012b. "Women, Peace, and Securing Human Rights." In *Activating Human Rights and Peace: Theories, Practices, and Contexts.* Ed. Goh Bee Chen, Baden Offord, and Rob Garbutt. Farnham, Surry: Ashgate, 201–216.

———. 2013. "Rethinking Women's Empowerment." *Journal of Peacebuilding and Development* 8(1): 1–14.

Porter, Elisabeth, and Anuradha Mundkur. 2012. *Peace and Security: Implications for Women.* Brisbane: University of Queensland Press.

Porter, Norman. 2003. *The Elusive Quest: Reconciliation in Northern Ireland.* Belfast: Blackstaff Press.

Quinn, Joanna R. 2009. "What of Reconciliation? Traditional Mechanisms of Acknowledgment in Uganda." In *Reconciliation(s): Transitional Justice in Postconflict Societies.* Ed. Joanna R. Quinn. Montreal: McGill-Queen's University Press, 174–206.

Ramsbotham, Oliver. 2010. *Transforming Violent Conflict: Radical Disagreement, Dialogue, and Survival.* London: Routledge.

Rawls, John. 1972. *A Theory of Justice.* Cambridge, MA: Harvard University Press.

Rifkind, Gabrielle, and Giandomenico Picco. 2014. *The Fog of Peace: The Human Face of Conflict Resolution.* London: I. B. Taurus.

Rigby, Andrew. 2001. *Justice and Reconciliation: After the Violence.* Boulder, CO: Lynne Rienner Publishers.

Robinson, Fiona. 1999. *Globalizing Care: Ethics, Feminist Theory, and International Relations.* Boulder, CO: Westview Press

———. 2006. "Methods of Feminist Normative Theory: A Political Ethic of Care for International Relations." In *Feminist Methodologies for International Relations.* Ed. Brooke Ackerly, Maria Stern, and Jacqui True. Cambridge: Cambridge University Press, 221–240.

Ross, Fiona. 2003. *Bearing Witness: Women and the Truth and Reconciliation Commission in South Africa*. London: Pluto Press.

———. 2010. "An Acknowledged Failure: Women, Voice, Violence, and the South African Truth and Reconciliation Commission." In *Localizing Transitional Justice: Interventions and Priorities after Mass Violence*. Ed. Rosalind Shaw and Lars Waldorf. Stanford, CA: Stanford University Press, 69–91.

Rudd, Kevin. 2008. "Apology to Australia's Indigenous Peoples." *Hansard*, February 13. http://parlinfo.aph.gov.au/parlInfo/search/display/display.w3p; query=Id%3A%22chamber%2Fhansardr%2F2008-02-13%2F0003%22, accessed September 22, 2012.

Rutayisire, Antoine. 2010. "Rwanda: Repentance and Forgiveness—Pillars of Genuine Reconciliation." In *Forgiveness and Reconciliation: Psychological Pathways to Conflict Transformation and Peacebuilding*. Ed. Ani Kalayjian and Raymond Paloutzian. Heidelberg: Springer, 171–187.

Sachs, Albie. 2009. *Strange Alchemy of Life and Law*. Oxford: Oxford University Press.

Sara, Sally. 2007. *Gogo Mama: A Journey into the Lives of Twelve African Women*. Sydney: Pan Macmillan Australia.

Sarkin, Jeremy. 2009. "The Role of the United Nations, the African Union, and Africa's Sub-Regional Organizations in Dealing with Africa's Human Rights Problems: Connecting Humanitarian Intervention and the Responsibility to Protect." *Journal of African Law* 53: 1–33.

Sarkin, Jeremy, and Erin Daly. 2004. "Too Many Questions, Too Few Answers: Reconciliation in Transitional Societies." *Columbia Human Rights Law Review* 35(3): 661–728.

Schaffer, Kay, and Sidone Smith. 2004. *Human Rights and Narrated Lives: The Ethics of Recognition*. New York: Palgrave MacMillan.

Schirch, Lisa. 2006. "Linking Human Rights and Conflict Transformation." In *Human Rights and Conflict: Exploring the Links between Rights, Law, and Peacebuilding*. Ed. Julie Mertus and Jeffrey Helsing. Washington, DC: United States Institute of Peace Press, 63–95.

———. 2012. "Frameworks for Understanding Women as Victims and Peacebuilders." In *Defying Victimhood: Women and Post-Conflict Peacebuilding*. Ed. Albrecht Schnabel and Anara Tabyshalieva. Tokyo: United Nations University Press, 48–76.

Schott, Robin May. 2004. "The Atrocity Paradigm and the Concept of Forgiveness." *Hypatia* 19(4): 204–211.

Sen, Amartya. 1999. *Development as Freedom*. New York: Knopf.

Sevenhuijsen, Selma. 1999. "Too Good to Be True? Feminist Thoughts about Trust and Social Cohesion." *Focaal* 34: 207–222.

Shklar, Judith. 1990. *The Faces of Injustice*. New Haven, CT: Yale University Press.

Simić, Olivera. 2014. *Surviving Peace: A Political Memoir*. Melbourne: Spinifex Press.

Sluzki, Carlos E. 2003. "The Process Toward Reconciliation." In *Imagine Coexistence: Restoring Humanity after Violent Ethnic Conflict*. Ed. Antonio Chayes and Martha Minow. San Francisco: Jossey-Bass, 21–31.

Smith, David. 2004. "Why I Befriended My Dad's Killer." *The Observer*, October 10: 10.

Smyth, Geraldine. 2008. "Telling a Different Story: Hope for Forgiveness and Reconciliation in Northern Ireland." In *Pathways to Reconciliation: Between Theory and Practice*. Ed. Philipa Rothfield, Cleo Fleming, and Paul A. Komesaroff. Aldershot: Ashgate, 67–78.

Smyth, Marie. 2003. "Putting the Past in Its Place: Issues of Victimhood and Reconciliation in Northern Ireland's Peace Process." In *Burying the Past: Making Peace and Doing Justice after Civil Conflict*. Ed. Nigel Biggar. Washington, DC: Georgetown University Press, 125–153.

Sooka, Yasmin. 2006. "Dealing with the Past and Transitional Justice: Building Peace Through Accountability." *International Review of the Red Cross* 88(862): 311–325.

Spelman, Elizabeth V. 1997. *Fruits of Sorrow: Framing Our Attention to Suffering*. Boston: Beacon Press.

Steans, Jill. 1998. *Gender and International Relations: An Introduction*. Cambridge: Polity Press.

Stern, Maria. 2005. *Naming Security—Constructing Identity: "Mayan Women" in Guatemala on the Eve of "Peace."* Manchester: Manchester University Press.

Steward, John. 2008. "Only Healing Heals: Concepts and Methods of Psycho-Social Healing in Post-Genocide Rwanda." In *After Genocide: Transitional Justice, Post-Conflict Reconstruction, and Reconciliation in Rwanda and Beyond*. Ed. Phil Clark and Zachary D. Kaufman. London: Hurst, 171–190.

Subotic, Jelena. 2009. *Hijacked Justice: Dealing with the Past in the Balkans*. Ithaca, NY: Cornell University Press.

———. 2011. "Expanding the Scope of Post-Conflict Justice: Individual, State and Societal Responsibility for Mass Atrocity." *Journal of Peace Research* 48(2): 157–169.

Sylvester, Christine. 2002. *Feminist International Relations: An Unfinished Journey*. Cambridge: Cambridge University Press.

———. 2013. *War as Experience: Contributions for International Relations and Feminist Analysis*. New York: Routledge.

Taylor, Charles. 1992. *Multiculturalism and "The Politics of Recognition."* Princeton, NJ: Princeton University Press.

Thakur, Ramesh. 2008. *The United Nations, Peace, and Security: From Collective Security to the Responsibility to Protect*. Cambridge: Cambridge University Press.

Thomson, Susan. 2011. "Whispering Truth to Power: The Everyday Resistance of Rwandan Peasants to Post-Genocide Reconciliation." *African Affairs* 110(440): 439–456.

Totten, Samuel, and Rafiki Ubaldo, eds. 2011. *We Cannot Forget: Interviews with Survivors of the 1994 Genocide in Rwanda*. New Brunswick, NJ: Rutgers University Press.

Tronto, Joan. 1993. *Moral Boundaries: A Political Argument for an Ethic of Care*. London: Routledge.

Tutu, Desmond. 1999. *No Future without Forgiveness*. London: Rider.

———. 2012. "Why I Had No Choice but to Spurn Tony Blair." *The Observer*, September 2: 31.

Tuyaga, Adrien. 2005. "Picking Up the Pieces: Jamaa in Burundi." In *People Building Peace II: Successful Stories of Civil Society*. Ed. Paul van Tongeren, Malin Brenk, Marte Hellema, and Juliette Verhoeven. Boulder, CO: Lynne Rienner Publishers, 157–161.

UN General Assembly. 1948. *UN Declaration of Human Rights*. Paris: United Nations.

———. 2008. *Nuremberg Declaration on Peace and Justice*, A/62/885. New York: United Nations.

United Nations Development Programme. 1994. *Human Development Report*. New York: UNDP.

UN Office of the High Commissioner for Human Rights. 2005. *Basic Principles and Guidelines on the Right to a Remedy and Reparation for Victims of Gross Violations of Human Rights Law and Serious Violations of International Humanitarian Law*. http://www.ohchr.org/EN/ProfessionalInterest/Pages/RemedyAndReparation.aspx, accessed September 15, 2013.

UN Office of Legal Affairs. 1998. *Rome Statute of the International Criminal Court,* July 17. http://untreaty.un.org/cod/icc/statute/romefra.htm, accessed September 8, 2013.

UNRISD. 2005. *Gender Equality: Striving for Justice in an Unequal World*. Geneva: UNRISD.

UN Secretary-General. 1999. *Prevention of War and Disaster*. Report of the Secretary-General on the Work of the Organization. A/541. August 31. New York: United Nations.

Ure, Michael. 2008. "Post-Traumatic Societies: On Reconciliation, Justice, and the Emotions." *European Journal of Social Theory* 11(3): 283–297.

US Department of State. 2012. *Country Reports on Human Rights Practices for 2012: Democratic Republic of Congo*. http://www.state.gov/j/drl/rls/hrrpt/humanrightsreport/index.htm?year=2012&dlid=204107#wrapper, accessed September 15, 2013.

van Tongeren, Paul, Malin Brenk, Marte Hellema, and Juliette Verhoeven, eds. 2005. *People Building Peace II: Successful Stories of Civil Society*. Boulder, CO: Lynne Rienner Publishers.

van Woerkom, Marieke. 2004. "Seeds of Peace: Toward a Common Narrative." *New Directions for Youth Development* 102: 35–46.

Verdeja, Ernesto. 2009. *Unchopping a Tree: Reconciliation in the Aftermath of Political Violence*. Philadelphia: Temple University Press.

Verwoerd, Wilhelm. 2003. "Toward a Response to Criticisms of the South African Truth and Reconciliation Commission," In *Dilemmas of Reconciliation: Cases and Concepts*. Ed. Carol A. L. Prager and Trudy Govier, Waterloo, Ontario: Wilfred Laurier University Press, 245-278.

Volf, Miroslav. 1996. *Exclusion and Embrace: Our Theological Exploration of Identity, Otherness, and Reconciliation*. Nashville, TN: Abingdon Press.

———. 2000. "The Social Meaning of Reconciliation." *Interpretations* 54: 158–172.

———. 2014. "Exclusion and Embrace: Reconciliation in an Australian Context." Public lecture, University of South Australia, Adelaide, March 16.

Walker, Margaret Urban. 2006. "The Cycle of Violence." *Journal of Human Rights* 5(1): 81–105.

Walzer, Michael. 1997. *On Toleration*. New Haven, CT: Yale University Press.

Warner, Marina. 2002. "Sorry: The Present State of Apology." *Open Democracy*. November 7: 1–17.

Waterson, Roxana. 2009. "Reconciliation as Ritual: Comparative Perspectives on Innovation and Performance in Processes of Reconciliation." *Humanities Research* 15(3): 27–47.

Weinstein, Harvey, Laurel Fletcher, Patrick Vinck, and Phuong Pham. 2010. "Stay the Hand of Justice: Whose Priorities Take Priority?" In *Localizing Transitional Justice: Interventions and Priorities after Mass Violence*. Ed. Rosalind Shaw and Lars Waldorf. Stanford, CA: Stanford University Press, 27–48.

Wibben, Annick. 2011. *Feminist Security Studies*. London: Routledge.

Wiesenthal, Simon. 1998. *The Sunflower: On the Possibilities and Limits of Forgiveness*. New York: Shocken Books.

Wolff, Stefan. 2006. *Ethnic Conflict: A Global Perspective*. Oxford: Oxford University Press.

Young, Iris Marion. 2006. "Responsibility and Global Justice: A Social Connection Model." *Social Philosophy and Policy Foundation* 23(1): 102–130.

Yovel, Yirmiyahu. 1998. "Tolerance as Grace and as Rightful Recognition." *Social Research* 65(4): 897–920.

Zorbas, Eugenia. 2004. "Reconciliation in Post-Genocide Rwanda." *African Journal of Legal Studies* 1(1): 29–52.

Index

Abbott, H. Porter, 32
Abe, Toshihiro, 190
Ackerman, John, 144
acknowledgment: apology and, 142; characteristics of, 142–143; examples of, 144–145; as first step to healing, 144; forgiveness and, 142; forms of, 144; of wrongdoing, 142–143, 144, 215
Acorn, Annalise, 177
Adams, Gerry, 101n2
agency: characteristics of, 49; definition of, 47–48; narrative approach to, 51–52
Agenda for Peace, An (Boutros-Ghali), 6
Ahmed, Sheikh Sharif, 122
Aiken, Nevin, 205
Akayesu case, 63
Allan, Pierre, 15, 16
Ambos, Kai, 67, 85
amnesties, 81–83
Amstutz, Mark, 141
Anderlini, Sanam Naraghi, 17, 29
anger, 136, 169–170
Annan, Kofi A., 6
Apiyo, Nancy, 41
apology: acknowledgment and, 142; ethical issues of, 22; examples of, 140–141, 151–152; as healing tool, 134; narrative dimension of, 134;

nature of, 132; obstacles to, 134–135; political, 139–142; power of, 23, 134; in relation to forgiveness, 139, 145–146; significance of, 138, 152, 155
Appleby, Scott, 8
Arendt, Hannah: on forgiveness, 150, 152; on humanization by speaking, 45; on humanly actions, 43; on importance of life stories, 34, 58; on interpretation of narratives, 59; on Nazi crimes, 61; on notion on evil, 64
Aristotle, 9
Ashrawi, Hanan Mikhail, 29
Assefa, Hizkias, 187
Asvat, Abubaker, 151
asylum seekers, 159
Atran, Scott, 127
Australian Greens, 180n1
Australian Human Rights Commission, 159

Bar-Tal, Daniel, 186
Baxi, Upendra, 43
Bekerman, Zvi, 149
Benhabib, Seyla, 49, 116
Benito, Odio, 64
Bennink, Gemma, 186
Berak village, 119, 131n3
Bernstein, Richard, 153, 156n4

About the Book

Can postconflict states achieve both peace and justice as they deal with a traumatic past? What role does reconciliation play in healing wounds, building trust, and rectifying injustices? This provocative book, incorporating the frameworks of both peace/conflict studies and transitional justice, explores the core challenges that war-torn states confront once the violence has ended.

The book is organized around a series of questions, each one the subject of a chapter, with each chapter presenting a wide range of practical examples and case studies. The author also stakes out a position on each question, encouraging readers to evaluate and respond to ideas, practices, and strategies. Narratives are a notable feature of the work, with the human consequences of war and peace highlighted throughout.

Elisabeth Porter is professor of politics and international relations at the University of South Australia. Her recent publications include *Peace and Security: Implications for Women* (with Anuradha Mundkur) and *Peacebuilding: Women in International Perspective*.